POSTMORTEM

ALSO BY JEFFREY ABRAMSON

We, the Jury
The Electronic Commonwealth
Liberation and Its Limits

POSTMORTEM

The O. J. Simpson Case

Justice Confronts Race, Domestic Violence,
Lawyers, Money, and the Media

Edited by Jeffrey Abramson

BasicBooks
A Division of HarperCollinsPublishers

FIRST EDITION

Designed by Elliott Beard

Library of Congress Cataloging-in-Publication Data

Postmortem : the O. J. Simpson case / [edited] by Jeffrey
   Abramson.
      p.   cm.
    ISBN 0-465-03319-9
      1. Simpson, O. J., 1947– —Trials, litigation, etc.
    2. Trials (Murder)—California—Los Angeles.
    3. Criminal justice, Administration of—California—Los
    Angeles.   I. Abramson, Jeffrey, 1947— .
KF224.73'02523'0979494—dc20   96-10423
[347.30525230979494]   CIP

96 97 98 99 00 ❖/HC 10 9 8 7 6 5 4 3 2 1

For Jackie

postmortem (pōst-môrtəm) *adj.* 1. occurring or done after death; *noun* 1. an examination of a human body after death; 2. an analysis or review of some completed event.

adapted from *The American Heritage Dictionary of the English Language*, ed. William Morris (New York: American Heritage Pub. Co. and Houghton Mifflin Co., 1969), p. 1024

Contents

PART II
Domestic Violence: The Disappearance of an Issue

PART III
Lawyers: Their Strategies and Their Ethics

PART IV
Reforms:
Proposals for Juries, Police, and Prosecutors

PART V
Cameras in the Courtroom?

PART VI
The Trial in Historical Perspective

List of Contributors

JEFFREY ABRAMSON is Louis Stulberg Professor of Law and Politics at Brandeis University and author, most recently, of *We, the Jury: The Jury System and the Ideal of Democracy*.

LORRAINE ADAMS is a reporter for the *Washington Post*, where her articles on the Simpson trial appeared.

ALBERT W. ALSCHULER is Wilson-Dickinson Professor at the University of Chicago Law School. Among his most recent writings on the jury is "Racial Quotas and the Jury" in the *Duke Law Journal* (1995).

BARBARA ALLEN BABCOCK is McFarland Professor of Law at Stanford Law School and former Director of the Public Defender Service in Washington, D.C. She is currently at work on a biography of Clara Shortridge Foltz, initiator of Public Defenders for the indigent accused.

PAUL BUTLER is Associate Professor of Law at George Washington University Law School and author of "Racially Based Jury Nullification: Black Power in the Criminal Justice System" in the *Yale Law Journal* (1995).

LINCOLN CAPLAN, a lawyer, writes about legal affairs for newspapers and magazines. His previous book was *Skadden: Power, Money, and the Rise of a Legal Empire*.

HARVEY COX, Professor of Divinity at Harvard University, is the author of *Fire from Heaven: The Rise of Pentecostal Spirituality and the Reshaping of Religion in the Twenty-First Century.*

STANLEY CROUCH is the author of *The All-American Skin Game, or the Decoy of Race: The Long and Short of It: 1990–1994,* nominated for the 1996 National Books Critics Circle Award in the field of criticism.

MICHAEL ERIC DYSON directs the Institute of African-American Research and is Professor of Communications Studies at the University of North Carolina, Chapel Hill. His latest book is *Between God and Gangsta Rap: Bearing Witness to Black Culture.*

ANDREW HACKER, Professor of Political Science at Queens College, is the author most recently of *Two Nations: Black and White, Separate, Hostile, Unequal.*

KENNETH JOST is a staff writer for the *Congressional Quarterly* and is the author of *The Supreme Court Yearbook.*

YALE KAMISAR is Clarence Darrow Distinguished University Professor of the University of Michigan Law School. He is the author of numerous articles on criminal procedure and constitutional law and co-author of *Cases in Modern Criminal Procedure.*

RANDALL KENNEDY is Professor of Law at Harvard Law School and is completing a book on race and criminal justice in America.

NANCY J. KING is Associate Professor of Law at Vanderbilt Law School. She is the author of numerous articles on the jury, including "Racial Jurymandering: Cancer or Cure? A Contemporary Review of Affirmative Action in Jury Selection" in the *New York University Law Review* (1993).

SERGE F. KOVALESKI wrote on the Simpson trial for the *Washington Post.*

HARLAN LEVY was a prosecutor for eight years with the Manhattan District Attorney's Office. He is the author of *And the Blood Cried Out: A Prosecutor's Spellbinding Account of the Power of DNA,* which draws on his own courtroom experiences.

MICHAEL LIND is a contributing editor to *The New Republic* and writes widely on current affairs.

JOSEPH D. MCNAMARA, a research fellow at the Hoover Institution, Stanford University, is the former police chief of San Jose. He is currently working on his fifth book on policing.

CHARLES J. OGLETREE, JR., Professor of Law and Director of the Criminal Justice Institute at Harvard Law School, is co-author of *Beyond the Rodney King Story: An Examination of Police Conduct in Minority Communities*. Professor Ogletree also served as a legal commentator for NBC News during the O.J. Simpson case.

DEBORAH L. RHODE is Professor of Law and Director of the Keck Center on Legal Ethics and the Legal Profession at Stanford Law School. She is the author of *Justice and Gender*.

ELIZABETH M. SCHNEIDER, Professor of Law at Brooklyn Law School, has written many articles on domestic violence and is co-authoring a law school casebook on domestic violence, and completing a book on domestic violence and social change.

JIM SLEEPER, author of *The Closest of Strangers: Liberalism and the Politics of Race in New York,* was a columnist for the *New York Daily News* during the Simpson trial.

GLORIA STEINEM, co-founder of *Ms.* magazine, is the author of *Outrageous Acts and Everyday Rebellions*.

DIANA TRILLING is the author most recently of *The Beginning of the Journey: The Marriage of Lionel and Diana Trilling*.

SCOTT TUROW, whose most recent novel is *Pleading Guilty,* was an Assistant United States Attorney for eight years.

PATRICIA WILLIAMS is Professor of Law at Columbia Law School. She is the author of *The Alchemy of Race and Rights*.

Preface and Acknowledgments

For Nicole Brown Simpson and Ronald Lyle Goldman, the postmortem examinations took place in a Los Angeles coroner's office on June 14, 1994. Their autopsies told us nothing about how they lived, only that they died from multiple slashes made by a single-edged knife. The principal wound on Nicole Brown Simpson's body was a deep gash running from the left side of her throat to just below her ear. According to the coroner's testimony at trial, a knife appeared to have been drawn across her neck like a ruler, severing arteries and nicking her spinal cord.

Ronald Goldman was stabbed and slashed to death after apparently resisting his killer. He suffered multiple cuts on his head, face, and lungs. The coroner speculated that Goldman's ability to resist his attacker lessened with loss of blood and that the murderer inflicted two deep knife wounds across Goldman's neck while holding the victim still.

Nearly two years have passed since these murders. The literal postmortem examinations are long over but the postmortems on the criminal trial of O. J. Simpson for killing his ex-wife and Goldman go on. The jury verdict pronouncing Simpson not guilty of the murders is entitled to respect but juries do not bind history. Juries never explain the reasons for their decisions; scholars must.

In this book, twenty-six scholars come together to ponder what went on at O. J. Simpson's criminal trial and what the long-range implications of the case are for criminal justice, race relations, domestic violence, jury reform, legal and media ethics in the United States. The idea for this book originated with the editorial staff at Basic Books, in particular Christopher Korintus, assistant to the publisher. When Chris asked me whether I would be interested in editing a collection of essays on the trial, I was skeptical at first: Was there anything left to say about the most media-covered trial in the history of the world? But after calling a number of people whose names now appear in the table of contents, I found a consensus that the trial was one thing, immediate reactions to the trial were another, and reactions to the reactions yet a third phenomenon. These scholars relished the opportunity to stand back from the flux of events and begin the long process of putting the trial in historical perspective.

As editor of this book, I owe principal thanks to the individual authors of the essays. In a few instances, I have chosen merely to reprint essays originally published elsewhere. But for the most part, the essays have either been written originally for this book or else substantially revised and enlarged from articles originally appearing shortly after the trial. The contributors worked under tight deadlines to submit their essays and I thank them for their cooperation and team spirit. Editing of their essays has been kept to a minimum, the better to let differences of opinion and approach speak for themselves.

At Basic Books, Chris Korintus shepardced the book through from beginning to end, dealing with everything from topic selection, recruitment of contributors, gathering of permissions, and manuscript production. Two hundred miles away, at my home university of Brandeis, Trudy Crosby helped me with administrative support and shuttled words to New York City by getting them on (and off) computer screens, faxes, and e-mail.

During the trial itself, my wife and I tried not to debate the case much in front of our children: we thought it a poor introduction to critical thought about men and women, whites and blacks, justice and injustice in the United States. One exception came when my daughter Sarah bravely asked me to speak about the trial to her seventh-grade social studies class. The seventh graders were already great skeptics about trials but were still floored by news that Simpson could never be tried a second time for murder, if the first jury pronounced him not guilty. Their hunger to understand basic justice has stayed with me during the course of putting this book together. My younger daughter, Anna, is more reticent about what lessons she takes away from all the Simpson talk. I'm hoping she will find this book quietly useful.

Jacqueline Jones, my wife, pushed me to take the high road in topic selection for this book. Her own pioneering work on the history of black women, work, and poverty in the United States is my model for scholarship at once passionate and yet impeccably researched. I dedicate this book to Jackie to honor the person she is.

As always, my parents, Al and Rose Abramson, served as invaluable if unpaid research assistants, keeping newspaper files for me regarding jury trials. When I wanted to have the practitioner's point of view of the trial, I had only to turn to my favorite law firm of Abramson, Newman and Abramson, where my brothers Harvey and Rick just happen to be partners.

For me, this book is a natural follow-up to my scholarly study of the jury (*We, the Jury*) completed just as the Simpson story broke. En route from that book to this one, I was invited to explore the implications of my jury research for the Simpson trial by a number of distinguished groups. I want to express appreciation to the federal judges at the 1995 Judicial Conference of the Sixth Circuit of the United States; the trial judges of the Massachusetts District and Superior Court; judges attending my jury seminar sponsored by the Flaschner Judicial Institute; students and alumni attending a jury symposium sponsored by The Harvard Law School Voluntary Defenders; and litigants attending a forum on jury selection sponsored by Decision Research. Special thanks to United States Judge Nancy Edmunds, Massachusetts judges Jonathan Brandt, Margot Botsford, J. Harold Flannery, and Nancy Kelly, and Flaschner Judicial Institute director, Robert Brink.

Thanks also to the following journalists for publishing commentary from me on the Simpson trial: David Corcoran and Julie Just of the *New York Times;* Henry Weinstein of the *Los Angeles Times;* Glen Nishimura of *USA Today;* Gail Cox of the *National Law Journal;* and Karen Winkler of the *Chronicle of Higher Education.*

My father-in-law, Albert H. Jones, would have enjoyed debating the themes of this book with me. He possessed a lively curiosity about the law that grew with age and kept us lawyers on our toes during conversation. I will miss him and his insights.

While president of Basic Books, the late Martin Kessler let me know he believed in the importance of my work on the jury. His death leaves a hole in the American publishing industry.

Decent respect for the memory of Nicole Brown Simpson and Ronald Goldman means remembering the difference between a physical and intellectual postmortem. But we owe to victims and defendants alike the obligation to make sure justice is done.

Jeffrey Abramson
Wellesley, Massachusetts
March 1996

Editor's Introduction

JEFFREY ABRAMSON

$\mathbf{D}$id the jury in *People v. Orenthal James Simpson* reach a true and accurate conclusion when it decided that the defendant was not guilty of murdering Nicole Brown Simpson and Ronald Goldman on the night of June 12, 1994? As the months pass and passions soften, many Americans on both sides of the color line have come to accept that reasonable jurors acting in good faith could have decided the state failed to prove Simpson's guilt beyond a reasonable doubt. But acknowledging that the state failed to meet its extraordinary burden of proof in criminal cases is not the same as believing Simpson is actually innocent. A plausible consensus has emerged that Simpson was "probably" guilty but the jury legitimately acquitted him nonetheless.

This consensus is not without its problems. Four hours of deliberation hardly gave the jury time to review nine months of testimony totaling over 45,000 pages of trial transcript. The DNA evidence alone warranted longer study: among other signs of Simpson's guilt, tests showed that fewer than one person in 170 million had the genetic characteristics found in a blood drop near the murdered bodies and O. J. Simpson was one of those people; that blood found on a sock in Simpson's bedroom could have come from only one person in 6.8 billion and Nicole Brown Simpson was one of those persons; that one blood stain on the infamous glove found at Simpson's estate could have come from only one in every 1.2 billion people and Ronald Goldman was one such person.

These are astoundingly incriminating findings, especially since they point toward a person with a prior record of abusing and stalking the murdered woman. But even those sure of Simpson's guilt have to concede that the evidence passed through the hands of some racist police (Mark Fuhrman), inept criminologists (no one discovered blood stains on socks found in Simpson's bedroom for weeks after the murders), and less than careful lab technicians (samples of crime scene blood may have been stored too close to blood samples taken from Simpson for comparison). These revelations lent credibility to defense arguments that some evidence could have been planted (the bloody glove, for instance), while other evidence was hopelessly contaminated. This is how probable guilt melts down to reasonable doubt.

The consensus that Simpson is guilty and yet the jury did the right thing to acquit him has permitted a mood of racial rapprochement to replace the competing, incendiary interpretation of the jury's verdict that dominated commentary right after the verdicts were read: as a deliberate act of muscle-flexing by mostly African-American jurors so fed up with official police racism that they subordinated their duty to convict a guilty murderer to their desire to send a message of protest.

Although legitimizing the jury verdict in terms of reasonable doubt has helped promote racial harmony, it has also robbed the trial of any moral closure. No one has ever been held responsible for two gruesome murders. The Los Angeles Police Department considers its investigation into the slayings closed, notwithstanding the jury's verdict. Simpson himself can never be retried for the killings, no matter what turns up in the future. But *60 Minutes* correspondent Andrew Rooney spoofed the notion that any other suspects are out there when he offered $1 million of his own money for information leading to the conviction of someone besides Simpson for the murders.

The lack of moral closure is equally great for those who believe that Simpson is truly innocent and the real murderers are on the loose. Simpson's most ardent defenders continue to ask how so savage a set of murders could have left so little blood on Simpson's person, his car, or his carpets—by the prosecution's own case, the murderer's shoes should have been soaking in blood. If the answer is supposedly that Simpson washed up and disposed of his clothes and shoes before returning home, Simpson's defenders point out that the prosecution's own time line gave him precious little time to have done the necessary scrubbing and changing. At the very least, there must have been an accomplice. Then, too, Simpson supporters hold to the mystery of why Simpson would have chosen the night of June 12 to commit premeditated murder, knowing that in about an hour a limousine was due at his home to take him to the airport.

Short of the murder weapon turning up, definitive proof of Simpson's guilt or innocence seems unlikely at this point. The civil trial, in which the victims' families are suing Simpson for the wrongful death of their loved ones, will give another jury another go at the events. Since civil juries only need to be convinced Simpson is the killer by a preponderance of the evidence (that is, a bare 51 percent of it), we may indeed end up with two conflicting jury verdicts. But losing a civil trial will cost Simpson only money, hardly a punishment fit for the crime.

Of course, there is always the possibility that definitive proof will come outside the courtroom. Critic Diana Trilling suspects that Simpson suffers from post-traumatic denial that he murdered two people—if so, the erased memory could return with the passage of time. Al Cowlings may ultimately tell us what Simpson had to say during the slow-speed Bronco chase. The minister/penitent privilege prevented the prosecution from asking Rosie Greer, former football star turned prison minister, whether Simpson confessed his guilt, but perhaps word of their confidential communications will leak out. Weeks after the jury verdicts, Paula Barbieri said she left a "Dear John" message on Simpson's answering machine the morning of the murders. Will this new detail make a difference during the civil trial? Five days before her murder, Nicole Brown Simpson apparently called Sojourn, a battered women's shelter. Citing confidentiality, Sojourn so far has refused to divulge why she called. Thus, neither the jury nor the nation heard the full extent of Nicole Brown Simpson's fear during the last days of her life.

I mention these details because they illustrate that the Simpson story is far from over. But whatever is still to come, the revelations so far are worthy of serious commentary. For fifteen months, the nation remained engrossed in the trial and what it told us about race relations, domestic violence, Othello-like tragedy, Los Angeles–style farce, the ethics of lawyers, the behavior of jurors, the racism of police, and the influence of the media. Of course, the trial also provided lighter fare for tabloid television, with its focus on the life styles of the rich and famous. At times, tabloid titillations overwhelmed the serious business of the trial and made one wonder about the moral sensibilities of a nation which could turn a grizzly double murder into fodder for late night television routines such as Jay Leno's skit on the dancing Judge Itos.

At its best and its worst, the trial offered important insights into the state of justice and democracy in America and this book brings together some of the best that has yet been written on the trial's broader social significance. Contributors include law professors, prosecutors, defense counsel, historians, political scientists, philosophers, journalists, cultural critics, a former police chief, and a theologian. Their essays cover four major areas. Issues about race and criminal justice are central to the discussions of law professors Paul Butler and Randall Kennedy, African-American studies and communications professor Michael Eric Dyson, journalist Jim Sleeper, and author Diana Trilling. Together, their essays discuss jury selection, the influence of race on jurors, the debate over reasonable doubt as the grounds for the jury verdict, and whether the Simpson jury engaged in jury nullification, a practice where jurors deliberately acquit a guilty defendant in order to protest some larger injustice.

Domestic violence is the subject of the second set of essays, including those by law professors Deborah L. Rhode and Elizabeth M. Schneider, and the remarks of *Ms.* magazine co-founder Gloria Steinem and law professor Patricia Williams in a televised interview with host Charlie Rose. These contributors ponder why Nicole Brown Simpson vanished as a victim in the case, why indeed the trial as well as the media became so thoroughly distracted from issues of domestic violence. The prosecution considered Simpson's prior abuse of Nicole Brown Simpson to be relevant to his motive for murder; the jury apparently thought the abuse irrelevant in a murder trial. These essays ask why the jury and much of the public were so disinterested in the domestic violence background.

The performance of the lawyers in the case, their strategic successes and blunders, and their ethics are discussed throughout the book but three essays offer detailed comment on the lawyers. Law professor Charles J. Ogletree, Jr. discusses whether we should view Johnnie Cochran and Marcia Clark as role models for future defenders and prosecutors. Reporters Lorraine Adams and Serge F. Kovaleski offer a synopsis of the strategic decisions that for many explain how the so-called defense Dream Team outmaneuvered the prosecution. DNA expert Harlan Levy provides exacting commentary on how the defense undermined crucial DNA evidence.

In Part Four, contributors turn to the subject of reform, with special attention to reforming or even abolishing the jury in articles by journalist Michael Lind, law professors Albert W. Alschuler, Barbara Allen Babcock, and Nancy J. King, jury researcher Kenneth Jost, and political scientist Andrew Hacker. Joseph D. McNamara, former police chief in San Jose, California, discusses how to reform the Los Angeles Police Department and novelist and former prosecutor Scott Turow adds some thoughts on procedures for warrantless searches and the role of the District Attorney's office in supervising the LAPD's search and seizure decisions.

The fifth cluster of essays tackles the pros and cons of cameras in the courtroom. I offer a brief survey of the debate, while journalist Lincoln Caplan couples his doubts about televised trials with larger qualms about the state of legal journalism in general.

The book concludes with some general reflections on the trial's overall significance. Law professor Yale Kamisar relates the hue and cry over Simpson's acquittal to previous moments in U.S. history where a crisis mentality caused many Americans to think the Constitution coddled criminals. Theologian Harvey Cox sees the trial as a metaphor for the city and as a "nasty parody" of multiculturalism. On the other hand, critic-at-large Stanley Crouch finds some "good news" in the multiracial cast of characters central to the trial: the interracial couple, the presiding Asian-American judge, black and Jewish lawyers working together in both sides of the aisle, witnesses from every class and race in America.

In the remainder of this introduction, I offer a more detailed summary of the views of the contributors on key trial areas, as well as my own assessments.

RACE: ITS INFLUENCE ON THE JURY AND PUBLIC OPINION

The Simpson trial raised deep and troubling questions about race and the American criminal justice system. Jeffrey Toobin, who covered the trial for *The New Yorker,* noted that "the only reason anyone will care about this case five years, ten years from now is because of what it illuminates about race in America—the yawning gap between black people and white people on more issues than many people thought."

On the surface, the Simpson trial did not involve issues of race—the defendant was no Rodney King–like symbol of black victimization and the victims clearly were not murdered because they were white. Nonetheless, public opinion about Simpson's guilt almost immediately split along racial lines. The first *Los Angeles Times* poll, taken three weeks after Simpson was charged with the murders on June 17, showed that African Americans in the city were almost twice as likely as whites to believe Simpson innocent. A nationwide Gallup Poll taken at the same time found that 60 percent of blacks thought Simpson innocent, while 68 percent of whites thought him guilty. Of course, anyone who had watched the strange hero's welcome freeway crowds gave Simpson during the famous slow-speed Bronco chase already knew that, through some strange alchemy, a rich and famous celebrity more at home on white golf courses than in the black community had emerged as symbolic of the plight of the black defendant in a racist society.

One of the first persons to detect that Simpson was becoming a cause célèbre in certain sectors of the African-American community was Dennis Schatzman, a journalist for the *Los Angeles Sentinel,* a black weekly newspaper. "The more vigorously Mr. Simpson has been pursued by the criminal justice system, the 'blacker' he has become," Schatzman noted. "A man who, in the minds of many, was either colorless or white has now been placed in a position of having to defend himself against a charge that he murdered a beautiful white woman and a white man. Everything is magnified and black people, irrespective of the fact that he never set foot in South Central, can identify with him."

In hindsight, it is noteworthy that Schatzman made this assessment before allegations of Detective Mark Fuhrman's racism were circulated. In July, months before the trial began, *The New Yorker* and *Newsweek* revealed that Fuhrman had once applied for a stress disability pension, accusing himself of harboring racial prejudices from his service on the streets of L.A. The LAPD denied Fuhrman's application and thought he was lying. Strangely enough, they put a cop whom they thought a liar back out on the streets with a gun. Once apprised of Fuhrman's dubious past, the defense began to plan its strategy suggesting that a rogue, racist cop had planted the damning bloody glove on Simpson's estate. At this point, any chance that race would be irrelevant in Simpson's trial vanished. Interestingly enough, Gerald Uelmen, co-counsel for Simpson, told the *Los Angeles Times* that the initial hunch Fuhrman might have planted the bloody glove came from another defense co-counsel, Alan Dershowitz, even before Johnnie Cochran, Jr. officially joined the defense team.

The early poll results showing a racially split city put Los Angeles County District Attorney Gil Garcetti in a bind. Under normal circumstances, a defendant is tried in the courthouse closest to where the crime occurred—in Simpson's case, this would have meant holding the trial in Santa Monica, about four miles from the Bundy address where Nicole Brown Simpson and Ron Goldman met their deaths. Since Los Angeles recruits jurors only within a twenty-mile radius of each courthouse, Santa Monica juries tend to be predominantly white. But Garcetti chose to mark the case up for trial in the downtown courthouse, where jury selection was far more likely to achieve a racially mixed jury.

Officially, the move was attributed to earthquake damage and inadequate security at the Santa Monica courthouse. Garcetti also wanted a grand jury to indict Simpson, and the L.A. grand jury sits only at the downtown courthouse. But Garcetti had deeper reasons to move the trial. In a city still suffering from the first Rodney King trial and the riots spawned by the refusal of a jury without blacks to convict four white cops videotaped beating a prostrate black man, the District Attorney wanted no part of convicting Simpson before a mostly white jury. Garcetti's sentiment may have been commendable but fear of another Rodney King was overblown. For one thing, the mistake in the first King trial was in moving the trial out of Los Angeles entirely—Garcetti could hardly be accused of manipulating the venue if he left the Simpson case where it belonged. Second, any prediction that blacks might riot if Simpson were convicted seemed silly, given how routine convictions of black men in Los Angeles are.

JURY SELECTION

Garcetti probably did not anticipate that sending the case downtown would result in an overwhelmingly black jury. According to Trial Logistics, a Pasadena consulting firm, downtown juries in recent years have averaged 46 percent white, 25 percent African-American, 19 percent Hispanic, and 10 percent Asian. Moreover, the initial pool of 900 persons from which the Simpson jury was selected was 40 percent white, 28 percent African-American, 17 percent Hispanic, and 15 percent Asian. African Americans are a decided minority even in the twenty-mile radius surrounding the downtown courthouse. Nonetheless, on November 3, a jury of eight African Americans, one white, two Hispanics, and one person of mixed race (white/Native American) was sworn in. On December 8, jury selection was completed when twelve alternates were selected—seven African Americans, four whites, and one Hispanic.

The full story of how the pool of jurors and alternates came to be so predominantly African-American has yet to be told. One factor, as reported by Lorraine Adams and Serge F. Kovaleski of the *Washington Post* in their essay for this volume, is that lead prosecutor Marcia Clark disregarded the advice of jury selection experts and welcomed the presence of African-American women on the jury, on the theory that they would approach the case more in terms of gender than race (the final jury was ten women and two men; eight of the women were African-American).

At the time, Clark had good reason to believe that domestic violence aspects of the case would ultimately trump racial factors— Nicole Brown Simpson was dead but jurors would hear her frightened 911 call to the police, with the rage-distorted voice of her ex-husband clearly audible as he bangs at her door. Although not officially admissible into evidence, selected jurors might have already heard that, even from the grave, Nicole accused her husband of her murder, through pictures of her bruises locked in a bank vault, and by telling friends that Simpson would murder her one day and get away with it. While African-American women could be expected to share with their men painful recollections of an era where innocent black men were lynched for supposedly attacking white women, Clark counted on the fact that these echoes of outrageous history would be faint and that the jury would put aside the black man/white woman circumstance as irrelevant in the Los Angeles of 1994–95.

Both the *Washington Post* and *Newsweek* have quoted Donald Vinson, head of the trial consulting firm Decision Quest, as saying the prosecution largely ignored his firm's advice on jury selection. Decision Quest conducted a computer analysis of answers given by

307 prospective jurors in their written questionnaires and during voir dire; it ranked them on a scale of 1 to 7, with 7 being the ideal prosecution juror. But the state was extremely wary of creating any public impression that it was trying to manipulate the jury selection process. John Martel, a prosecution adviser, told *Time* magazine that prosecutors in fact asked Vinson to leave the courtroom the first day of trial and ignored most of Decision Quest's profiles. Of the nine African Americans on the final jury, four had been rated 2s and two were 3s; the one Hispanic was a 4, and one white was rated a 7.

The final configuration of the jury also included only two persons with college degrees. In highly publicized cases, jury selection almost always works to lower the educational level of the jury, as daily newspaper readers in particular are eliminated for following pretrial events too closely. Sequestering a jury only aggravates the problem, as self-employed persons and professionals successfully claim financial hardship. In a case involving technical forensic evidence and complicated DNA calculations, the prosecution would have hoped for a more educationally representative jury. For instance, Decision Quest's research found a clear correlation between belief in Simpson's innocence and deriving information about the case mostly from tabloid television shows. It was not a hopeful sign, therefore, when none of the initial jurors had answered "yes" to a question about reading a newspaper regularly.

On the defense side, jury selection expert Jo-Ellan Dimitrius thought it crucial that jurors, regardless of race, be receptive to a defense built around charges of police misconduct and incompetence. Beyond the Fuhrman factor, the defense strategy called for attacks on the competence of the coroner who performed the autopsy, the criminologist who collected evidence at the crime scene, and the labs which tested the blood evidence. Dimitrius's surveys of the Los Angeles population showed that the Rodney King trial had increased negative attitudes toward the L.A. police among all demographic groups, but African Americans were off the chart. "In the life experience of any African American, I don't think any of us understands the problems they face on a daily basis," she told the *Washington Post* by way of explaining defense strategy during jury selection. "So are [African Americans] predisposed to distrust law enforcement? You bet they are. There are a lot of other groups that have that attitude—[but] not to that extent."

From the moment a predominantly black jury was seated, the media reported a consensus among experts that the prosecution had already lost the case—the only question was whether the jury would deadlock or acquit Simpson. One widely cited poll of practicing lawyers showed nearly a two-thirds majority convinced that at least some African Americans on the jury would vote to acquit for reasons of racial loyalty, regardless of the evidence. Of course, these same lawyers were betting that whites were equally locked into a race-driven conviction of Simpson: hence widespread predictions that the jury would hang. But, as Vanderbilt law professor Nancy J. King shows in her essay, the evidence for race-based voting by jurors is mixed. While there are race-charged cases where appeals to racial solidarity seem to have trumped the evidence (King mentions an all-black jury's failure to convict Washington, D.C., Mayor Marion Barry of using crack cocaine in a D.C. hotel, even after seeing a videotape of the mayor using the drug in the hotel, or the refusal of a Crown Heights jury to convict a black teenager of killing a visiting Jewish student, even though the dying victim identified his killer and the suspect was arrested with the murder weapon on him), she concludes that "a fair reading on the correlation between race and verdict reveals that juror race probably does not matter in most cases."

For reasons to be discussed, the Simpson case may be one of the exceptions. But cavalier attributions of the jurors' verdict to their race conveniently forgets that the two white members of the jury and the one Hispanic quickly agreed with the other nine on unanimous verdicts of not guilty. The brief time for deliberation indicates that the three nonblacks had no desire to hold out and were not beaten down into returning a verdict against their will. And while one African-American juror showed a political attitude toward the case when he raised his fist in the clenched black power salute following the verdicts, we know that another African-American juror, Brenda Moran, had served on five previous juries and on two of them had joined with her fellow jurors in finding the defendants—one of them African-American—guilty of murder.

In general, the media exaggerates the importance of jury selection, because reporters cover trials as mere games of strategy, not rational events moving slowly with the force of evidence. Without bothering to cite anyone in particular, *Newsweek* quoted jury selection experts as concluding that "poor black women may be more tolerant of spousal abuse" and that they might turn on Marcia Clark "as a white woman who was trying to emasculate Simpson." These were irresponsible accusations for which there is no basis. Moreover, although the paucity of college graduates on the jury was a cause for concern, the final jury included a computer technician, an insurance claims adjuster, an environmental health specialist, a postal worker, and a city tax collector. The jury was more than qualified to hear and judge the scientific evidence. Law professor Paul Butler, in his essay, is right to suspect that, had a mostly white jury with only two college graduates convicted Simpson, we would not have heard similar complaints about the jury's incompetence.

Of course, there were two juries who heard and decided the case, and we know far more about the influence of race on the television audience "jury" than on the actual twelve persons in the jury box. The two juries did not see the same trial—much of what the television audience saw or heard (for instance, the full run of Mark Fuhrman's tape-recorded racism or Rosa Lopez's week on the stand), the jury did not fully receive. On the other hand, few of us sat all through the trial, the way the actual jury did. This makes it dangerous to assume that the same racial split occurring in the general public was happening inside the jury. In April 1995, dismissed juror Jeanette Harris fueled media speculation that racial tension was rampant on the jury with her allegations of shoving matches and favoritism of white jurors by the mostly white sheriffs. We now know that these charges were highly exaggerated.

Still, it would be odd if twelve persons selected randomly from the community were wholly immune to racial forces rocking the rest of the public. We ignore at our peril what the Simpson trial revealed about the racial fissures in the foundations of our democracy. Following the jury's not guilty verdicts, 80 percent of African Americans polled by the *Washington Post* agreed with Simpson's acquittal, including 66 percent who expressed strong approval. Fifty-five percent of whites disagreed with the verdicts, including 40 percent who strongly disapproved. After fifteen months of preliminary hearings, pretrial motions, and trial testimony, the racial split in public opinion over O. J. Simpson remained pretty much what it had been on the day of his arrest. This racial split in public opinion is troubling, whether or not it seeped into the jury room.

REASONABLE DOUBT

Contributors to this volume sort through two different explanations for the influence of race on judgments about the defendant, the first centering on reasonable doubts in a minority community long mistreated by the police, the second on unreasonable solidarity even on behalf of a guilty murderer. (American law does not require jurors to give reasons for their verdicts—a feature of jury trials that might be worth changing, on the assumption that the need to justify a verdict in public would push jurors to be more rational in their deliberations. As things stand now, the famous "inscrutability" of jury verdicts lets jurors escape public accountability for their decisions. It also frees the rest of us to put our own spin on the verdict.)

Reasonable doubt exists, Judge Ito instructed the jurors, when they "cannot say they feel an abiding conviction of the truth of the charge" against the defendant. With varying degrees of reluctance, several professors of law contributing to this volume concede that jurors and onlookers acting in good faith rather than racial anger could have found reasons to doubt Simpson's guilt: Barbara Allen Babcock, Paul Butler, Randall Kennedy, and Patricia Williams all make this point, even while expressing their personal belief that Simpson was probably guilty. For Butler, the refusal of a majority of white onlookers to accept a reasonable doubt verdict as legitimate is itself symptomatic of racial problems in the United States: as if only ignorant or racist black jurors could have found the evidence lacking against Simpson.

The reasonableness of reasonable doubt in the Simpson case flows from a number of difficulties. Certainly the principal one was the apparent perjury and racism of Detective Mark Fuhrman, calling into question the truthfulness of his claim to finding blood spots on the door of Simpson's Bronco or finding the bloody glove in a walkway behind the guesthouse on Simpson's estate. One juror, Gina Rosborough, specifically mentioned being bothered that no blood was detected in the walkway leading up to the bloody glove. But defense counsel Alan Dershowitz told a Boston public radio station after the trial that this was a "Vannatter, not Fuhrman" case, referring to lead detective Philip Vannatter. The jury heard Vannatter's painfully false explanation of why he ordered police to scale the walls of Simpson's estate without a search warrant (he did not think Simpson was a murder suspect, he was worried for Simpson's own safety). Later, they heard how Vannatter did not immediately book samples of Simpson's own blood drawn from the accused at police headquarters on June 13 but took the unusual step of driving the blood samples out to Simpson's estate, where he delivered them to the criminologist gathering other blood evidence at the estate. Juror Brenda Moran commented on this oddity in her posttrial interviews, apparently receptive to defense suggestions that the police may have framed Simpson by sprinkling his blood around. Suspicions about police handling of the blood evidence received another boost when a prosecution witness initially conceded that a few centiliters of the blood drawn from Simpson on June 13 could not be accounted for. Yet another suspicious detail was the belated discovery of blood on socks in Simpson's bedroom and on the gates to the walkway where the murders took place—crucial evidence that Dennis Fung, the police criminologist called to the scene on June 13, did not notice in his initial investigation.

The defense also zeroed in on Collin Yamauchi, the DNA analyst for the Los Angeles police. According to the defense, Yamauchi contaminated most of the blood evidence by somehow allowing blood collected from the crime scene to come in contact with samples of Simpson's blood provided to the police and kept in the same lab. Harlan Levy's contribution to this volume rebuts this defense claim.

The defense never clarified whether they were accusing the police of manufacturing evidence or merely contaminating it. Nor did they have to separate out their twin attacks. Grueling cross-examination of criminologist Fung in particular showed a number of careless mistakes. Fung failed to secure Simpson's Bronco at the crime scene and he permitted a police officer to compromise hair fiber evidence by covering Nicole Brown Simpson's body with a blanket from inside the condominium that conceivably could have been an innocent source of Simpson's hairs found near the bodies.

If the jury needed more illustrations of sloppy investigative work, the autopsy provided them in abundance: the contents of Nicole Brown Simpson's stomach were discarded—with them went the chance to set a precise time of murder through examination of the progress of digestion. Knowing from the preliminary hearing just how disastrous a witness the pathologist who performed the autopsy was, the prosecution never called him to the stand during the actual trial. Then too, recounted one juror after the trial, it didn't help that the gloves did not fit Simpson. A cardinal rule for prosecutors is never to ask a question whose answer you do not know, never carry out a demonstration whose results are not preordained. Prosecutor Christopher Darden violated that rule when he asked Simpson to put on the gloves and his gamble lost big time.

In light of these serious evidentiary lapses, Randall Kennedy speaks for many when he concedes the legitimacy of a reasonable doubt verdict in the Simpson case. Still, in a case with nine months of testimony, it was hardly possible that the jury had shifted through all the significant evidence in less than four hours of deliberation. Diana Trilling notes that the speed of the verdict alone suggested that reasonable doubt was a springboard for racial passions. Moreover, there remains the question of why so many more African Americans than whites found it reasonable to doubt the state's evidence? Here Kennedy gives a carefully balanced answer. On the one hand, historical recollection and modern life experiences make minority community members properly suspicious of the criminal justice system, especially when it comes to trials of black men accused of attacks on white women. The jury system is bankrupt if it does not represent these rational suspicions and force often too trusting white jurors to put the state's evidence to the test.

On the other hand, Kennedy fears that some segments of the African-American community have now moved from reasonable to unreasonable doubts about law enforcement. He writes that "there is a paranoid, conspiracy-minded sector of the population that would honestly though irrationally have rejected the state's argument virtually without regard to the evidence" and "even in the absence of Mark Fuhrman's racism and the L.A. police department's incompetence." Patricia Williams echoes this point in her remarks to Charlie Rose about just how large and complicated a conspiracy it would have taken to frame Simpson and to plant so many different pieces of physical evidence. (Although Kennedy and Williams do not draw the comparison, segments of the white community share this paranoid-style thinking about the police, as recent events in Waco, Texas, Ruby Ridge, Idaho, and Oklahoma City show.)

Experts on DNA testing also told the jury that Fung's carelessness was not of the sort that could have produced "false positive" results implicating Simpson. At most his mistakes (for instance, storing blood samples in plastic bags) would have caused the samples to deteriorate and to produce "false negative" results. In other words, tests on a deteriorated sample might have failed to match Simpson's DNA to the sample but they would never have falsely implicated him. The jury must have disregarded this testimony, if they relied on Fung's mistakes as a predicate for reasonable doubt.

Babcock and Trilling separately note the possibility that the jurors misunderstood Judge Ito's instructions on reasonable doubt. Correctly understood, reasonable doubt means that, taking the evidence as a whole, the jury must be convinced to the ultimate level. But the jury may have thought that it should disregard each separate piece of evidence if it had reasonable doubts about it standing alone. This misunderstanding would at least explain the bizarre ending of the trial where the jury asked to have the testimony of Allan Park, the limousine driver, read back to them. Apparently, the jurors decided they had reason to doubt all of Park's otherwise damning testimony simply because he hadn't noticed any white Bronco drive up.

JURY NULLIFICATION

Beyond racial differences over reasonable doubt and police work, contributors to this volume discuss a second, more virulent way in which race may have influenced the jury and trial onlookers. In his closing argument, Johnnie Cochran urged jurors to "police the police" by sending a message that official police racism and misconduct would no longer be tolerated. The implication of Cochran's remarks was that delivering such a message was more important than convicting even a guilty murderer. In this sense, Cochran was suggesting that the jury engage in a practice known as "nullification."

Nullifying juries acquit a defendant they know to be guilty in order to protest either an unjust law (the acquittal of Dr. Jack Kevorkian for violating Michigan's ban on assisted suicide may be an example) or else the unjust behavior of those enforcing otherwise valid laws (the issue in Simpson). There is no concrete evidence that the jury responded to the call for nullification—one of the two white jurors has said she found the argument ludicrous. But what should we make of the cheering crowds outside, mostly African-American, who welcomed the verdicts with a hoopla usually reserved for political victories? Referring to pictures of students at Howard University celebrating the not guilty verdicts, Trilling compares their exhilaration to the "fever of delight" that once possessed witnesses to the fall of the Bastille. This may be putting the point too strongly—whites have a bad habit of telling blacks how to behave—but certainly many celebrants were expressing more than dispassionate satisfaction that reasonable doubt had triumphed.

A more persuasive interpretation of the shouts of joy and scenes of hugging is that segments of the African-American community welcomed the not guilty verdicts as a proud instance of racial solidarity and "racial muscle-flexing" (Kennedy's terms). Here at last was a case where a mostly African-American jury had taken power into its own hands and delivered a retaliatory blow against a pernicious system. Simpson may have been an odd choice to rally the troops around. But few African-American defendants have the clout to take on the system and win. That clout permitted long, overdue payback to the system for all the wrongs suffered by other, undeniably innocent, defendants.

If the Simpson jury did nullify, it would be hard to justify the moral calculations that led them to ignore evidence of Simpson's guilt. Jurors have no higher duty than to convict murderers when proof is there. Nullification should always be a position of last resort, when a vote to convict would be a vote against deep commitments of conscience. But no juror needed to violate his or her conscience to convict Simpson, so long as the evidence warranted conviction. As Kennedy points out, neither juror nor onlooker needed to choose between convicting murderers and protesting police racism: both could and should have been done. If there was rhetorical genius in Johnnie Cochran's closing argument, as critic Stanley Crouch thinks there was, it was in Cochran's ability to sway jurors into thinking they had to choose between standing up for their race and convicting Simpson.

Journalist Jim Sleeper, who covered the trial for the *New York Daily News,* regards Cochran as one of a growing number of "impresarios of racial theater" who wins cases by creating these kinds of false moral dilemmas. While the facts of racism are undeniable, so too for Sleeper are the cynical manipulations of our racial differences. Before O. J. Simpson and Johnnie Cochran, Sleeper maintains, there was the Tawana Brawley episode in New York where the Rev. Al Sharpton and lawyer Alton Maldox for too long supported the lie that Brawley had been abducted and raped by a white police officer. Sleeper quotes the late William Kunstler, perhaps the greatest impresario of trial as racial theater, as saying that "it makes no difference anymore whether the attack on Tawana really happened. It doesn't disguise the fact that a lot of young black women are treated the way she said she was treated."

Trilling echoes Sleeper's indictment when she accuses the defense of "a cruel play upon the feelings of black Americans, adding a bad dream to bad-enough reality." The bad-enough reality is that police such as Mark Fuhrman exist. Still, for Trilling "the story of Simpson's victimization by the police was the creation of his own counsel."

We will never know for certain whether the Simpson jury deliberately engaged in nullification. But what about other cases—is there evidence of any trend toward African-American jurors refusing to convict African-American defendants despite strong evidence of guilt? In his essay, *Congressional Quarterly* researcher Kenneth Jost reports on one post-Simpson case where an African-American juror seemed influenced by the Simpson verdicts to expect an unreasonable amount of proof. The case involved an African-American man arrested by two police officers, both of whom testified to finding both narcotics and a firearm on the defendant. Eleven jurors, some white and some black, were convinced of the defendant's guilt but the twelfth juror, an African-American man, hung the jury. He was annoyed that the police did not bother to corroborate their testimony by presenting fingerprint evidence linking the defendant to the gun. Absent such corroboration, the juror refused to trust the word of the arresting officers.

The day after the Simpson verdicts, the *Wall Street Journal* ran a front-page article suggesting that mostly African-American juries in several urban areas (the Bronx, Detroit, and Washington, D.C.) acquit defendants at a rate far higher than the national average. The *Journal* suggested that the disparity in acquittal rates is evidence of a growing reluctance of African-American jurors to convict fellow blacks. But, as Nancy King points out, the *Journal* numbers are hard to evaluate without information about the proportion of defendants acquitted who are of different racial backgrounds, and whether defendants of different racial backgrounds elect jury trials at the same rate. Moreover, King points out that during the last two decades when the number of African Americans on federal juries was increasing, the acquittal rate of federal juries actually declined. The fact of the matter is that African-American jurors vote to convict African-American defendants all the time.

Since the Simpson verdict, the debate over jury nullification has taken on new urgency. In his essay, Paul Butler defends nullification as an appropriate exercise of black power in certain kinds of cases. Butler is careful to rule out nullification on behalf of persons guilty of crimes of violence—his position is not meant to ratify the Simpson verdict. But for certain nonviolent, "victimless" crimes, especially drug possession, he concludes that incarceration imposes more costs than benefits on the community affected by such crimes. In such cases, "it is . . . the moral responsibility of black jurors to emancipate some guilty black outlaws."

Such a position, Kennedy responds, underestimates "the extent to which the black community in particular needs vigorous, efficient, enthusiastic law enforcement." Police misconduct harms black communities but that harm "pales in comparison to the misery that criminals (most of whom are black) inflict upon black communities." While Kennedy would not rule out nullification entirely (there could be compelling moral reasons to refuse to enforce a law), he is "wary of supporting anything that further depresses law enforcement's ability to apprehend and convict those who prey upon their neighbors."

The debate about whether race unduly influenced jurors to acquit Simpson is likely to continue for some time. But the essays in this volume can help history get its verdict right about the trial, by showing how both evidentiary difficulties and racialized loyalties haunted the case from beginning to end.

DOMESTIC VIOLENCE:
THE DISAPPEARANCE OF AN ISSUE

In the weeks after Nicole Brown Simpson's murder, complaints filed in Los Angeles courts by women alleging they had been beaten nearly doubled. The Los Angeles Commission on Assaults Against Women, accustomed to handling an average of 1,300 calls per month, was flooded with 3,000 calls in June 1994.

In the weeks following the jury's acquittal of Simpson, the number of battered women seeking help was still at higher than pre-Simpson levels. Yet hope seemed far lower. Gloria Steinem told television host Charlie Rose that she had visited battered women in shelters who essentially said their husbands or boyfriends had cut out stories of Simpson's acquittal, put them on refrigerators and said, "See, I can do anything I want to you." Elizabeth M. Schneider reports similarly fearful remarks from battered women who saw the verdict as saying "violence against women is okay." To be fair to the jury, Schneider points out, they probably did not mean to say this at all—we don't know what would have happened had the outrages of police racism not eclipsed the outrages of domestic violence. But that eclipse did occur and a case which promised to bring problems of domestic violence out into the light of day ended up casting a dark shadow over the issue.

By contrast to its initial flurry of concern for data on domestic violence, the media soon lost interest and covered Nicole Brown Simpson less as a battered women than, in Patricia Williams's words, a "sexy, blond bombshell." Deborah L. Rhode quotes a news director at National Public Radio as saying of the domestic violence aspects of the trial that "there's no new angle on that topic."

The media's disinterest in connecting the plight of Nicole Brown Simpson to ordinary victims of battering was so obvious that Patricia Williams fumed to Charlie Rose that the Simpson case would never have been heard from if Simpson had killed a plain, black woman. Michael Eric Dyson shares that sentiment.

Rhode and Schneider make the telling point that, however atypical O. J. Simpson was of African-American defendants, Nicole Simpson was all too representative of battered women failed by the legal system. Here was a woman who reported her abuse on time and yet the most she could get from a court of law was a meaningless sanction that Simpson undergo counseling over the telephone. Simpson's employers took no action at all, even after he pled guilty to one instance of assaulting his wife.

Rhode faults the prosecution for "soft-pedaling" Simpson's extensive record of spousal abuse, out of fear that overemphasis would backfire. Indeed, as Schneider shows, although Judge Ito ruled that nineteen separate incidents or statements involving abuse or stalking were admissible into evidence, the jury never heard about more than a few of them. Even at this late date and after all that has been written on the case, it is an educational eye-opener to read Schneider's list of the full record of O. J. Simpson's abuse and stalking of Nicole Brown Simpson.

To be fair to the prosecution, they did make a strategic decision to lead off their case with key incidents of past abuse. A portrait of Simpson the batterer, the prosecution hoped, would correct his public, "good guy" image and prepare jurors to hear why he murdered his ex-wife.

From what we know of juror reactions, even this limited attention to the past history of Simpson's violence backfired. One juror, Brenda Moran, told reporters she had dismissed evidence of abuse as "irrelevant" to a murder trial—if they wanted to convict Simpson of abuse, she said, they should have sent him to a different courtroom. Michael Knox, a juror who was removed from the panel in March, reports his own reaction to Simpson's beatings of his wife: part of the "ups and downs with spouse and girlfriends." Juror Jeanette Harris was dismissed in April after it was discovered that she had hidden the fact that she had once sought a restraining order against her husband. Ironically, her remarks after dismissal indicated she was favorably disposed toward Simpson.

Brenda Moran's apparent failure to see any connection between Nicole's prior abuse and her murder was a frightening form of denial. "I don't know what's in her heart," Gloria Steinem told Charlie Rose. "[M]aybe she experienced domestic violence and she doesn't want to believe she could be killed. Or maybe she sees it in her neighborhood, and she doesn't want to believe it can escalate."

It may be true that most women who are abused do not end up being murdered by their abuser. But the more apt question for the jury should have been "How many abused women who are murdered are killed by someone else than their abuser?" In this regard, statistics cited by Rhode and Schneider are chilling: about one-third of all female homicide victims are killed by a husband or boyfriend.

The case developed in such a way that many of the eight African-American women on the jury may have felt as if they had to choose between identifying with their race or their gender. As stated earlier, there is no general evidence that African-American women equivocate on issues of domestic violence, a point made by Patricia Williams to Charlie Rose. But Williams also thought it possible that the more the media eroticized Nicole Brown Simpson, the harder it may have become for African-American women to identify with her or not to resent the prurient interest the public took in a case precisely because the battered woman was white and pretty. Moreover, Williams speculates that African-American women jurors may have been reluctant to convict Simpson, because the trial played into loaded stereotypes about the "hypersexualized" black male preying upon white women. In short, the trial walked into a symbolic mine field that posed a false choice between standing by your man and convicting a murderer.

Steinem holds out hope that reactions to Simpson's acquittal might yet have positive results for battered women. In accusing Supreme Court nominee, now Justice Clarence Thomas, of harassing her, Anita Hill lost before the Senate but prevailed in public opinion over the years. History and public opinion may accomplish the same transformation of the Simpson legacy. But this raises a nagging question. When all those people cheered Simpson, they knew for certain that he was a self-confessed batterer of women even if they did not know he was a murderer. This knowledge has not prevented some segments of the community from regarding Simpson as a hero.

LAWYERS: THEIR STRATEGIES AND THEIR ETHICS

In the beginning, Robert Shapiro; in the end, Johnnie Cochran: *sic gloria transit mundi.* Media and public fascination with lawyers as personality figures was rampant: in a case with two butchered bodies, what difference did it make how Marcia Clark wore her hair? But if anything illustrates Lincoln Caplan's condemnation of the quality of legal journalism today, it was the cult of personality showered on the lawyers. Not only the TV tabloids portrayed lawyers as celebrities but the venerable *New York Times Magazine* ran a lead story on Robert Shapiro, declared him the most famous lawyer in America, told us everything about his private life, and all just in time to watch him retire into a swivel chair for the duration of the trial.

Cochran's influence on the jury is debatable, but his stature in the outside community is undeniable. Cultural critic Michael Eric Dyson explains why so many African Americans came to regard Cochran as a modern-day Joe Louis: another slugger showing that black men have what it takes. In this sense, it was as important that Cochran win as that O.J. win and their fates became entwined for onlookers. Victory confirmed that Cochran could outsmart and outtalk the white lawyers in their own arena. Critic Stanley Crouch agrees, remarking that "in the heat of battle, the man was extraordinary" and that "to bellow and whine about 'the race card' is to deny the fact that this man proved, day by day, that he is the best lawyer in the whole town."

A great misfortune is that prosecutor Christopher Darden did not emerge as a similar source for black pride and a role model for African Americans aspiring to be lawyers. The importance of recruiting minorities into prosecutorial positions is as crucial as recruiting minorities onto the police force. Yet Darden was predictably left out in the cold, suspected by many of being assigned to the case only to lend a black face to the prosecution. Darden deserved a better public reception. His rhetorical skills may not match those of Cochran but his performance was steady throughout, his demolition of Rosa Lopez superb, and his closing argument, with its appeals to juror rationality, was powerful.

Although the trial did much to enhance the reputation of a few lawyers, it may end up damaging the standing of lawyers in general. An American Bar Association Journal/Gallup poll found that respect both for lawyers and for the criminal justice system as a whole dropped dramatically after the trial was under way. Trilling is critical of the bad manners lawyers on both sides displayed throughout the trial, treating both the judge and their opponents without even minimal civility. What the public saw, she bemoans, was that the lawyers themselves treated the trial as a circus and trampled on the sense of decorum without which the rule of law is impossible.

The whole issue of the "race card" was another debating point about the behavior of the lawyers. As the trial dragged on, the defense became more successful in putting the LAPD on trial and in focusing attention on the horror of police racism rather than the horror of the murders themselves. The question for many Americans is what to make of lawyering whose skill had much to do with turning the tables so that Simpson the defendant became Simpson the victim.

Cochran is on record as saying that "race plays a part of everything in America" but he irately insisted after the trial that race was introduced into the case by the prosecution when it put a known racist such as Fuhrman on the stand. At that point, Fuhrman's credibility was a key and legitimate issue in the case. Cochran is certainly right to complain that any defense lawyer who did not attack the credibility of a racist cop with a hatred of interracial couples and who bragged about planting evidence in other cases would have been guilty of malpractice. Robert Shapiro's sudden attack of conscience after the trial ("Not only did we play the race card, we dealt it from the bottom of the deck") seemed more the remark of a wounded ego than a serious student of legal ethics.

In our adversary system of justice, it fell to the prosecution to convince the jury that even a rogue, racist cop such as Fuhrman did not have the opportunity to plant all the evidence incriminating Simpson. Clark, Darden, Brian Kellogg, and the rest of the prosecution struggled mightily to do just that, and introduced a mountain of physical and statistical evidence that the media had a hard time summarizing for the public. For instance, prosecutors presented DNA evidence showing that blood found in Simpson's Ford Bronco matched not only his own but also that of both victims. The likelihood that even a racist cop could have planted Ronald Goldman's blood inside Simpson's Bronco seems infinitesimally small. And there was an avalanche of similarly damning evidence presented by the prosecution—hair fibers matching those of Simpson's found in a knit cap at the murder scene; bloody footprints matching the size and kind of shoes Simpson wore; the one in billion odds that blood found on one of the gloves came from anyone besides Ron Goldman, the one in many billions odds that blood on socks in Simpson's bedroom came from anyone else than Nicole Brown Simpson. Judged rationally, the cumulative force of this evidence certainly outweighed the Fuhrman factor and prosecutors did a first-rate job of walking jurors through the meaning of DNA testing.

But the prosecution never succeeded in giving the jury the will to follow the evidence. Here the work of defense lawyers Barry Scheck and Peter Neufeld was crucial. As one Los Angeles defense lawyer put it, Cochran won the contest for the jury's will: he made them *want* to disbelieve the evidence. Scheck and Neufeld followed up by showing the jury why it was legitimate to act on that desire.

In one sense, Scheck and Neufeld were the real hired guns in the case. Whereas much of their past work focused on using DNA test results to prove the innocence of convicted prisoners, this time they attacked the reliability of the DNA evidence. Of course, their claim was that the LAPD's handling of the evidence compromised blood samples even before they could be shipped out for DNA testing at a Cellmark laboratory in Maryland or the state lab at Berkeley. For many onlookers, Scheck's relentless cross-examination of criminologist Dennis Fung was the turning point in the trial, when the defense finally made its case that contamination of the blood samples made DNA test results unreliable.

Could the prosecution have done anything which would have changed the verdicts? Probably not. But certain questions linger. Among them are why the prosecutors decided not to introduce into evidence Simpson's original statement to the police on June 13 or his rambling "farewell" note left on the day he took off in Al Cowlings's Bronco? In the June 13th statement, police ask Simpson how blood got on and in his car on the night of the murders and Simpson explained he had cut himself. When Simpson was arrested, he was photographed with cuts on his fingers but he claimed those cuts came only after he learned of his wife's death while in a Chicago hotel room. These two versions of where and when he cut himself are not consistent and it is not clear why the prosecution elected not to use the June 13th statement where Simpson admits to bleeding the night of the murders.

It is also a mystery why the prosecution did not make use of Simpson's "farewell" letter and his subsequent flight. While there are many innocent explanations for flight, the letter's remarks about "loving Nicole too much" and being a "lost" person betray some level of guilt, especially when coupled with the fact that Simpson took off with a passport, $8,000, and a disguise.

REFORMS: PROPOSALS FOR JURIES, POLICE, AND PROSECUTORS

The Simpson trial has spawned a number of proposals for jury reform, as essays by Albert W. Alschuler, Barbara Allen Babcock, Andrew Hacker, Kenneth Jost, Nancy J. King, and Michael Lind show. Lind urges the most radical reform: he would abolish the jury as we know it and substitute the civil law system where a panel of professional and lay judges together decides cases. Alschuler lists twelve particular reforms that might make juries work better. Babcock argues the jury system is not broken. She warns that the pieces of the jury system form an organic whole and one feature cannot be lopped off without threatening the whole. Some reform proposals—chiefly the move to eliminate peremptory challenges and unanimous verdicts—strike her as motivated by a "bald desire for more convictions." This desire ignores just how unusual Simpson's acquittal was and the fact that the jury conviction rate has remained steady in the 60 to 70 percent range for the last half-century.

Drawing on his own service on five juries, Andrew Hacker also agrees that juries work well, even if the textbook description of juries deciding facts but leaving the law to the judge is a fiction. Hacker turns to the first Menendez trial to illustrate the complexity jurors in murder cases often face and he finds in dismissed Simpson juror Michael Knox's book a firsthand account of why not to sequester juries.

King and Jost provide two of the most comprehensive surveys available on the myriad of jury reform proposals spawned by the Simpson trial. Bills to permit nonunanimous verdicts in certain criminal cases have been introduced in the legislatures of California, New Jersey, New Mexico, and New York. The Illinois legislature has pending before it a bill prohibiting the use of any nonlawyer jury consultants. New York and Louisiana are debating proposals to reduce the number of peremptory challenges available to litigants. Louisiana, New York, and Tennessee are considering bills that would make sequestration of juries even less likely than it currently is—nationally only one jury out of every hundred is sequestered.

The Simpson trial certainly demonstrated the need to speed up trials and to treat jurors with more respect. Babcock is especially critical of Judge Ito for wasting so much of the jurors' time and urges judges to hear motions in the evenings and to hold court on Saturdays to keep trials moving along. Alschuler and Jost outline recent reforms aimed at giving the jury a more active role in trials. These include the right to take notes (something Judge Ito did allow), to ask questions of witnesses (submitting them first to the judge) and to discuss the evidence during trial, so long as jurors reserve final judgment.

None of these jury reforms would prevent a recurrence of the racial drama enacted during the Simpson trial. That would require fundamental changes in police treatment of minorities and minority attitudes toward police. In his essay, Joseph D. McNamara, former police chief of San Jose, urges the LAPD to abandon its traditional style of "military policing" that so alienates minorities. He finds insufficient contact and communication between rank-and-file police officers and the neighbors they patrol. This could change if the LAPD would follow the example of other big-city departments and engage in a more community-oriented police style, where officers leave their patrol cars to walk the beat, to attend various neighborhood meetings, to go into the schools, and in general to "hear what the people think of them."

In regard to drugs, McNamara believes the greatest challenge is to be found. The military model advocates declaring war on drugs and taking the assault right into the inner city. The predictable result is that African Americans experience themselves as living in a police state. The key to real change in relations between police and minorities, McNamara concludes, is in ending the drug war and involving the police in partnerships with other service agencies that provide treatment and prevention programs.

For such a partnership to emerge, attitudes in minority communities toward the police also have to change. McNamara echoes points made by Randall Kennedy when he writes that "the minority community, which has the highest crime rates, must come to realize that it suffers the most when law enforcement fails to punish violent criminals."

The Simpson case also exposed difficulties in the District Attorney's Office. When I served as an assistant district attorney in Middlesex County, Massachusetts, it was standard practice for police officers to come to us for advice on searches with or without a warrant. The District Attorney for whom I worked had put police departments on notice that, to the extent time and circumstances allowed, they should seek legal advice before conducting a warrantless search. The acclaimed novelist Scott Turow, himself a former federal prosecutor, makes a similar point about the working relationship between the United States Attorney's Office and federal agents in Illinois. But apparently, the LAPD and District Attorney's Office did not have even this minimal safeguard in place. In Turow's judgment, this permitted the LAPD to conduct a palpably illegal search of Simpson's estate. Instead of rejecting illegally obtained evidence, the L.A. District Attorney greedily made use of it, especially the bloody glove, and suffered the consequences. Common sense alone would have alerted jurors that the police were liars when they said they went to Simpson's house the night of the murders without a thought in the world that he might be a suspect—even though they knew he had formerly beaten his ex-wife. These initial police illegalities conditioned the jury to look at the police work in the case with a jaundiced eye. Had the District Attorney's Office done its job of policing the police, Turow concludes, the jury might not have felt it was left to them to do the job.

CAMERAS IN THE COURTROOM?

An estimated 150 million Americans watched the reading of the jury verdicts, surpassing all previous television viewing records. Court TV provided gavel-to-gavel coverage throughout the trial. CNN devoted some 631 hours of coverage to the trial, attracting an audience five times the size of its normal viewership.

Was it good or bad that people could avoid the media spins on the trial, turn on their TV sets, and judge the trial and defendant for themselves? The cases for and against cameras in the courtroom are both straightforward. Supporters claim that cameras do not change what goes on in the courtroom—they just show home viewers what has been taking place all these years in their absence. Cameras thus serve the public's right to know about the judiciary and can also be an important forum of civic education. In the Simpson case, for instance, viewers would have learned about grand juries, preliminary hearings, motions to suppress evidence, search and seizure law, selecting juries and the role of jury consultants, admissibility of prior bad acts, scope of open and closing arguments, rules of discovery, hearsay, relevance of dreams, qualifying expert witnesses, validity of DNA evidence and hair fiber samples, establishing chain of custody, and deciding whether the defendant should testify. Georgetown law professor Paul Rothstein considers the videotapes of the trial to be such a valuable teaching tool that he is devising an "All O.J." evidence course.

Court TV, which provided the cameras for live coverage of the Simpson case, has 24 million subscribers nationwide and has televised more than 400 trials in the past four years. Supporters of televising trials make a number of arguments for expanding the presence of cameras in the court. First, televising the Simpson trial served its purpose in a democracy by making the public question various aspects of the system. Second, to the extent the Simpson trial was atypical, the solution is to broadcast more trials, not to pull the plug entirely. Court TV emphasizes it is dedicated to showing ordinary criminal and civil cases, as well as sensational ones. Third, the real "garbage coverage" of the Simpson trial stemmed from out-of-court sources concentrating on anything other than the mundane details of the trial testimony itself. Gavel-to-gavel coverage gives us "the most truthful depiction of what actually happens in court" and is a check not only on government but bad journalism as well.

The argument against cameras in the courtroom is that their presence inevitably changes what goes on during the trial, as lawyers and judges play to the camera, and as jurors off camera learn the whole world is watching. Critics say much valuable time was wasted as big egos such as Cochran or Clark or F. Lee Bailey soaked up as much camera time as possible, and found it necessary to spar with one another over issues that had no trial importance but plenty of importance for the lawyers' own reputations with the television audience. In her essay, Barbara Allen Babcock particularly faults Judge Ito for losing control over the trial and speculates that he was intimidated by the presence of cameras.

Perhaps the most serious indictment of televised trials has to do with its effect on the public, not trial participants. Public confidence in justice demands that courtrooms remain places of decorum and of quiet and rational procedure. But televising a trial attracts all kinds of tabloid sideshows into the vicinity. Coverage of the actual trial becomes an excuse for titillating kiss-and-tell stories or lurid looks at the lifestyles of the rich and famous. Inevitably, a circuslike atmosphere thus descends upon the televised trial in ways that pollute the public perceptions of justice.

By contrast, when television cameras were barred from the South Carolina trial of Susan Smith for drowning her two children, the pack of journalists covering the trial thinned, the trial proceeded at a brisk pace, and the public was given direct coverage of the trial without the carnival atmosphere. A similar sense of quiet and decorum surrounded the retrial of the Menendez brothers in Los Angeles, when the judge barred cameras from the court.

Lawyer and journalist Lincoln Caplan offers a criticism of legal journalism that goes beyond television cameras. The Simpson trial showed what the "new" journalism does at its best and its worst. At its best, it expands trial coverage enormously—in addition to TV blanket coverage, the major news magazines ran ten cover stories on the Simpson trial just between June 1994 and April 1995. At its worst, the "new" journalism shuns ideas in favor of personalities and treats trials as games of strategy rather than debates about serious issues of justice. Television coverage may be the biggest culprit in delivering "information without knowledge" but Caplan faults print journalists as well for being captives of the cult of lawyers as celebrities. The end result is that legal reporting "has become increasingly like sports and political reporting, a form of play-by-play" consumed by the narrowest of concerns with who's winning and losing.

MONEY

For Trilling, the "m" word was more important than the "n" word at Simpson's trial. Employing up to sixteen different lawyers and countless assistants and investigators, Simpson spent a reported $10 million on his defense. Few fault Simpson for purchasing the best justice he could afford or lawyers for charging him their high fees, but Trilling suggests we should tell the truth about money buying justice by requiring expert witnesses to inform the jury what they are being paid for their testimony.

Every contributor to this volume agrees there is something fundamentally wrong with a criminal justice system that leaves the average criminal defendant poorly represented while lavishing extravagant resources on the few. Simpson got a lucky break when tape recordings of Mark Fuhrman's racism surfaced in North Carolina but money paid to a private investigator made that luck possible. The ordinary defendant rarely has the resources to scour the country for exonerating evidence—as Rhode points out, the average legal fee a court-appointed attorney bills the government in many jurisdictions is $400. That is why, even on the same evidence, the poor get convicted but the rich buy reasonable doubt.

For some time to come, O. J. Simpson is likely to be a convenient reference for those who think the system coddles criminals or that trial procedures somehow favor the defense. As Yale Kamisar, Rhode, Babcock, and Williams argue in particular, these would be extremely wrong conclusions to draw about a system where nine of every ten persons charged with a crime does not even elect a trial but pleads guilty. In particular, lessons are being drawn that make the poor black defendant more invisible than ever. Functionally speaking, the Simpson trial as spectacle served to divert public attention for over a year from the real issues of poverty and justice as they affect ordinary defendants. By substituting O. J. Simpson for all defendants, particularly those who are poor or African-American or both, policymakers continue to milk the trial as an excuse for pursuing reforms that would make life harder on defendants. Kamisar's historical essay shows just how old and repetitive are these cries of "we are living through a crime crisis and cannot afford rights for criminal defendants anymore."

Whether we approve or not, the Simpson case became an occasion for a national conversation about race relations, police work, lawyer ethics, jury behavior, domestic violence, and televised trials. That conversation is still ongoing and the contributors to this book are important voices to hear.

PART I

Race

Its Influence on the Jury and Public Opinion

Reasonable v. Unreasonable Doubt

RANDALL KENNEDY

The acquittal of O. J. Simpson brought to an end an extraordinary criminal trial that attracted, like a magnet, anxieties over crime, sex, race, and the possibility of reaching truth and dispensing justice in an American courtroom. Even after many months, the jury's not guilty verdict is difficult to interpret since juries are not required to give reasons for the conclusions they reach and since, even if jurors do articulate their reasons to reporters, there remains the problem of deciphering them and distinguishing expressed views from real bases of decision.

My own view is that the verdict represented a combination of three beliefs. One is that the prosecution simply failed to prove that O. J. Simpson was guilty beyond a reasonable doubt. Reasonable people could have come to this conclusion. After all, police investigators displayed remarkable incompetence, the prosecution erred mightily—remember the gloves that did not fit!—and, of course, there was the despicable Mark Fuhrman. Even with help given by several questionable judicial rulings before the trial and near the end, the prosecution did permit a reasonable juror to vote to acquit on the basis of the evidence presented. I disagree with that conclusion. But I do concede that it could have been reached reasonably and in good faith.

If this belief is what prompted the decision of all twelve of the jurors who acquitted Simpson, their decision has little broader cultural significance than that reasonable jurors sometimes come to different conclusions than those which many observers favor. I doubt, though, that this belief was the only or even the dominant predicate for the acquittal. I say this based on what I have heard many people say and write about the evidence presented at the trial and also on the remarkably short time that the jury deliberated. If the jury was at all representative of the American public, particularly that sector of the public which leaned toward acquittal, it was probably influenced considerably by two other beliefs.

The first is characterized by an unreasonable suspicion of law enforcement authorities. This is the thinking of people who would have voted to acquit O. J. Simpson even in the absence of Mark Fuhrman's racism and the L.A. police department's incompetence and even in the face of evidence that was more incriminating than that which was produced at trial. There is a paranoid, conspiracy-minded sector of the population that would honestly though irrationally have rejected the state's argument virtually without regard to the evidence.

One of the things that nourishes much of this community, particularly that part comprised of African Americans, is a vivid and bitter memory of wrongful convictions of innocent black men and wrongful acquittals of guilty white men. A key example of the former were the convictions of the Scottsboro Boys in the 1930s for allegedly raping two white women. Now it is widely believed that these young men were framed. A key example of the latter was the acquittal of the murderers of Emmett Till forty years ago. In the face of overwhelming evidence of guilt, an all-white jury in Sumner, Mississippi, took an hour and seven minutes to acquit two white men who later acknowledged that they had killed Till for having whistled at the wife of one of them. Asked why the jury had taken an hour to deliberate, one of the jurors declared that it would not have taken so long if they hadn't paused for a drink of soda pop.

Some readers may find it hard to believe that these despicable events of sixty and forty years ago influence the way that people now evaluate people and events. But just as some in the Balkans remember battles fought 600 years ago as if they happened yesterday, so too do many blacks recall with pained disgust the racially motivated miscarriages of justice that they have helplessly witnessed or been told about. That recollection, refreshed occasionally by more recent outrages, prompts them to regard prosecutions against black men— especially black men accused of attacking white women—with such an intense level of skepticism that they demand more than that which should convince most reasonable people of guilt beyond a reasonable doubt.

A third belief is that to which Johnnie Cochran appealed directly in his summation when he pleaded with jurors to help "police the police." This belief animates jury nullification. By nullification, I mean the act of voting for acquittal even though you know that, in terms of the rules laid down by the judge, the evidence warrants conviction. A nullifier votes to acquit not because of dissatisfaction with the evidence but because, in the phrase of choice nowadays, he wants "to send a message." In many locales, black people in particular want to send a message that they are way past tolerating anti-black racism practiced by police and that they are willing to voice their protest in a wide variety of ways, including jury nullification. Frustrated, angry, and politically self-aware, some black citizens have decided to take their protest against racism in the criminal justice system to the vital and vulnerable innards of that system: the jury box.

In a certain way, the specter of this sort of jury nullification represents an advance in American race relations. Not too long ago, blacks' dissatisfactions with the criminal justice system could often be largely ignored without significant immediate consequence because whites, on a racial basis, excluded them from decisionmaking. Invisible in courthouses, except as defendants, blacks could safely be permitted to stew in their own resentments. Now, however, because of salutary reforms, blacks are much more active in the administration of criminal justice and thus much more able to influence it.

Notwithstanding this advance, however, the current state of affairs as revealed by the Simpson case is marked by several large and tragic failures. The first and most important is the failure on the part of responsible officials to clearly, publicly, and wholeheartedly abjure racism of the sort that Mark Fuhrman displayed during his hateful career as a police officer. Fuhrman's prejudice and his ability to act on it likely had much to do with O. J. Simpson's acquittal. His bigotry provided a vivid basis for the argument that the police framed Simpson. His bigotry also provided an emotionally satisfying basis upon which to follow Cochran's invitation to "send a message" by voting to acquit. In other words, the state inflicted upon itself a grievous wound when its representatives failed to establish a rigorous, anti-racist personnel policy that might have obviated the problem that ultimately crippled the prosecution most. Perhaps more headway on this front will now be made; practicality and morality dictate a more vigorous push against racism in law enforcement circles.

A second failure has occurred within the ranks of those who cheered the acquittal. I have no objection to cheers based on the assumption that the jury system worked properly, that is, cheers based on an honest and reasonable perception that the acquittal has freed a man against whom there existed too little evidence for a conviction. I get the impression, though, that there are other sentiments being voiced in the celebrations of some observers, including feelings of racial solidarity, yearnings to engage in racial muscle-flexing, and a peculiar urge to protect the hero status of a man whose standing within the black community rose precipitously by dint of being charged with murder.

The failure of those moved by these sentiments is twofold. First, such feelings can only predominate by minimizing the stark fact that two people were brutally murdered and by resisting the claim that *whoever* committed that dastardly deed ought to be legally punished, regardless of his color and regardless of the racism of Mark Fuhrman and company. To subordinate the need to convict a murderer to the need to protest the intolerability of official racism is a moral mistake. Both could have been done and should have been done. Contrary to the logic of Johnnie Cochran's summation, neither jurors nor onlookers were trapped in a situation in which they had to choose one imperative over the other. Second, as a practical matter, it cannot be emphasized too frequently the extent to which the black community in particular needs vigorous, efficient, enthusiastic law enforcement. As bad as racist police misconduct is, it pales in comparison to the misery that criminals (most of whom are black) inflict upon black communities. After all, blacks are four times as likely as whites to be raped, three times as likely to be robbed, twice as likely to be assaulted, and seven times as likely to be murdered.

The problem of criminality perpetrated by blacks is the one that many black political leaders appear to have trouble discussing thoroughly. A good many prefer condemning white racist police to focusing on ways to render life in black communities more secure against ordinary criminals. That Simpson allegedly killed two white people makes him in some eyes far easier to rally around than had he allegedly killed two black people. This difference in sympathy based on the race of victims is itself a profoundly destructive racialist impulse, one deeply rooted in our political culture. But there is yet another difficulty with this particular racialist response. Like so much else about the Simpson case, the racial demographics of those who were killed was atypical. Because the more typical scenario features black victims of murder, those who claim to speak on behalf of blacks' interests should be extremely wary of supporting anything that further depresses law enforcement's ability to apprehend and convict those who prey upon their neighbors.

In the days immediately after the jury acquitted Simpson, I wrote that the result, like so much of the trial itself, left me—normally an optimist—overcome by a sense of profound gloom. Although it will take years to place the trial into proper perspective, nothing I have learned so far lifts the gloom entirely.

Black Jurors: Right to Acquit?

PAUL BUTLER

When I heard the verdict in the O. J. Simpson case I wanted to cheer, but I was the only black person in the room. When I saw the long faces of my colleagues on the law faculty, I thought: Here we go again. More evidence of the cold war between whites and blacks. But when I saw how angry some of my fellow law professors were, I got angry too. Why don't so many white people get it? Are they racist or just stupid?

On television, many white people watched with horror as some of my sisters and brothers, bolder than me, publicly rejoiced over the verdict. Among themselves, some whites asked a question like mine: Are black people racist or just stupid? We are neither. We were applauding not so much for the Juice as for justice. At last the criminal justice could work for an African-American man. Even one charged with violence against a white woman, an allegation with historical resonance in the United States—go look at the strange fruit on the limbs of Southern trees. Many of us do not doubt that O.J. bought himself that reasonable doubt with a lot of cash, but we also know that's how criminal justice works in the United States. Most white people did not seem to take it so personally when it worked that way for rich white men like John DeLorean, William Kennedy Smith, and Claus von Bulow.

For people who think criminal justice failed because O.J. was acquitted, I guess the system only would have worked right if he had been convicted. That makes me wonder why those persons wanted a trial at all.

Ironically, the jurors who rendered the verdict were among the least demonstrative of any of the African Americans who were televised reacting to it. Most of them did not even look at the defendant when they announced their decision to free him. I think the reason those jurors were not so happy is because, like me, they thought he *probably* did it. Nonetheless, like me, they also had reasonable doubt. "Probably guilty" is not good enough under the Constitution, so in returning the verdict those jurors are heroes—the truest American patriots.

Simply because the jury rightfully acquitted on reasonable doubt doesn't mean that race was not a factor in the jury's verdict. What is reasonable to a black person may not be reasonable to a white person, especially in matters involving the police.

There was reasonable doubt about the integrity of the evidence. When I was a federal prosecutor in Washington, D.C., we spent weeks learning about the importance of the chain of custody of evidence—precisely because a lot of jurors do not and should not trust the evidence when police work is as sloppy as it was in the Simpson case. As well, there may have been reasonable doubt about Simpson's motive, the timing of the sequence of events, and what the DNA really proved.

And obviously there was reasonable doubt about Mark Fuhrman. Why should any juror believe anything from a prosecution team that embraced a racist cop so warmly? Recall prosecutor Christopher Darden's original questioning of Fuhrman: "Oh, Mr. Police Officer, sir, isn't it awful when those mean defense attorneys call you a racist? I feel your pain." And when the defense revealed what the prosecution should have known all along—namely, that Fuhrman is a proud white supremacist with a license to kill black people—the government's strategy changed, although it still defied logic. We heard Marcia Clark's new theory of the case in her closing argument: Okay, Mark Fuhrman is a racist, and he especially hates interracial couples, and sometimes he plants evidence and then he lies under oath, but what does that have to do with the O. J. Simpson case?

When Johnnie Cochran pointed out the ridiculousness of this argument, some white people had the temerity to accuse him of injecting race in the case. They could not see race had been there all along, or at least as soon as Fuhrman reported to the scene of the crime. They could not see because they do not believe what black people tell them about race and criminal justice until they see or hear it for themselves, as they saw with Rodney King and heard with Mark Fuhrman. And even when they hear it they don't know what to make of it: the police were nice to them when they came to get the cat out of the tree.

My earliest encounter with a police officer occurred when I was ten years old and foolish enough to ride my bike to an all-white neighborhood. A white policeman drove his car next to me and asked if the bike I was riding was mine. I answered yes, and as I sped off I asked the cop if his car belonged to him. When I got home and told my mother what I had done, she spanked me good. Didn't I know what happened to black boys who talked to the police like that?

If that is my most unpleasant experience with a police officer, I am one lucky black man. That is why I understood the power of Johnnie Cochran's closing argument, when he told the jurors to acquit O.J. to send a message to the police. The message that racism is wrong is one the police badly need, but jurors in a violent murder case are not the best messengers. Cochran's argument encouraging an acquittal on this basis was unfortunate. The jurors who have spoken to the press suggest this argument was also unnecessary, in light of the government's failure to prove its case.

Let's be realistic: if black jurors could be inflamed to disregard evidence and render verdicts based on emotion, then many defense attorneys would play the race card every day. In the District of Columbia, for example, there are mostly black jurors and mostly black defendants. There also is a conviction rate of over 70 percent for violent felonies, so it is clear that black jurors don't always use their jury vote to make a political point.

My experience tells me, however, that sometimes they do. For the remainder of this essay I make an argument as to why I believe, in selected cases, this practice is in the best interests of the African-American community.

In 1990 I was a Special Assistant United States Attorney in the District of Columbia. I prosecuted people accused of misdemeanor crimes, mainly the drug and gun cases that overwhelm the local courts of most American cities. As a federal prosecutor, I represented the United States of America and used that power to put people, mainly African-American men, in prison. I am also an African-American man. During that time, I made two discoveries that profoundly changed the way I viewed my work as a prosecutor and my responsibilities as a black person.

The first discovery occurred during a training session for new assistants conducted by experienced prosecutors. We rookies were informed that we would lose many of our cases, despite having persuaded a jury beyond a reasonable doubt that the defendant was guilty. We would lose because some black jurors would refuse to convict black defendants whom they knew were guilty.

The second discovery was related to the first but was even more unsettling. It occurred during the trial of Marion Barry, then the second-term mayor of the District of Columbia. Barry was being prosecuted by my office for drug possession and perjury. I learned, to my surprise, that some of my fellow African-American prosecutors hoped that the mayor would be acquitted, despite the fact that he was obviously guilty of at least one of the charges—an FBI videotape plainly showed him smoking crack cocaine. These black prosecutors wanted their office to lose its case because they believed that the prosecution of Barry was racist.

There is an increasing perception that some African-American jurors vote to acquit black defendants for racial reasons, sometimes explained as the juror's desire not to send another black man to jail. There is considerable disagreement over whether it is appropriate for a black juror to do so. I now believe that, for pragmatic and political reasons, the black community is better off when some nonviolent lawbreakers remain in the community rather than go to prison. The decision as to what kind of conduct by African Americans ought to be punished is better made by African Americans, based on their understanding of the costs and benefits to their community, than by the traditional criminal justice process, which is controlled by white lawmakers and white law enforcers. Legally, African-American jurors who sit in judgment of African-American accused persons have the power to make that decision. Considering the costs of law enforcement to the black community, and the failure of white lawmakers to come up with any solutions to black antisocial conduct other than incarceration, it is, in fact, the moral responsibility of black jurors to emancipate some guilty black outlaws.

Why would a black juror vote to let a guilty person go free? Assuming the juror is a rational, self-interested actor, she must believe that she is better off with the defendant out of prison than in prison. But how could any rational person believe that about a criminal?

Imagine a country in which a third of the young male citizens are under the supervision of the criminal justice system—either awaiting trial, in prison, or on probation or parole. Imagine a country in which two-thirds of the men can anticipate being arrested before they reach age thirty. Imagine a country in which there are more young men in prison than in college. Such a country is a police state. When we think of a police state, we think of a society whose fundamental problem lies not with the citizens of the state but rather with the form of government, and with the powerful elites in whose interest the state exists. Similarly, racial critics of American criminal justice locate the problem not with black prisoners but with the state and its actors and beneficiaries.

The black community also bears very real costs by having so many African Americans, particularly males, incarcerated or otherwise involved in the criminal justice system. These costs include the large percentage of black children who live in female-headed, single-parent households; a perceived dearth of men "eligible" for marriage; the lack of male role models for black children, especially boys; the absence of wealth in the black community; and the large unemployment rate among black men.

According to a recent *USA Today*/CNN/Gallup poll, 66 percent of blacks believe that the criminal justice system is racist. Interestingly, other polls suggest that blacks also tend to be more worried about crime than whites; this seems logical when one considers that blacks are more likely to be victims of crime. This enhanced concern, however, does not appear to translate into black support for tougher enforcement of criminal law. For example, substantially fewer blacks than whites support the death penalty, and many more blacks than whites were concerned with the potential racial consequences of the strict provisions of last year's crime bill. Along with significant evidence from popular culture, these polls suggest that a substantial portion of the African-American community sympathizes with racial critiques of the criminal justice system.

African-American jurors who endorse these critiques are in a unique position to act on their beliefs when they sit in judgment of a black defendant. As jurors, they have the power to convict the accused person or to set him free. May the responsible exercise of that power include voting to free a black defendant whom the juror believes is guilty? The answer is "yes," based on the legal doctrine known as jury nullification.

Jury nullification occurs when a jury acquits a defendant whom it believes is guilty of the crime with which he is charged. In finding the defendant not guilty, the jury ignores the facts of the case and/or the judge's instructions regarding the law. Instead, the jury votes its conscience.

The prerogative of juries to nullify has been part of English and American law for centuries. There are well-known cases from the Revolutionary War era when American patriots were charged with political crimes by the British Crown and acquitted by American juries. Black slaves who escaped to the North and were prosecuted for violation of the Fugitive Slave Law were freed by Northern juries with abolitionist sentiments. Some Southern juries refused to punish white violence against African Americans, especially black men accused of crimes against white women.

The Supreme Court has officially disapproved of jury nullification but has conceded that it has no power to prohibit jurors from engaging in it; the Bill of Rights does not allow verdicts of acquittal to be reversed, regardless of the reason for the acquittal. Criticism of nullification has centered on its potential for abuse. The criticism suggests that when twelve members of a jury vote their conscience instead of the law, they corrupt the rule of law and undermine the democratic process that made the law.

There is no question that jury nullification is subversive of the rule of law. Nonetheless, most legal historians agree that it was morally appropriate in the cases of the white American revolutionaries and the runaway slaves. The issue, then, is whether African Americans today have the moral right to engage in this same subversion.

Most moral justifications of the obligation to obey the law are based on theories of "fair play." Citizens benefit from the rule of law; that is why it is just that they are burdened with the requirement to follow it. Yet most blacks are aware of countless historical examples in which African Americans were not afforded the benefit of the rule of law: think, for example, of the existence of slavery in a republic purportedly dedicated to the proposition that all men are created equal, or the law's support of state-sponsored segregation even after the Fourteenth Amendment guaranteed blacks equal protection. That the rule of law ultimately mended some of the large holes in the American fabric is evidence more of its malleability than its goodness; the rule of law previously had justified the holes. If the rule of law is a myth, or at least not valid for African Americans, the argument that jury nullification undermines it loses force.

A similar argument can be made regarding the criticism that jury nullification is antidemocratic. This is precisely why many African Americans endorse it; it is perhaps the only legal power black people have to escape the tyranny of the majority. Black people have had to beg white decisionmakers for most of the rights they have. Jury nullification affords African Americans the power to determine justice for themselves in individual cases, regardless of whether white people agree or even understand.

At this point, African Americans should ask themselves whether the operation of the criminal law system in the United States advances the interests of black people. If it does not, the doctrine of jury nullification offers African-American jurors an opportunity to "opt out" of American criminal law.

How far should they go—completely to anarchy, or is there someplace between here and there that is safer than both? I propose the following: In cases involving violent malum in se (inherently bad) crimes, such as murder, rape, and assault, jurors should consider the case strictly on the evidence presented, and if they believe the accused person is guilty, they should so vote. In cases involving nonviolent, malum prohibitum (legally proscribed) offenses, including "victimless" crimes such as narcotics possession, there should be a presumption in favor of nullification. Finally, for nonviolent, malum in se crimes, such as theft or perjury, there need be no presumption in favor of nullification, but it ought to be an option the juror considers. A juror might vote for acquittal, for example, when a poor woman steals from Tiffany's but not when the same woman steals from her next-door neighbor.

How would a juror decide individual cases under my proposal? Easy cases would include a defendant who has possessed crack cocaine and an abusive husband who kills his wife. The former should be acquitted and the latter should go to prison.

Difficult scenarios would include the drug dealer who operates in the ghetto and the thief who burglarizes the home of a rich white family. Under my proposal, nullification is presumed in the first case because drug distribution is a nonviolent malum prohibitum offense. Is nullification morally justifiable here? It depends. There is no question that encouraging people to engage in self-destructive behavior is evil; the question the juror should ask herself is whether the remedy is less evil. (The juror should also remember that the criminal law does not punish those ghetto drug dealers who cause the most injury: liquor store owners.)

As for the burglar who steals from the rich white family, the case is troubling, first of all, because the conduct is so clearly "wrong." Since it is a nonviolent malum in se crime, there is no presumption in favor of nullification, but it is an option for consideration. Here again, the facts of the case are relevant. For example, if the offense was committed to support a drug habit, I think there is a moral case to be made for nullification, at least until such time as access to drug-rehabilitation services are available to all.

Why would a juror be inclined to follow my proposal? There is no guarantee that she would. But when we perceive that black jurors are already nullifying on the basis of racial critiques (i.e., refusing to send another black man to jail), we recognize that these jurors are willing to use their power in a politically conscious manner. Further, it appears that some black jurors now excuse some conduct—like murder—that they should not excuse. My proposal provides a principled structure for the exercise of the black juror's vote. I am not encouraging anarchy; rather I am reminding black jurors of their privilege to serve a calling higher than law: justice.

I concede that the justice my proposal achieves is rough. It is as susceptible to human foibles as the jury system. But I am sufficiently optimistic that my proposal will be only an intermediate plan, a stopping point between the status quo and real justice. To get to that better, middle ground, I hope that this essay will encourage African Americans to use responsibly the power they already have.

Obsessed with O.J.

MICHAEL ERIC DYSON

When O. J. Simpson took that long, slow ride down the L.A. freeway in A. C. Cowlings's Bronco, it wasn't the first time he used a white vehicle to escape a black reality. I'm not referring to interracial marriage per se. Compatibility in love doesn't respect race, height, sex, color, age, culture, religion, or nationality. Transgression and affection often team up to knock down artificial conventions built on bias and ignorance. But sex between blacks and whites is an especially volatile instance of interracial intimacy. Every gesture of crossover and exchange between blacks and whites indexes the bitter history of American race. When many interracial couples forge ahead against social taboo, they often act courageously to undermine rigid racial beliefs.

Some blacks, though, pursue white lovers and lifestyles in a way that only reinforces the rules of race. White identity signifies for them the desirable, the healthy, the stable. Black identity, by contrast, symbolizes the undesirable, the unhealthy, the unstable. Although I cannot know for sure, I imagine that O.J., however unconsciously, may subscribe to these beliefs. He apparently belongs to that fraternity of black men who "have-to-have-a-white-woman-at-all-costs." There's a difference, after all, between preference and obsession. (Of course, even preferences don't jump at us out of a cultural void; our deepest desires bear the imprint of the society that shapes them.)

O.J. wanted to get as far away from his ghetto roots as his legs, wealth, fame, and diction could carry him. Good for him. But because he appears so uncomfortable with the idea that you can be identifiably black and have all those things, he has drowned his racial identity in an ocean of whiteness.

O.J.'s current condition has added his name to a growing list of (in)famous black men whose personal problems have made them poster boys for the perversions of patriarchal culture. Mike Tyson and date rape. Clarence Thomas and sexual harassment. Michael Jackson and child molestation. And now, O. J. Simpson and spousal abuse. Each of these problems merits serious action, and these men, if guilty, should be held responsible and punished accordingly. But these maladies are ancient. How is it that these black men have managed to do in disrepute what most black men can't do in honest achievement: transcend race to represent America?

Make no mistake. O.J. is not Rodney King. In the racial firmament, the King case can be considered a supernova, illuminating the ground of race relations beneath its harsh but powerful light. Millions of poor black men can identify with Rodney King because police brutality is a staple of their adolescence and adulthood, a ritual of initiation into a fraternity of black male pain. Despite his working-class hustling roots, the meaning of Rodney's beating could nevertheless travel in an upwardly mobile fashion: even well-to-do black males understood King's horror because it could be directed toward any black man on any given day.

O.J.'s case, by contrast, is considerably more narrow. Most black men charged with a capital crime have little money to seek responsible representation. Most do not count the police as their friends, even lackeys. Nor do they have the use of fame as a powerful deterrent to their conviction. If Rodney King is an exploding star, it may be that O. J. Simpson is a black hole, a collapsed star of such immense gravity that no light can escape.

Johnnie Cochran has been called a modern-day Joe Louis. In part, I can see that. He has fought tough legal battles for some of our most beleaguered black brothers: Jim Brown, Todd Bridges, Michael Jackson, and now O.J. Rascals all, in their own ways. In representing them, Cochran has slugged it out with a justice system that often punishes black men with frightening consistency.

Unlike the Brown Bomber, though, Cochran's gifts spill forth from his golden throat. He is smooth and silky, an orator of great skill whose rhetoric reflects his Baptist roots and his early days as an insurance salesman. He performs the law, dramatizing its arcane rituals of argument and translating its esoteric dogmas into stirring, poetic declaration. For many blacks Cochran *is* the law, masterfully taming the chaos of white contempt camouflaged in legal language and protected by obscure codes and regulations.

The pride so many blacks feel in Cochran's performance has a lot to do with an ancient injury to black self-esteem that not even Joe Louis could relieve: the white challenge to black intelligence and its skillful defense in eloquent black speech. Among his many racial functions, the black orator lends credence to claims of black rationality. When black folk in barbershops and beauty salons say of Cochran that "the brother can talk," what they mean in part is that the brother can think. Thinking and speaking are linked in many black communities. And neither are abstract reasoning and passionate discourse often diametrically opposed in such circles. Like all great black rhetoricians, Cochran makes style a vehicle for substance.

When *Time* blackened O.J.'s face on its cover, it was a gesture full of irony and, yes, dark humor. *Time*'s act raises several questions. Was their artificial enhancement of O.J.'s natural hues, which forced us to be more conscious of his color, a signifying move, suggesting that O.J. needed help with his color consciousness? Was it a subversive move, motivated by *Time*'s hidden ties to skin nationalists who argue a link between pigment and personality? Were they demonizing him by darkening him, making O.J. a Darth Vader where many once believed he was a Luke(warm) Skywalker? Was *Time* trying to help a brother out by boosting his melanin count to swing public sentiment his way? Or were they vilifying O.J.'s vanilla vision of black identity? Were they extending the spookification of black public faces? Or were they simply doing with O.J. what the media have done to countless other black men: giving him the benefit of the lout?

The riveting and repulsive drama of O. J. Simpson's freakish unraveling before our very eyes contains many ironies. An athlete whose brilliant moves on the football field were marked by beauty and grace now left an international audience aghast at his ungainly flight from the law. A champion who played Prometheus to a nation of Walter Mittys now shrank in stature to a shriveled, self-defeating parody of his former strength. An icon with an ingenious talent for turning gridiron glory into Hollywood fame and fortune was now bedeviled by the media that helped make him a national figure. And a man whose face and initials were broadly familiar became in an instant a stranger with a secret history of spousal abuse.

One of the most remarkable features of the initial commentary around Simpson's sad situation is the way in which race, in its deliberate denial, was made even more present. Like Poe's purloined letter, race lay hidden in plain sight.

On the face of things, the denial of race in the Simpson case signaled a praiseworthy attempt by the media to balance its racially skewed reporting of news events. That's not easy when politicians and pundits are obsessed with negatively linking race to everything from welfare reform to crime. But in denying the role of race in the Simpson ordeal, media critics showed that you can't get beyond race by simply pretending it's not there.

The goal should not be to transcend race, but to transcend the biased meanings associated with race. Ironically, the very attempt to transcend race by denying its presence reinforces its power to influence perceptions because it gains strength in secrecy. Like a poisonous mushroom, the tangled assumptions of race grow best in darkness. For race to have a less detrimental effect, it must be brought into the light and openly engaged as a feature of the events and discussions it influences.

In the case of O. J. Simpson, the fingerprints of race are everywhere. O.J.'s spectacular rise to fame was aided not only by his extraordinary gifts, but because he fit the mold of a talented but tamed black man, what was known in his youth as a "respectable Negro." O.J. received brownie points throughout his playing career as much for who he wasn't as for how he performed. He wasn't considered, like football-star-turned-actor Jim Brown, a black "buck," an "uppity nigger," an arrogant, in-your-face threat because of his volatile presence and unpredictable behavior.

From the beginning of his career, O. J. Simpson was marketed to white society as a raceless figure whose charisma drew from his sophisticated, articulate public persona. In this light horrified, disbelieving gasps of "not him" unleashed at O.J.'s initial public disintegration take on new weight. Let's face it. The unspoken, perhaps unconscious belief of many whites is that if he's guilty, if this could happen to O.J.—the spotless embodiment of domesticated black masculinity—it could happen to any black man. Translation: No black male can really be trusted?

At first, the fact that Nicole Brown Simpson was a beautiful blonde white woman went virtually unremarked upon. Now, of course, her ubiquitous picture has made it hard not to notice. The fact that O.J. married Nicole made a lot of people mad.

When a black man marries a white woman, it irks white supremacists ("he's spoiled one of *our* women"). It grieves many black mothers ("when a black son brings home a white woman, it's an insult to his mama"). It angers many white men ("she's throwing her life away"). It disappoints many black women ("with all these single black women, why would he choose a white woman?"). It unnerves some white women ("I could never see myself with a black man"). And it raises some black men's ire ("why all these brothers, when they get successful, got to marry a white woman?"). This small sample of anecdotal responses to interracial relationships provides a glimpse of the furious passions and unresolved conflicts that continue to haunt love in black and white.

Were O.J. and Nicole completely immune to such concerns? Probably not. Does the fact that O.J. was charged with killing his *white* wife make a difference in our world? Probably so. Can we seriously doubt that if O.J. had been accused of murdering his *black* wife, and not a symbol of ideal white beauty, we wouldn't be learning of it with a similar degree of intensity, its details so gaudily omnipresent?

Many argue that Simpson's troubles have nothing to do with race, that his fall is instead an *American* tragedy. Of course it is, because all black citizens are Americans, and all of our problems, therefore, are American problems. But we don't have to embrace our American identity at the expense of our race. The two are not mutually exclusive. We simply have to overcome the limitations imposed upon race, to make sure that neither privilege nor punishment are viciously, arbitrarily assigned to racial difference. To erase race is to erase ourselves, and to obscure how race continues to shape American perceptions and lives.

O.J.'s handsomeness has played a large part in his appeal over the years. He has long been the object of the "safe" eroticization of black masculinity by white women. His pretty face has been beamed everywhere. His facial expressions have been deconstructed around the globe. Once the master of his image in a medium where he adroitly projected a cool persona, O.J. has now lost himself, at least his public self, in the infinite gaze of international television. O.J.'s every glance is now filtered through the theories of thinkers with names like Derrida, Sartre, and Foucault. What could he mean by looking up? How could his failure to regard photos of his dead ex-wife possibly signify his guilt or angst? What were the possible meanings of his intense glare at jurors?

Before his demise, O.J. spoke with authority, breaking stereotypes of black sports icons' severe inarticulateness. His precise diction rebutted the vicious subculture of parody that dogged the verbal skills of his boyhood idol Willie Mays. During his trial, and for the most part since his acquittal, O.J. sat mute. He has been forced to minstrel his meanings by bucking his eyes like Rochester or Stepin Fetchit.

For many black men *and* women, the problem of domestic violence in the Simpson case was subordinated to race. In fact, for many it almost didn't exist. This denial was achieved by insisting that Nicole was "trash," that she was sexually loose, that she was a party girl who played O.J. for material gain. On this reading, Nicole got what she deserved.

But even if this portrait of Nicole is accurate (and a strong case can be made that it was), it still doesn't justify O.J.'s brutal beating of Nicole. Nor should it have cost her life. After all, a stronger case can be made that O.J. was extraordinarily promiscuous, a man of enormous appetites for varied substances, and beneath the public sheen of class, a brazen bully of women. O.J. and Nicole equally embodied the ugly lives of pretty people.

The truth is that black male violence against black women is a mainstay of relations between the two. The oppressive silence black women have observed in deference to race loyalty, or had imposed on them out of fear, remains a tragically underexplored issue in black life. Domestic violence against women is a concealed epidemic in black communities. It needs to be exposed.

If any good can come out of O.J.'s case for black women, it is that violent behavior should not be tolerated for any reason, racial or domestic. The male sexual ownership of women, the presumption of male discretion over women's bodies that feeds obsession and domination, must simply desist. Plus, sisters, when O.J. walked, he didn't come for you. Does he, or any black man who doesn't display the utmost respect and admiration for black women, really merit such profound loyalty?

During the trial, the polls continually showed that blacks and whites were divided on how they viewed this case. The wonder is that so many white folk were surprised. Why? Race remains the primary prism through which Americans view reality. Yet you only see the ruinous results of race when your perspective of reality is affected.

For instance, when I appeared on television and radio, commentators frequently asked me about the "race card"—a flawed way to understand race, to be sure. They were invariably referring to Mark Fuhrman's testimony and the charges that he is a bigot who might have planted evidence to frame O.J. While Fuhrman may have been the ace of all race cards, the deck had been shuffled, and many hands dealt, long before his appearance for the prosecution.

The choice to field Christopher Darden on the prosecution was a clear nod to race in this case. Darden seems oblivious to the fact that he was added to blacken up the prosecution's public face. His value derived not from his lawyerly demeanor or his rhetorical skills, which remain remarkably mediocre, but from his metaphysical presence in countering the incantatory powers of blackness invoked by Johnnie Cochran. The presence of Darden was meant to show that the prosecution was not racially insensitive. That O.J. and Cochran and Carl Douglas don't exhaust the resources of authentic black identity. The "race card" was played from the very beginning.

Marcia Clark is a brilliant attorney, a wonderfully disturbing presence. She is a woman with guts, whose fortitude and chutzpa are refreshing. The fact that she had to cut and restyle her hair, be harassed about the length of her skirts, and have her nearly nude picture plastered in a tabloid magazine underscores the hypocrisy of gender double standards.

It is odd to consider Marcia Clark as David to Johnnie Cochran's Goliath. After all, the state has enormous resources usually denied to the run of the mill client that it prosecutes. Perhaps that's one reason people were pulling for O.J.: finally here's a guy who can literally afford to fight back. However, there were strident class divisions as well. Marcia Clark and her cohort were unglamorous, underpaid public prosecutors in battle with glamorous, highly paid private counsels. Clark was clearly the underdog, the woman who when she slugged it out with the guys on the defense was considered "whiny." Who when she stood up to the defense's shenanigans was considered aggressive. And who when she strategized with cunning was considered disingenuous. (Think of her babysitting chores the night possible defense witness Rosa Lopez was to give taped testimony. Spurred by the rancor caused by Cochran's rather rude, even sexist rebuke, Clark brilliantly, implicitly employed her domestic responsibility as a metaphor for how female identity had been unjustly hammered by the defense that night, and by extension, by their client O. J. Simpson throughout his entire relationship to Nicole Brown Simpson.)

Even Clark's attempt to identify with the undernamed victims, Nicole Brown Simpson and Ron Goldman, by wearing an angel on her lapel, was winning. To be sure, it showed poor judgment. But that's the quality that endears: a lawyer, a prosecutor no less, exposes the futility, the impossibility, even the undesirability, of objectivity by casting her lot with the deceased's families. Even though she lost her bid to keep the pin, Clark's gesture gave morality priority over legality.

Now that Clark's husband has waged a public war to wrest their children away from her, she has come to symbolize the ultimate contradiction of women working: if you don't work like a man, you'll lose your job. If you work like a man, you'll lose your family. Too often working women are punished by what are supposed to be their rewards. During the trial—and before her $4.2 million book deal—had Marcia Clark been a partner in a prestigious firm like Johnnie Cochran's, she could have afforded a nanny.

I have visited the crime scene. It is immediately the touchstone of my obsession with O.J. I view the impossibly small spot where Ron Goldman lost his life. I am able to even more vividly imagine the fierce struggle he waged to remain alive. And to see the landing on which Nicole breathed her last breath is numbing. I feel I have crossed some void, offended some greatly observed taboo against polluting privacy, even in death, especially in death. And yet strangely, I feel a tie to their lives. In the end, though, I realize that it is a bond produced by little more than a fetish for what television has made falsely familiar.

Why is it that some black people spend so much energy denying the impact of race on their lives, only to embrace it when their backs are against the wall? Clarence Thomas employed this ruse. He insisted that he had not relied upon race as a crutch to succeed. Still, when he was caught in the heat of battle with Anita Hill, he fell back on race. He used it in ways that only days before he would have disdained as cowardly and dishonest.

The same may be said about O.J. He always aspired to get beyond race, to be neither white nor black, to be human. That damnable equation has stumped many who have failed to understand that it sets up a false dichotomy. There is no such thing as being black and not already being a human being. The two are not diametrically opposed. Taken separately, at least for black folk, they are impossible.

When I read in O.J.'s book, *I Want to Tell You*, that as he faced racism in the past he either ignored or denied it, I am even more saddened. This sort of person is well known in many black circles. They protect themselves from racism by turning their backs on its most hateful expressions. They hide its most brutal effects in their spiritual or moral trunks. Or they cover the wounds racism inflicts with the temporary balm of diversion or avoidance. But sooner or later they must confront themselves and the choices they have made, particularly when the peace pacts they have negotiated with their psyches have disintegrated.

It used to be—or was it ever the case?—that the dead were safe, protected by their sleep beneath the ground. Nicole Brown Simpson and Ron Goldman have gained posthumous notoriety, for no other reason than their murders may have been committed by a fallen hero, a tarnished celebrity. It is the ultimate act of violation, a gesture of profound obscenity. Their deaths have been emptied of the inherently private meaning of grief to their circle of intimates and family. Their murders have given them a life beyond their bodies, but not a life respected by tabloid media or former friends looking to turn Nicole and Ron's murders into money. The bottom line seems to be: it's not that they died, but that they were the persons that a famous man may have killed, that makes Nicole and Ron important.

It may be that football provided O.J. a public context to wrestle the demon of violence that haunted his private life. The pure art of his

movements on field may have countered, driven, or even comple-
mented his desperate scrambling for escape from inner turmoil. The
ritualized cleansing of violent passions that brutal sports are alleged
to achieve may only in the end lead to greater violence. The irony is
that Nicole Brown Simpson benefited from the public face of O.J.'s
acceptable aggression—a luxurious lifestyle as the wife of a sports
star—but its private expression may have killed her.

Commentators have called the Simpson case the "trial of the century." What's intriguing about the case is how its major players are a
virtual rainbow of color, gender, ethnicity, and class. Judge Lance A.
Ito is Asian American. Johnnie Cochran is African American. Marcia
Clark is a white woman. And Robert Shapiro, like Clark, is Jewish. A
judicial landmark was constructed by people who a few decades ago
couldn't stand equally together in the same court.

In the aftermath of the O. J. Simpson verdicts, I must confess that
I'm saddened. In this case—and it's true, of course, for many facets
of our national lives, though we're still not ready to admit it—race
ruled, gender disappeared, and justice was exiled to the Island of
Ambiguity.

I'm sad because, in legal terms at least, the brutal murders of two
human beings remain painfully unresolved. I'm sad because the criminal justice system (in this case epitomized by former Detective Mark
Fuhrman) has once again proved to be hostile to black folk. Sure, it
worked like a charm for O.J. That's because he had the fame and fortune to expose the callous attitudes and cavalier practices that routinely mock fairness for millions of anonymous minorities. I'm sad
because the issue of domestic violence was shattered and swept away
by a hurricane of legal strategies and maneuvers. The bodies of battered women simply don't count where they should matter most—in
the public imagination, and in private spaces where they live, work,
and play, and too often, where they die.

Though this case has been highly touted for the lessons it teaches
Americans about our national psyche, many of the lessons we have
learned from this ordeal are bad ones. One bad lesson is that faulty
metaphors are used to simplify the complex problems that plague
our country. The race card metaphor, for instance, fails to show how
bigotry blinds us to the worth of human beings who are not like us.

The metaphor falls short, too, in portraying how racism poisons the wellsprings of civic confidence in the positive contributions of black intelligence and moral vision to our country's welfare.

Race is not a card. It is a condition shaped by culture and fueled by passions buried deep in our history that transcend reason. That's why many white folk are angry at the verdict, while many black folk feel joy. Their differing responses are a pithy but painful statement about the stalemates and contradictions that race offers. And rest assured, all the reasons for their differences will never be completely explained to either side's satisfaction.

Unfortunately, a bad case of either/or thinking has clouded our understanding of the complexity of the Simpson trial. Either we pay attention to the effects of race, or we look at gender. Either we note the privileges of wealth, or we track the effects of domestic violence. It's just not that simple. This case was precisely about how nefarious social forces intersect and collide, and how they shove people into artificial choices about what issue is most important. Unfortunately, when Robert Shapiro said in a postverdict interview that the Holocaust stands alone in human suffering, implicitly negating the equally vicious ordeal of slavery, he fell right into the trap.

As I see it, most white women get the domestic violence part, but they just don't understand how race gives their pain more visibility than the suffering of black women. Most black men understand the plague of racism, but they're woefully indifferent to the sexism and domestic violence that haunt (black) women. Many white men feel in their guts that O.J. got away with murder, but they fail to see how thousands of innocent blacks are routinely prejudged to be guilty. Most black women identify with their blackness and their womanhood, but many of them subordinate gender to race because they fail to see how both factors shape the quality of their lives. Only if we begin to see how race, gender, domestic violence, and money are intimately bound will light begin to appear at the end of our collective tunnel. Perhaps then the O. J. Simpson case can have a salutary effect upon our national debate about the ugly social problems we have yet failed to resolve.

Racial Theater

JIM SLEEPER

Asked by a New York television interviewer just after O. J. Simpson's acquittal whether the uproar over the verdict reflected differing perspectives on race, the Reverend Al Sharpton replied, "It's not the *perception* of race; it's the *experience* of race in the criminal justice system," where blacks have been treated so differently for so long. A long road does run from the Scottsboro Boys, the Southern black teens falsely accused of raping two white women in the 1930s, to Simi Valley, where a mostly white jury acquitted Rodney King's assailants, for reasons perhaps more dubious than those a mostly black jury seemed to use in acquitting Simpson. Such experiences of racist mistreatment have become archetypes, seared into collective black memory.

But Sharpton and his onetime attorney Alton Maddox, Jr.—New York's Johnnie Cochran—know better than anyone how black "perceptions of race" sometimes distort even the bitter experience of it. In many blacks' reactions to the Simpson trial and to other recent, racially tinged acquittals of blacks by predominantly black juries, "the experience of race" has been deformed by its dubious *reenact-*

ment in a public, primal racial theater staged by impresarios such as Sharpton, Maddox, and Cochran. That politics of paroxysm has helped to create bitter experiences of race for *whites,* experiences that are now seared into a larger, more ominous collective memory.

Some of us in New York first sensed the drift toward courtroom psychodrama in 1987, when Maddox nearly won acquittal for a black man who had slashed a young white model, Marla Hanson, on the street outside her apartment in Brooklyn. Maddox told a racially mixed jury that Hanson had framed the defendant in order to protect her white landlord, who, he insisted without evidence, had assaulted her after they'd had an affair. Hanson was "a girl from Texas [with] a lot of racial hangups," Maddox proclaimed. "Just the simple sight of two black men [walking toward her on the street] and she went absolutely nuts."

In 1990, years after a grand jury found no evidence that white law enforcement authorities abducted and raped Tawana Brawley, Sharpton brought Brawley to a Manhattan courthouse to shake hands publicly with young black and Hispanic men then on trial for raping and bludgeoning the "Central Park jogger," a young white woman whom they had attacked on her evening run. Although some of the youths had confessed on videotape, newspaper polls found that many blacks were not reconciled to their convictions; Wilbert Tatum, editor of the black weekly *Amsterdam News,* proclaimed them the victims of a "lynching." Outside the courtroom, at least, archetypes had overwhelmed evidence in the hands of the impresarios of racial theater.

Then in 1992 Lemrick Nelson, a black teenager charged with murdering the Australian Jewish scholar Yankel Rosenbaum during Brooklyn's Crown Heights riots, was acquitted by a mostly black jury whose members then went out to dinner with him to celebrate their verdict. The evidence against him had been damning, but, as in the Simpson trial, the defense accused police of having manipulated it. The jurors bought this line, in a climate of recriminations about the Crown Heights and Los Angeles riots and the then recent acquittals of Rodney King's police assailants. Nelson, freed, moved out of the city; two years later, he was convicted of stabbing a youth in Atlanta.

Extensive though police racism has been and can be, what struck me and other journalists who followed these and similar cases years before the Simpson trial was the sheer psychodramatic momentum that carried Sharpton, Maddox, and celebrants of their theatrics almost serenely through lie after lie. "In cultural perspective," wrote the anthropologist Stanley Diamond of the Brawley case, "it doesn't matter whether the crime occurred or not. . . . It was described with skill and controlled hysteria by the black actors as the epitome of degradation, a repellent model of what actually happens to too many black women. The perpetrators supposedly included more than one white law enforcement officer, also echoing a social fact and creating the occasion for indicting once again the system of white justice. . . . It may be asking too much of the white community to excuse the Brawley deceit; but they misunderstand it at their peril."

William Kunstler was giving out much the same line. "It makes no difference anymore whether the attack on Tawana really happened," he told a reporter. "It doesn't disguise the fact that a lot of young black women are treated the way she said she was treated. . . . I don't think Maddox [and his colleague C. Vernon] Mason are further inflaming racial tensions in the city. But maybe there has to be some sort of cataclysm before anything constructive can happen. The more the white community is afraid of the black community, the better off the black community will be."

Thus did racial memory, triggered by little more than theatrics turning on defendants' and victims' skin colors, displace evidence as the determinant of innocence or guilt, just as it has done when white juries have acquitted guilty whites or convicted innocent blacks. Yet surely reaching a verdict on the basis of racial-group membership opens a door back to the old South—especially now that, according to conviction data and victim reports compiled by the federal Bureau of Criminal Justice Statistics, white women are raped by black men at least five times more often than black women are raped by white men.

Kunstler wasn't wrong to observe that the force of black collective memory cannot be denied. The question is how that force should be deployed, and to what ends. Why couldn't Diamond, a distinguished anthropologist, find in the Brawley psychodrama even a faint echo of the fable of the boy who cried wolf? As it leaps from the Brawley story, that fable reminds us that while there may indeed have been a wolf of racism in her community, crying out that it was there at a moment when it wasn't would only convince some defensive whites that it wasn't there at all. Diamond misunderstands the relationship of factual truths to mythmaking in public discourse. By his logic, it wouldn't have mattered if the Scottsboro Boys had indeed committed the rapes of which they were accused in 1931.

A better way to direct collective memory emerges from the way

Jews' most nightmarish experience of anti-Semitism was recalled in 1960, dispelling more than fifteen years of a kind of public amnesia about the Holocaust. After Israeli agents captured Adolph Eichmann in Argentina and brought him to Tel Aviv to stand trial for the mass murder of European Jews, life in Israel came virtually to a stop as thousands jammed the streets around the court, listening to the proceedings on loudspeakers and opening the floodgates of memory.

It may be that here in America, which is the scene of blacks' primal violation, some black jurors are groping for a definitive, purging conviction of white society akin to the conviction of Nazism through Eichmann. If such a cathartic reckoning means putting Los Angeles Police Detective Mark Fuhrman in the dock instead of Simpson—however unofficially and at whatever cost to justice for the actual victims of the crime with which Simpson was charged—so be it; the force of collective memory, once stirred, cannot be denied. After Simpson's acquittal, several of his jurors insisted that they hadn't even discussed race. But then, did they have to? Archetypes run deeper than evidence.

Archetypes ran deep in Israel, too. But because Eichmann was tried by institutions that Jews had constructed in the real world according to essential and universal principles of justice, and because his trial was legitimately a "class action" case brought on behalf of his many thousands of actual victims, the verdict did not pervert and degrade his accusers. However powerful, the dramatization of collective memory inherent in the trial was thus ancillary to its conclusion. In contrast, the Nelson and Simpson verdicts were reached by eclipsing the actual victims and some of the actual evidence; the relationship between memory and justice was broken in order to vindicate collective memories that, like those of Brawley's claimed violation, should have been reenacted in a church or communal theater, not in courtrooms where other people's lives (or justice for their deaths) hung in the balance.

Blurring the boundary between communal drama and courtroom justice based on transracial truths—and between group myth and individual dignity that is sustained by interracial organizing and discourse—means suborning new injustices and lengthening the list of bitter "white" memories. To what end? Such a politics of paroxysm resembles a neurotic person's reenactment of old grievances and hurts, using the wrong targets. It brings only fitful, temporary release while making new enemies; one is condemned to repeat it, again and again, in a world that comes increasingly to resemble the nightmare one means to escape. It is almost as if one has found it perversely more satisfying to hurt than to hope. That is certainly the case with black demagogues and their more devoted followers.

One cannot acknowledge too often that it is whites who have most often blurred the boundaries between racial resentments and criminal trials, submerging black individuals' rights beneath skin color in defiance of the Constitution. But that is precisely why a tit-for-tat response by black juries cannot banish the terrors of the past. It is, rather, a fateful turn off the high road taken by the civil rights movement during the Emmett Till and Medgar Evers cases of the 1950s and 1960s. The early movement's awesomely disciplined, even more awesomely loving marches shamed white America by insisting on embracing a shared civic culture, not trashing it as inherently, eternally racist. The movement sowed seeds that bore fruit even in last year's retrial and conviction of the white man who in 1963 had assassinated Evers, a leader of the NAACP in Mississippi.

That strategy and the philosophy behind it was succeeding, wrote *New York Post* editor James Wechsler in 1960, because blacks "have refused to do wrong. They . . . have been the victims of sadistic violence, legal subterfuge, government betrayal; in the face of every rejection and rebuff they have said simply that they will seek new recourse within the framework of our Constitution." The movement showed that the Constitution cannot countenance the displacement of evidence by collective memory; if it does, it cannot sustain anyone's freedom for long.

Yet archetypes do die hard. Only seven years after Wechsler wrote, a young Alton Maddox, then a student in Newnan, Georgia, suffered a brutal beating at the hands of local police when he protested their order to move his car. Twenty years later in Brooklyn, an almost maniacal Maddox managed to win a mostly black jury's acquittal of Andre Nichols, a nineteen-year-old black man who'd confessed to murdering the Rev. Frederick Strianese, a white priest. Nichols said the priest had invited him into his car in a known "pickup" area. The priest had been unarmed; Nichols had had a gun, which he said he used because the priest had tried forcibly to detain him. Maddox got the jury to acquit Nichols by trading heavily in the worst sort of reverse racism and hostility to homosexuals, replete with imagery of white sexual exploitation of blacks that presaged his charges in the Brawley case. The priest, he said, had enjoyed "good food, good wine . . . and now he wanted some good flesh."

Perhaps the priest's conduct had been reprehensible, even immoral. But had that justified *murder?* It took Maddox's race-baiting theatrics to seal the judgment, which even acquitted Nichols of gun possession. A year later, Nichols was convicted of armed robbery in another case; Maddox went on to dubious glory with Sharpton in the Brawley case (but was later suspended from practicing law by a judicial panel investigating his counseling Brawley's mother to refuse to answer a subpoena).

It is against this background—quite as much as against the background of the Los Angeles Police Department's sordid history of racist abuses—that the Simpson case is best understood. Like Maddox, Johnnie Cochran did play the race card fast and low, as his own defense teammate Robert Shapiro has charged. Like Maddox, Cochran—escorted in and out of the courtroom by Louis Farrakhan's guards—manipulated black memories of violation by white authorities; unlike Maddox, he did it not on behalf of an otherwise hapless Andre Nichols or Tawana Brawley, but on behalf of a wealthy celebrity whom whites had befriended and loved—and whom some blacks had disowned until he took the stage in a Los Angeles public racial theater. Cochran's own acting on that stage was more decorous than Maddox's and Sharpton's, but it veered even more sharply off the high road of the civil rights movement into a road strewn not only with Till, Evers, and Rodney King but also with Reginald Denny, Marla Hanson, the Central Park jogger, the Rev. Strianese, Yankel Rosenbaum, and, of course, the innocent victims of Brawley's false witness.

Where do the impresarios of collective memory think this road leads? Why do they cynically conflate legitimate grievances against racism in the criminal justice system with false charges like Brawley's against white law enforcement officers, or even with more plausible but extenuated accusations against Fuhrman in the Simpson case itself?

Racism is the obvious answer, but perhaps not quite in the way Maddox or Cochran might expound it. Archetypal racism is indeed one reason why the black community has a long, often irresistible tradition of rhetoric divorced from responsibility to the larger society. Until the late 1950s, when Adam Clayton Powell, Jr., James Baldwin, and Martin Luther King, Jr. began to write and speak politically in ways that truly got under the skins of whites, black political rhetoric tended (with some notable exceptions, such as Frederick Douglass, W. E. B. Du Bois, and Booker T. Washington) to be flamboyant precisely because it was weightless, of no consequence, unable to move the high and mighty walls of white ignorance and indifference. For all the difference men such as Powell, Baldwin, King, A. Philip Randolph, Roy Wilkins, and others made, the older tradition surfaces from time to time, even in Jesse Jackson's claim to be "a tree shaker, not a jelly maker." Although Simpson, not Fuhrman, was the defendant in this particular trial, it was as if some blacks were still saying: "It is our duty only to evoke and provoke; it is someone else's [the real grown-ups'?] duty to put matters to rights. We will spin our webs of narrative and metaphor." Someone else, always someone else, will have to turn them into serious politics and policy.

Ignorance and economic exploitation or exclusion might also be cited to explain why some blacks do not assume more responsibility. But, as Wechsler noted, blacks in the Jim Crow South showed the world that even poor, uneducated, and marginalized people could shoulder great burdens on behalf of the larger society, and some of this country's greatest black leaders have arisen amid conditions far more dire than those that obtain now. They proved, as many blacks do daily, that there are ways, perhaps mythically less satisfying but pragmatically more rewarding, to reduce racism in the criminal justice system.

One way is to apply a community's electoral muscle, in concert with other communities that share at least some common goals, to elect judges and district attorneys who feel a political as well as moral obligation to racism's victims. Another is to persevere, in colleges and law schools, toward professional careers that are not circumscribed so tightly by racial preferences, posturing, and myths. A third way, in times of crisis, is to organize demonstrations that embarrass whites into decency by *embracing them* in the process of confronting them, as the civil rights movement at its best did so brilliantly. To watch Howard University Law School students cheer the Simpson verdict was to understand how thoroughly these roads, too, have been abandoned by a critical mass of young blacks. And that prompts one to ask again: Where do they think the road they are taking leads?

Notes on the Trial of the Century

DIANA TRILLING

Although, like most of the white population of America, I think that O. J. Simpson murdered Nicole Brown and Ron Goldman, I was not surprised by his acquittal. Almost everyone with whom I spoke about the case expected a hung jury; no one anticipated a conviction. Not only was the defendant a black sports hero; he was uncommonly charming, worldly, wealthy, and he was being tried in Rodney King country. Even at our distance from Los Angeles, the brutal beating of King, and its consequences both inside and outside the courtroom, was still fresh in our memory.

But if we were prepared for Simpson's acquittal, we were anything but prepared for the speed with which the jury reached its verdict. It had taken nine months to present the evidence in the case, much of it highly complicated; it was not possible for the jury to have sifted through it and deliberated on it in less than four hours. It was the speed of the verdict, indicating as it did that the case had been decided on the basis of race rather than by the testimony, that sent a shock through the nation. Alert as we might be to the problems of race in present-day America, we had failed to realize that our racial discord had reached the point where it could announce itself this baldly and boldly.

Simpson is said to have sneered at Marcia Clark as he left the courtroom, a free man. By the speed with which the jury in his case reached its decision, it sneered at our legal system and the state, and at Judge Ito, who had been so much its friend and sympathizer.

Confronted with the racial solidarity of the jury, Simpson's lawyers have reminded us that it was an integrated jury. There were nine black jurors but also two Caucasians and an Hispanic. In the press conference that juror Brenda Moran called on the day after the verdict, and again in a television interview, she offered us similar assurances: the jury was integrated. It may be, of course, that the nonblack minority in the jury deferred to reasonable arguments of its black majority, just as it may be that among the black jurors Ms. Moran was not unique for either her powers of persuasion or the force of her feeling for Simpson—we now know, for instance, that another of the jurors was once a Black Panther; as he left the courtroom, he saluted Simpson with upraised fist. But as I watched Ms. Moran on television, I asked myself for how long I or anyone I knew could have withstood her.

I wait for someone to mention the Dreyfus case in connection with the Simpson case but, to my knowledge, this has not yet happened. For France, the Dreyfus case was its trial of the century. Dreyfus was a Jewish captain in the French army, and he was accused of spying for the Germans. France reeled under the impact of his trial. He was found guilty as charged and sent to Devil's Island where he remained for more than four years until eventually, after a retrial in which he was again declared guilty, he was pardoned. The rift in French society caused by the Dreyfus case makes a central theme in Proust's great novel, *Remembrance of Things Past;* just as a madeleine triggered his personal memory, the Dreyfus case triggered his social memory. Good books will no doubt be written about the Simpson case, but will it ever produce the monumental work of fiction that it demands? I suspect that for a Simpson novel to be truly great it will have to be written by a black writer who, while transcending the divisions of color, will bring to the story all the racial pain that went into its making. To me, a white viewer, the fever of delight with which the students of Howard University greeted Simpson's acquittal was the most disturbing feature of the trial. The students hugged each other and jumped with joy, like witnesses at the fall of the Bastille.

Was Johnnie Cochran guilty of incitement in his final address to the jury? In the summation, the evidence was argued by Barry Scheck; the main thrust of Cochran's argument was its impassioned appeal to the jury to carry the message of racial injustice to the world and to help restore the American Constitution. But where was the American Constitution threatened in the Simpson trial? In what way was Simpson deprived of his Constitutional rights? By his own admission, detective Mark Fuhrman was in violation of the Constitution—he told an aspiring screenwriter that when it suited his purpose he planted evidence against black suspects. With other members of the Los Angeles Police, he was accused by the defense of having planted evidence against Simpson. But though repeatedly stated, this was never proved. Defense counsel did not invent Mark Fuhrman. Fuhrman and his kind exist. But it is important to keep it in mind that, whatever discrimination is practiced against blacks in our country, the story of Simpson's victimization by the police was the creation of his counsel. This represented a cruel play upon the feelings of black Americans, adding a bad dream to a bad-enough reality.

Judge Ito is said to regard the Simpson trial as the best and worst experience of his life. He is most usefully viewed, I think, as an archetypal product of our present-day progressive culture. I do not mean this as wholly discreditable—there is much to be praised in his unyielding effort to be fair-minded, but his wish not merely to *be* fair-minded but to be *perceived* as fair-minded caused this trial to last twice as long as it should have. He ran the trial like the permissive parent of a rambunctious household, teetering back and forth between indulgence and discipline, and demonstrating in the process that permissiveness is of as little service in a courtroom as in the rearing of children. Although he often seemed to lack sufficient awareness of his authority, he seemed also to be overly conscious of it, but with what D. H. Lawrence would have called "mental consciousness" rather than "blood consciousness." To the end, his personal uncertainty encouraged the lawyers to flout his orders: although during closing argument he cautioned the lawyers on both sides against grimaces or other shows of displeasure with the statements of their opponents and warned that any such demonstration would be severely punished, not moments later Barry Scheck returned to his elaborate head shakings and facial expressions of dismay with nothing done to stop him.

At the end of the trial, Judge Ito repeatedly instructed the jury in its duty to weigh all the evidence with which it had been presented. But the jurors were also instructed that where there was reasonable doubt on a single issue, it warranted acquittal. Does this mean that the chain of evidence in a criminal trial is no stronger than its weakest link?

According to juror Moran, it was the testimony of Allan Park, the driver who came to take Simpson to the airport, which provided the jury with its reasonable doubt. I myself saw nothing to doubt in Park's testimony; no one having answered the doorbell at Simpson's Rockingham residence, Park had waited for him to appear. While waiting, he saw a black man of Simpson's height and build, dressed in dark clothes, enter the house. He saw no white Bronco at the Rockingham address. In her summation, Marcia Clark reasonably described Park's testimony as testimony which no one had questioned or could question.

I try to recollect who it was who first spoke of the "L"-word. Probably it was someone in Washington; perhaps it was Dan Quayle. (Remember him?) The Simpson trial acquainted us with a new obfuscation, the "n"-word. No one has yet thought to introduce the "m"-word into our vocabulary, but we have need of it. Certainly money was everywhere in this trial: the lawyers' fees, the costs to both sides for their teams of investigators and researchers, the expensive exhibits, the fees to the expert witnesses. On one of the nightly programs which Larry King devoted to the case, he bravely brought up this neglected subject with Simpson's close friend, Robert Kardashian. He asked Kardashian how much O.J. had spent on the trial. O.J. couldn't be luckier than to have a friend as steadfast as Kardashian. Without a quiver, he conceded that it had probably been more than a million. More than a million, indeed! Closer, I should guess, to $10 million.

It was worth, of course, every penny if it bought Simpson his freedom. But how could this trial have failed to communicate to the world how important it is to be rich if one is going to come up against the law? We can only speculate upon how many mean deals may have been cut for impoverished criminals or how many went to jail while Simpson sat in court surrounded by his dream team of lawyers. We have often heard it said that there is one system of justice for the rich and another for the poor. We have now had nine months in which to contemplate the truth of this cynical statement.

Since the close of the Simpson trial, we have heard many proposals for change in our legal system: the sequestration of jurors must be abolished; a jury must no longer be required to reach a unanimous decision; new rules for the presentation of evidence must be formulated in order to save time in a trial. I have suggestions of my own. They have to do with the "m"-word. I propose that not only all lawyers involved in a trial but all expert witnesses be required to declare at the start what they are being paid for their services. Mr. Herbert MacDonell—Professor MacDonell, as this expert in blood spatters prefers to be called—candidly admitted on the witness stand that he had already been paid $10,500 and that he would be receiving more. He made this admission without embarrassment, and I liked him for his frank acknowledgment that he was in the blood business for the "m."

Robert Heidstra earns his modest living by detailing cars in the Brentwood vicinity. He was called by the defense, but he uncomfortably developed into a witness for the prosecution when he reported that, walking his dogs on the night of the murders, he was in the alley at the rear of Nicole's condo and heard a youthful male voice say, "Hey, hey, hey!" On cross-examination it was disclosed that he had also heard an older male voice, that of a black person. The reference to a black voice drew from Johnnie Cochran the hottest passion of this heated trial. How, he demanded of Judge Ito, was such blatant racism possible in this country at this point in time?

Cochran's rage was perhaps fueled by the fact that Heidstra had also testified that he heard the rear gate on Nicole's property being shut and that he had seen a white car or van—yes, it could have been a Bronco—speed away from the scene.

But even with this provocation, Cochran's protest was absurd. In an enlightened society, is one not to be permitted to recognize a national or regional or racial accent? Are we no longer to be allowed to identify a French person or an Italian by his speech, or an American Southerner?

Although what Christopher Darden elicited in his cross-examination of Heidstra remained on the record, the sound of a black male voice was not again referred to in the trial, not even by Marcia Clark in her summation.

It is my guess that Simpson is convinced that he didn't murder his former wife and her friend Goldman. He may be a gifted actor, but it is not on his acting ability that his management of himself now relies. I believe that he is now in denial, deepest denial—I use the word as it is used in psychoanalysis to connote the complete eradication of fact. Because he is so thoroughly in denial, he is able to convince those who are close to him of his guiltlessness. Whether we realize it or not, we all of us employ this phenomenon of denial in our lives. When it is too disturbing for us to admit something into our consciousness, we blot it out as if it had never been. We all of us have had the experience of accusing someone of a wrongdoing and having this wrongdoing denied. The person who denies our charge is most frequently speaking the truth as he now sees it. He is in psychological denial. While this may be viewed as a pathology, it exists as a psychological safety net for even the sanest and most competent of us. The mechanism comes into use without our conscious dictate.

Yet, even if we accept the premise that Simpson is no longer conscious of what actually took place on the night of Nicole's murder, we have also to understand that there remains to him the entire consciousness that his former wife, the mother of two of his children, was brutally slaughtered. During the trial, he was careful to look away from the screen when the details of the murder were too vividly displayed. But how do we account for his demeanor (that much-worn word) when he tried on the glove before the jury? The glove was soaked with Nicole's blood, yet he smiled broadly at its apparent misfit—it provided him with his moment of triumph over the prosecution. I was reminded of Jean Harris studying the blood stains on the bed sheets of her murdered lover, Dr. Tarnower. Mrs. Harris didn't smile as she examined the bedclothes, which were soaked with her lover's blood, but she had no hesitation in handling them. Psychiatry also identifies such inappropriate emotional detachment: it represents a lack of affect.

In the last days of the trial, Johnnie Cochran had a bodyguard in court, five members of the Nation of Islam. He said that he had received death threats. Questioned on television after the trial, he shrugged off the suggestion that there might be political significance in this connection with the Nation of Islam leader Louis Farrakhan.

I am returned to the racial tensions of the late '60s. For several weeks at the close of that decade, there hung down the side of the Riverside Church a huge banner demanding $5 million in reparations for blacks. I live near the Riverside Church, and as I passed this banner each day, I thought of my father and of how, were he alive, he would respond to it. My father was born and reared in Warsaw. As a child in the late nineteenth century, he had known pogroms. He was little and quick and he had been sent out by his parents to see if the Cossacks were gone and to scout for food. Did the Poles owe him reparation for their mistreatment of the Jews? Do the Poles owe me reparation for their treatment of my father? I speak, of course, not of repayment of property rights but only of the infringement upon human decency.

The political repercussions of Simpson's trial have yet to manifest themselves. President Clinton spoke promptly and sensibly: the decision of the jury must be respected; it was a time for racial healing; an end must be put to spousal abuse. Jesse Jackson appeared on television, but disastrously; it was clear that he had been left behind in the fast current of public events. Those most communicating of public characters, Dole and Gingrich, were suddenly all but silent.

More than hope lay behind the civil rights movement of the '60s. This social revolution of our time was importantly fueled by white liberal guilt and black anger. It also had its infusion of fear. We never intended ourselves to be led where we have been led by this explosive mixture nor, unhappily, have our last thirty years enabled us to separate out the explosive elements in this progressive movement or shown us how to bring them under intelligent control.

Until Simpson's trial, I had had but a single experience of a courtroom, and that was Jean Harris's trial for the murder of the Scarsdale diet doctor. I was writing a book about the case and attended the trial each day. It was held in the White Plains Courthouse and lasted for the better part of a year. In fact, as of that date it was the longest murder trial in the history of New York state.

The two trials are notably unrelated by rule or tradition. There were no racial elements in the Harris case and no cameras in the White Plains courtroom. Still, it was a famous trial and a major media event. The press rows were a tight squeeze, and there were as many spectators at the trial as the spacious courtroom could accommodate. Especially as the trial neared its close, the lobby of the courthouse became jammed with sightseers, reporters, camera people eager to catch a glimpse of the defendant entering or leaving the building.

Despite the popularity of the Harris case, there was a decorousness in the White Plains courtroom which one longed to see reproduced in Judge Ito's court. Only one lawyer appeared for each side, and this was a help. But it cannot account for the mood of courtesy and quiet seriousness that was maintained in White Plains but that was so dismayingly absent in Los Angeles. The opposing attorneys in the Harris trial never addressed each other except in entire politeness, and they never addressed the judge except with deference. The judge never scolded opposing counsel or threatened them with punishment—he had no reason to. No one played to the jury as Barry Scheck so openly did throughout the Simpson trial. Nothing of a personal nature intruded itself upon the legal situation. Everyone in the White Plains courtroom—judge, counsel, defendant, witnesses, scientific experts—was quietly, unostentatiously respectful of the power and dignity of the law.

Where has this decorousness disappeared to? How has it happened that in the space of fourteen years a criminal trial has come to be generally viewed as a circus? Were the bad manners of the attorneys in this trial an accurate reflection of a general deterioration of manners in the last decade and a half? This is frightening to think about.

Even more frightening, however, is the thought that with the passage of these few years we have lost this much of our respect for our legal system. Law is the foundation of our society and the guarantor of the rights which we all of us are supposed to cherish and guard. Without law, tyrants can exist but democracy cannot. If the Simpson trial teaches us nothing else, surely it must remind us of the root connection between civility and the sustaining processes of law.

PART II

Domestic Violence

The Disappearance of an Issue

What Happened to Public Education about Domestic Violence?

ELIZABETH M. SCHNEIDER

In June 1994 I was in Phoenix, Arizona, at an academic conference, participating on a panel on violence against women when Nicole Brown Simpson was found murdered and O.J. went on his freeway run. The panelists shared their perceptions that the facts which had begun to unfold about the history of the Simpsons' relationship were shockingly familiar to anyone who had done work with battered women and battering men, indeed, a "textbook case."

I am grateful to the many activists and advocates doing public education on the issue of domestic violence, with whom I discussed the ideas presented in this essay. I am also grateful to Kristin Bebelaar and the students in my Fall 1995 class on Battered Women and the Law at Brooklyn Law School, whose collective discussions on the Simpson case are reflected here, and who have reminded me why education on these issues can be so powerful and transforming. Thanks also to Susan N. Herman, Minna Kotkin, Sylvia Law, Michael Madow, and Myrna Raeder for helpful comments.

In the discussion that followed, activists and educators felt simultaneously emboldened by the opportunity that the case presented to do serious national public education about the severity of the problem of battering and afraid that domestic violence would get lost in the other issues that seemed likely to emerge—the cult of O. J. Simpson's celebrity status, the role of racism, and the media circus which the freeway run presaged. The possibility that the issue of domestic violence would explode in the media and then be so easily subverted in the legal process seemed potentially worse than silence. It was frightening to consider how much public knowledge of battering would depend on a series of events and factors over which advocates had so little control. Little did we know then how right we were to be worried.

In January 1995, in the middle of the trial, I participated in a meeting of scholars and activists working on domestic violence convened by the Ford Foundation, to discuss directions for reform. The impact of the Simpson trial on our work wove in and out of the discussion. Many people working in service organizations said that the case had led to an increase in calls for help from battered women, and that the early media attention had led to some increased public and legislative response. At the same time, we bemoaned the fact that the issue of domestic violence had been submerged in the trial. The fact that the case fit the familiar scenario of woman abuse, separation, and homicide seemed to have been ignored, and an initial media blitz on domestic violence had stopped dead. We worried about the impact that an acquittal would have on the lives of many battered women, on public education about the issue of domestic violence, and on our work.

By October 1995, the trial had ended with little focus on the issue of domestic violence. Although Nicole Simpson's chilling call to 911 and the "telephone counseling" that the court had sanctioned had been heard by the jury, the full history of abuse, and the role that Nicole's separation might have played in exacerbating O.J.'s violence and providing a motive for the homicide had not.

As the Simpson jury went into deliberation I joined other battered women's advocates at the White House to hear President Clinton's historic proclamation of October 1995 as the first Domestic Violence Awareness Month. Sitting in the East Room next to a Senatorial legislative aide, who told me about the positive changes in congressional attitudes toward domestic violence, I cautioned (not knowing that the jury had already reached a verdict) that we should wait to see what the Simpson jury did. The next day told all.

I begin with these stories because I think they highlight an important lesson underscored by the Simpson trial; a lesson about the limited role that major public cases, particularly cases that go to trial, can play in public education on serious social issues, like domestic violence. Like any major public case, the Simpson case contained the seeds to educate the public about serious social issues, albeit in the context of particular facts and circumstances. But those seeds never took root.

The first set of reports about the case focused on the issue of domestic violence. Newspaper accounts emphasized the fact that O.J. had beaten Nicole in 1989, that Nicole had called the police (and that the call had been taped), that O.J. had received a slap on the wrist as a sanction: counseling by phone and no criminal penalty. The media reported other beatings, that Nicole and O.J. had separated months before, that O.J. had been angry at the separation, and that O.J. had tried to break her door down. There were reports that Nicole had expressed fear for her life to a number of people, that she had called a local battered women's shelter for help shortly before she died, and that she had left a photograph and note expressing her fear that O.J. would kill her, in a safe deposit box to be opened after her death. The press reported that on the day of the homicide Nicole and O.J. had been together at a school recital of one of their children, and that the children had gone home with Nicole and then out to dinner with her family and friends, a dinner to which O.J. was not invited. To experts knowledgeable about battering, as well as about the fundamental issue of maintenance of power and control that underlies battering and the degree to which battered women's assertion of separation and independence heightens the likelihood of the batterer's lethal violence, the homicide was tragically explicable.

Domestic violence is the major health issue facing American women. Nearly four million women are physically battered each year in this country. The FBI estimates that more than 1,500 women are murdered by their husbands or boyfriends each year, and nearly 33 percent of all women murdered are killed by husbands or boyfriends. Battering fits within a larger picture of abuse of power and control; men who batter are frequently described as charming, controlling, seductive, jealous, and possessive, and they want control over "their" women. Men who batter also verbally abuse, stalk, threaten, and coerce.

From the beginning, the story that unfolded of the history of Nicole and O. J. Simpson's relationship manifested a common pattern within battering relationships, including the fact that when O.J.'s battering was ultimately reported to the police, there was no serious sanction by either the court system or his employers. Indeed, the history of abuse, the fact of the separation, rumors that Nicole had developed another relationship, and the circumstances that day presented a powerful motive for the homicide. Battered women recognized the facts of the Simpson case in their own experiences—particularly the 911 call. Battering men recognized themselves in O.J.'s rambling suicidal letter.

But in order for the jury to be able to consider, no less accept, this history of domestic violence as the context of the crime, and O.J.'s anger at his loss of control over Nicole and jealousy as the motive for the homicide, the jury had to understand the crucial link between domestic violence and homicide. They had to be presented with the full history of abuse within Nicole and O.J.'s relationship and, most important, to be sufficiently educated about domestic violence to be able to really hear this evidence. Of course, they would also have had to overcome public glorification of O.J., the racism and incompetence of the Los Angeles Police Department, and a host of other factors, none of which may have been possible in this trial.

Public recognition of the problem of domestic violence has certainly increased over the last fifteen years. A recent poll conducted for The Family Violence Prevention Fund and The Advertising Council showed that 80 percent of the American public consider domestic violence an extremely or very important social issue. Twenty years ago, there was no such concept as a "battered woman" and women who were battered did not admit the fact of abuse. Largely as the result of a national movement of battered women's advocates and shelter workers over the last twenty-five years, there are now laws protecting against abuse on the books in every state, and a federal Violence Against Women Act. Violence against women has been recognized as an international human rights violation. Yet at the same time, the traditional view that domestic violence is a "private" matter persists. Empirical studies of jurors in cases involving battered women who have killed their assailants suggest that jurors harbor widespread misconceptions about domestic violence. Jurors tend to blame the woman for the abuse, and for failing to leave the abuser, do not recognize the risks of escalated violence in leaving, and trivialize the abuse. Jurors have trouble accepting the pervasiveness of the problem, and recognizing it as important. Indeed in a wide range of legal cases where issues of battering come into play, it has now been recognized that in order to overcome commonly held myths and misconceptions about battering, jurors need to be presented with expert testimony to assist them in considering these issues.

In the Simpson case, the full history of domestic violence that might have explained why O.J. would have killed Nicole was not presented to the jury. The only significant evidence concerning domestic violence that the jury heard was the 1989 incident that resulted after he pleaded no contest, Nicole's 911 call, and one stalking incident. Although there was an extensive history of abuse, and of other circumstances that corroborated the abuse and suggested that, at the time of her death, Nicole was in fear for her life, much of this history was not presented to the jury.

For example, evidence that Judge Ito ruled admissible, but that the jury did not hear, included the following:

- A 1982 incident in which O.J. allegedly smashed photos of Nicole's family, threw her against a wall, and threw her and her clothes out of the house.
- A 1985 call to a private security officer in which a crying, puffy-faced Nicole alleged that O.J. had bashed her car with a baseball bat.
- A 1987 incident in Victoria Beach in which O.J. allegedly struck Nicole and threw her to the ground.
- A 1989 incident in which O.J. allegedly slapped Nicole and pushed her from a slow-moving car.
- Several statements made by O.J. in 1993 and 1994. These include one incident in which O.J. showed a friend the secret back way into his ex-wife's home. "Sometimes she doesn't even know I'm here," Simpson allegedly said.
- Several allegations of "stalking behavior," including two times that O.J. allegedly followed Nicole to restaurants with another man, as well as one incident in which he claimed to have observed them having sex on a couch in her home.
- A 1994 incident in which O.J. saw Nicole with Ronald Goldman and another man having coffee, allegedly stopped his car and angrily motioned her to come over. Judge Ito said the episode

was relevant because it connected Simpson to Goldman and was "evidence of jealousy and motive."

Evidence that Judge Ito barred included:

- A 1977 incident in which neighbors said they heard O.J. beating Nicole and saw her with black eyes.
- Seven statements made by Nicole, including entries in a diary and a telephone call that she allegedly made to the Sojourn house shelter for battered women five days before she was killed. Among these statements was Nicole Simpson's remark to her mother that her ex-husband was following her to the gas station.

However, even if this fuller range of evidence had been presented, it would still have had to be explained to the jury. Although the prosecution did not introduce any expert testimony about the abuse, the defense clearly anticipated that the prosecution would seek to present testimony about the common characteristics of batterers. Johnnie Cochran announced in his opening statement that the defense would have an expert, Lenore Walker, testify that O.J. did not fit the common characteristics of batterers (which outraged battered women's advocates around the country because Walker is an expert on battered women, not battering men, and has testified in many cases for battered women). Although the prosecution apparently submitted a motion to introduce expert testimony on battering on rebuttal, it did not press this motion, and Judge Ito apparently never ruled on it. The defense never called Lenore Walker.

We know that some of the jurors had personal experience with domestic violence. One juror was dismissed when she came to court with visible bruises inflicted by her boyfriend; another was dismissed when it was discovered that she had filed a restraining order against her husband in 1988 accusing him of forcing her to have sex against her will and she had not previously disclosed the incident on voir dire. However, statements made by some of the jurors after the verdict that they did not understand why domestic violence was even "relevant" to the case, since Simpson was charged with homicide, not battering, suggest the depth of the inclination to minimize the evidence and the need for countervailing explanation.

As the trial went on, the initial issue of domestic violence presented in the prosecution's case got lost, lost in the defense exploration of the

DNA evidence, in the incompetence of the Los Angeles Police Department and Mark Fuhrman's racism, in the defense's direct appeal to racial solidarity. Without any effort to affirmatively educate the jury on domestic violence early in the prosecution's case in order to overcome the likely trivialization of the issue, there wasn't much chance for the jury to understand the connection between domestic violence and homicide. Even if there had been a more serious effort, and even if the jury had understood the connection, and accepted it, who knows? The jury would still have had to find no reasonable doubt.

From the standpoint of many battered women and domestic violence advocates, the jury's speed in arriving at a verdict, and the verdict itself, was frightening and disheartening. During the trial, many battered women reported that men battered and threatened them with a greater sense of impunity because "O.J. could get away with it" and they read the verdict as further support for the view that men would continue to "get away with it." One battered woman survivor interviewed after the verdict said, "My fear is that this verdict is sending a message that violence is okay." Another said that she feared that her husband and other battering men would use the Simpson case as justification to treat women more violently. Jurors' comments suggested that the jury had not taken the issue of domestic violence seriously or understood its relevance to the charge of homicide. Moreover, the degree to which the acquittal was celebrated, despite the fact that O.J. had previously been convicted of abuse, was troubling. For though Simpson was acquitted of murder, it is indisputable that he was a batterer who was not held duly accountable for his use of violence and threats early on—by a judge who allowed counseling by phone, by police who applied a double standard, and by employers like Hertz and NBC who ignored an arrest for a violent crime. The trial may also have reinforced false and misleading stereotypes, since domestic violence is unquestionably a considerable risk factor for female homicide, and a batterer's public persona or even loving relationship with children is not inconsistent with abuse or domestic homicide. Nonetheless, the case did not only involve the issue of domestic violence, and it was not a social referendum on the significance of the problem. There were many other issues in the case, most significantly the degree to which racism and incompetence within the LAPD had irreparably tainted the prosecution's case and raised reasonable doubt for the jury.

The acquittal challenges us as a society to seriously address and remedy the problem of domestic violence. Certainly the initial media blitz on domestic violence was useful, and a significant amount of public education was accomplished. It is heartening now to see posters addressing domestic violence in subways, and hear public service announcements on TV, such as the one in New York, which shows a couple ignoring sounds of abuse in the apartment upstairs, and saying, "It *is* your problem!" National public education programs such as "There's No Excuse for Domestic Violence" include television, radio, and print public service announcements designed to increase public awareness of battering. As an August 1995 *Sports Illustrated* special report shows, the case has also focused positive attention on the link between the glorification of male athletes and domestic violence.

Education for change on domestic violence is a long haul; domestic violence is deeply ingrained in our culture, reflected in historic concepts of women as male property. It is also threatening to our concepts of the family as "a haven in a heartless world" and there is much social denial. What is most important now is how we as a nation respond to the problem of domestic violence, and how we send the message that both individuals and government must take responsibility to stop it. Police, prosecutors, doctors, teachers, employers, and religious leaders must do more to address this epidemic. We must hold batterers accountable from the first sign of abuse and support domestic violence victims when they reach out for help.

The public education on domestic violence that we need as a society can't happen in the "quick fix" of a trial. It isn't on Court TV, but in every elementary school and high school, every hospital and law school, every court and welfare office. It has to be the recognition of the everyday deaths of so many women, here and around the world, not just one high-profile case, that animates us to change.

Simpson Sound Bites

What Is and Isn't News about Domestic Violence

DEBORAH L. RHODE

By the time the Simpson spectacle wound its way to a verdict, many Americans felt as Samuel Johnson reportedly did about Milton's *Paradise Lost:* No one ever wished it had been longer. Yet even as millions overdosed on O.J., still more remained in hot pursuit of larger truths. A cottage industry of commentary emerged to ponder not just the verdict, but the reactions to the verdict, and the reactions to the reactions. Among legal scholars, the question pummeled to death was "what does this case tells us about American law and lawyers?" But in the rush to generalize, it is critical to remind ourselves what is and is not typical about the Simpson prosecution. This case tells us little about the problems of America's criminal justice system as most defendants, particularly black men, experience it. But the facts leading up to the prosecution speak volumes about the inadequacies of law enforcement that most battered women encounter.

AN ATYPICAL DEFENDANT

An obvious point, but one that many Americans can't keep in focus, is the difference between Simpson's defense and the defense available in most felony proceedings. The United States has, in fact if not in law, a two-tiered criminal justice system with separate but by no means equal forms of legal representation.

For clients like O.J., attorneys will leave no stone unturned; after all, they charge by the stone. But the vast majority of defendants receive nothing close to the due process we witnessed in this or in other televised trials. About three-fourths of individuals in felony cases cannot afford lawyers. They receive court-appointed private counsel or public defenders who are grossly overworked and underpaid. Statutory fee ceilings often set ludicrously low limits on what private defense attorneys can bill the government. In many jurisdictions, the average fee for a felony case is under $400. That total is less than what one of Simpson's lawyers typically charges by the hour.

So too, public defenders generally handle between 200 and 500 felony cases per year and lack adequate time or resources for investigation and expert testimony. By contrast, in the Simpson case, trial-related expenses alone are estimated at more than a million dollars and the complete defense bill, including legal fees, may have reached $10 million. That figure exceeds what some states spend on appointed counsel for thousands of indigent defendants.

For most of these individuals, an extended trial is out of the question. Lawyers are under enormous pressures to convince poor clients to accept plea bargains, and these clients often believe that they have no real alternative but to accept. Over 90 percent of criminal cases are settled without trial, and frequently without significant pretrial legal investigation.

Contrary to the claims of many politicians, the Simpson prosecution is not a reliable guide for evaluating reform proposals, particularly those imposing further limits on trial advocacy and publicity. For the vast majority of criminal cases, the problem is too little public scrutiny and zealous advocacy rather than too much. Among poor defendants, the small minority of cases that proceed to trial often involve a real question of guilt or innocence, and they provide crucial opportunities to detect and deter misconduct by law enforcement officials. Protecting the rights of the defendants who demand a jury proceeding helps also to protect the vast majority of defendants who do not.

This is not to imply that the conduct of Simpson's defense attorneys should be the model for all cases. But much of what observers found most troubling is already punishable under existing rules. And the most serious problem that the Simpson case highlighted in our criminal defense system is not the one now attracting reform proposals. Where policymakers should focus is on our double standards of justice. The current structure bears an awkward resemblance to the one parodied in a well-known *New Yorker* cartoon. There, a well-heeled lawyer asks his anxious client, "So, Mr. Smith, how much justice can you afford?" As William Julius Wilson notes, "[t]here's something wrong with a system where it's better to be guilty and rich and have good lawyers than to be innocent and poor and have bad ones." Yet virtually none of the post-Simpson reform efforts focus on reducing our double standards of criminal defense.

Indeed, the dominant political forces are all pushing in the opposite direction. The federal government is cutting funds for legal aid centers that provide back-up assistance for poor defendants. States similarly are reducing criminal defense expenditures by relying less on public defenders and more on private lawyers who submit competitive bids for specified groups of cases. Often these bidding systems impose no caseload limits per attorney and provide no significant oversight of their services. For anyone who truly cares about the quality of American justice, these initiatives point in precisely the wrong direction.

Americans like to believe that their legal system provides extensive safeguards for individuals facing criminal prosecution. "It is better," we still claim, "that a thousand guilty men go free than that one innocent man be convicted." Yet the public reaction to the Simpson proceeding points up the gap between our rhetorical ideals and our political inclinations, at least when race and class enter the picture. Many Americans appear far more troubled by the possibility that one rich black man got off than the certainty that many poor black defendants risk unjust convictions. Without adequate legal assistance, these individuals have no way to expose tainted evidence or racist police practices.

If there are broader lessons to be drawn from the Simpson prosecution, they are not the ones that most policymakers are drawing. So atypical a case cannot justify the move to curtail defendants' rights or media scrutiny. Rather, this proceeding should focus our attention on the United States' increasing acceptance of apartheid justice.

A REPRESENTATIVE CASE OF DOMESTIC VIOLENCE

While the Simpson case is extremely atypical in the legal representation available to the defendant, it is all too typical in the legal responses available to the victim. Nicole Simpson's experience was quite representative, except in the amount of publicity it eventually received. And even in the Simpson proceeding, the blitz of media coverage was relatively brief; after the first weeks, the domestic violence issue largely dropped from view until the trial concluded. As the *New York Times* noted, prosecutors "soft-pedaled" Simpson's record of spousal abuse, "apparently considering it too risky" for full exposure.

The media followed suit, and for much of the trial turned its attention to more diverting issues, including Marcia Clark's hairstyles and squabbles among defense counsel. In commenting on the lack of coverage concerning domestic violence issues, one news editor interviewed on National Public Radio explained, "There's no new angle on that topic." Only the same old ones: inadequate sanctions, shelters, support services, and treatment programs. And millions of women brutalized as a result.

Those aging angles are the ones that more commentators and policymakers need to pursue. They need to ask about domestic violence the same question that so many politicians are asking about criminal defense: "What does this case tell us about the need for reform?" The answer is all too much. Until Nicole Simpson's murder, the law enforcement system failed to take seriously her repeated pleas for help. And that is equally true for most battered wives.

The statistics are sobering. Domestic violence is the leading cause of injury to women and claims an estimated four million victims each year. Between one-third and one-half of all women will experience brutality from a spouse or partner at some point during their lifetime. According to 1994 U.S. Department of Justice data, one-third of all female homicide victims are killed by a husband or boyfriend. The American Medical Association estimates that the cost of domestic violence totals somewhere between five and ten billion dollars per year in health care, absences, lost wages, litigation, and incarceration. Despite recent improvements, virtually every study finds serious deficiencies in the way that prosecutors, police, judges, and the public respond to spousal abuse. Although few individuals put it so directly, many share the view that Simpson expressed to arresting officers: "This is a family matter. Why do you want to make a big deal of it?"

In fact, most Americans don't. And the reasons have much to do with widespread patterns of denial that emerged in the Simpson case. We deny—often until it is too late—both the seriousness of women's injuries and men's responsibility for inflicting them.

The trivialization of injuries was all too apparent in the Simpson proceedings. The euphemisms that surfaced to describe the defendant's history of violence are illuminating, and illustrative of broader patterns. Simpson himself described his brutal marital assaults as "get[ting] physical." His lawyer, Johnnie Cochran, referred to the beating that led to Simpson's earlier conviction as an "unfortunate incident" and noted that "nobody's perfect." A dismissed juror, Michael Knox, was equally forgiving of the same incident, which he saw as part of the "ups and downs with spouse and girlfriends." The trial judge who imposed sentence for that assault seemed to share these views; Simpson escaped without jail time and was allowed to complete his required counseling sessions by telephone.

Such attitudes are all too common. Virtually every study of male batterers and every state report on gender bias in the courts finds widespread denial and devaluation of domestic violence. Men trivialize women's injuries even as they describe them. Assaults become "whacks," "physical responses," "misbehavior," and "unfortunate" exceptions to otherwise "umblemished" records.

Police and prosecutors often share those attitudes. Many law enforcement personnel see domestic "incidents" as diversions from their "real" criminal work, and are particularly unsympathetic to calls from low-income and minority women. Other officials acknowledge the seriousness of the problem but are unwilling to give it priority when judges refuse to do so. In surveyed jurisdictions, about 90 percent of family violence cases are never prosecuted. Over two-thirds of such complaints are classified as simple misdemeanors, even though most involve serious injuries. In some cities, no more than 1 percent of men arrested for assault are convicted or serve any jail time.

The trivialization of women's injuries is not lost on women themselves, who often have their own reasons to discount abuse. Many women—and Nicole Simpson was no exception—depend on batterers for economic support, social identity, and emotional attachment. Acknowledging the true extent of violence in their relationships can be extremely difficult. That difficulty is compounded by the negative stereotypes associated with battered women—passivity, helplessness, and disfiguring injuries. Many women who actively resist violence also resist labeling themselves as victims and their partners as abusers.

The pressures for denial are particularly great for certain groups of women. Some immigrants come from cultures where private violence is rarely a matter for public intervention, and many of these women fear contact with American governmental agencies. Lesbians often are reluctant to risk the homophobia and lack of gay community support that may accompany disclosure of an abusive same-sex relationship. These concerns help account for the gross underreporting of domestic violence; most surveys estimate that well under 10 percent of battering incidents reach police attention.

The reluctance of women to report abuse helps perpetuate a related pattern of denial—one that holds women accountable for the brutality they suffer and that denies, dismisses, or discounts the responsibility of men. Sometimes this entire process of denial gets lost in the subtleties of syntax. Reliance on the passive voice allows abusive men to remain out sight and out of mind. Women are victimized by "cycles of violence," or trapped in "dysfunctional families." In emergency room records, female patients are ambushed by abstraction. In one representative survey, four-fifths of medical case files suggesting risks of abuse included no information about the assailant.

In other contexts, the relocation of responsibility is more overt. Batterers blame alcohol, drugs, and most often, their victims. Abusive men often claim that they don't "want to get violent." It's just that "booze" causes their "temporary insanity," or that wives "provoke" the problem by nagging, cooking lousy meals, taking interest in other men, or refusing sex on demand. O. J. Simpson's *I Want to Tell You: My Response to Your Letters, Your Messages, Your Questions* offers a representative sampling of the "mental abuse" and verbal "tortures" that assertedly provoke physical responses by long-suffering men.

Of course, male batterers are not the only people who blame battered women. So do police, prosecutors, judges, and the rest of us. While we agree in principle that it is wrong for men to beat women, we often make allowances in practice for men who do. We condemn women for being "cold," "emasculating," "provocative," "self-destructive," and "dependent."

Such attitudes prominently figured in public and media responses to the Simpson proceedings. Many press accounts painted Nicole Simpson as a promiscuous gold digger who provoked her own abuse. "Poor Nicole," wrote one irritated reader in *People*'s March 13, 1995, letters to the editor. "I'm tired of hearing it. . . . [She chose to remain] a player in a high stakes game and lost big time." One of my own op-editorials prompted a similar response. The author was annoyed enough to write me personally to point out that Nicole Simpson had had eight opportunities to file assault charges. In his view, either she was still sexually attracted to Simpson or she did not want to "threaten the earnings power that provided her with a 'rich' and easy life." To other observers, the problem was not Nicole's passivity but her assertiveness. According to one radio talk show caller, "if men murder their wives in cold blood, it's because women murder their husbands with words."

Such attitudes persist in part because it is simpler to blame women than to question the conflicting signals that women receive. Friends, family, clergy, and the media remind wives that good marriages require work, that good men are hard to find, that children need a father, that welfare dependency is a sin, and that "for better or worse" means what it says. We tell women to stay married and then damn them for trying. As one African American notes, "I put up with violence all those years trying *not* to be the welfare mother white folks hate and then those same white folks . . . tell me I should have left my husband." Other women caught in similar double binds blame only themselves. Our questions become their questions. Why can't they avoid provoking the violence? Why don't they just leave?

But the questions more policymakers ought to be asking are whether women have somewhere safe to go, and whether they will be able to support themselves and their children. The answers in most jurisdictions are scarcely reassuring. Half of all interspousal homicides and most of the serious injuries occur after the woman attempts to leave. Although individuals at risk of violence are entitled to protective orders, these mandates are routinely violated. Battered women's shelters and related social services are chronically underfunded. Despite some recent improvements, including modest federal subsidies in the 1994 Violence Against Women Act, we are nowhere close to providing adequate assistance. About half of all counties have no formal resources for battered women. Existing programs meet only a fraction of survivors' needs for housing, child care, vocational training, legal aid, and related assistance. Our current system provides least for those who need help most: low-income, poor, nonwhite, elderly, disabled, and immigrant women. If someone like Nicole Simpson is unable to escape abuse, what does that say about millions of other battered women who have far fewer opportunities?

The Simpson case has attracted public attention to domestic violence, but not the resources necessary to address it. And the immediacy of our needs suggests one bridge across the racial divide that separated Americans following the verdict. Whatever our other differences, all of us have a stake in reducing the enormous toll that such violence continues to exact. That will, in turn, require more effective law enforcement responses to battering and far more social services for those who otherwise cannot escape it. The challenge remaining is to build the coalitions that can translate our shared concerns into social priorities.

Two larger lessons of the Simpson case are when money matters and how often we spend it in the wrong places. Wealth doesn't save women like Nicole Simpson but it often frees men like her former husband. A society that invested adequately in domestic violence prevention and law enforcement strategies might escape the price tags of prosecutions like Simpson's, which cost Los Angeles an estimated $10 million. And a society that took seriously its rhetorical commitment to equal justice under law would not tolerate apartheid in legal representation.

Nicole Simpson's experience was typical; O.J.'s is not. And we need to learn from both.

Race and Gender

Charlie Rose Interviews
Gloria Steinem and Patricia Williams

[Editor's Note: The following are edited and abridged excerpts from a transcript of *Charlie Rose*, broadcast on October 9, 1995; they may be out of context.]

CHARLIE ROSE: The O. J. Simpson verdict exposed a fault line between race and gender. While many white women identified with the issue of spousal abuse, many African-American women joined their male counterparts in cheering Simpson's acquittal. What does the Simpson verdict mean to women and the nation's attitude toward domestic violence? Joining me now, *Ms.* magazine founding editor, Gloria Steinem and Patricia Williams of the Columbia University School of Law. I am pleased to have both of you here, and my attention was struck this weekend by this story: "Whose Side to Take? Women Outraged and the Verdict on O. J. Simpson." And I read: "Perhaps the last time in an extraordinary week that Americans shared a single emotion was the cool second before the verdict in the Simpson case. That was before "not guilty" undraped a racial fault line between blacks and whites so deep that it seemed that the two groups had been watching different movies. Nowhere was that divide more stark than it was between black women and white women. And then it goes on to say, "Black women, pulled by competing loyalties, tended to see Mr. Simpson as a black man framed by the system even if he had been indifferent [to the] black community and even if they thought he might be guilty. White women tended to identify with Mrs. Simpson as an abuse victim."

What's going on here? Do you experience this kind of fault line, in which race and gender are cutting against each other? Pat?

PATRICIA WILLIAMS: I think that it is unfair to say that women were cheering, in fact anybody was really cheering this verdict one way or the other. I think there were two things going on. One was a trial in a courtroom, and one was an extraordinary spectacle, in which issues other than those on trial in the courtroom were being negotiated, including the issue of police behavior, including for many in other communities, domestic violence. And so in black communities, I think the issue of Mark Fuhrman and the abuse of—the abuses of the police department became uppermost in people's minds.

CHARLIE ROSE: Yeah.

PATRICIA WILLIAMS: There's a second level, in terms of your specific question about the response of black women. I think you customarily find some reluctance, some difficulty among black women to speak about issues of domestic violence, as well as issues of public harassment because it's in such a loaded symbolic field. It's—take, for example, Mike Tyson. On the one hand, you have Mike Tyson, real rapist, something that nobody approves of, nobody—black women, white women, black men, anybody. On the other hand, you have a hypersexualized image of the glistening black body that's also symbolically at reference in any discussion, and the question when you're talking about the combination of violence by black men is whether or not you can successfully narrow it down to the issue of domestic violence, which is a national problem among black and white, or whether or not it plays into the sort of excessive spectacle and theater that any time black men are involved tends to disproportionalize and terribly eroticize the result. And I think that's the sense of difficulty that you hear in black women speaking [out] too forcefully in the public arena. I don't think there's any equivocation in terms of the condemnation among black women of domestic violence, if that's what you're asking.

Jeffrey Abramson m. to
Jacqueline Jones
author of
<u>Labor of Love, Labor</u>
<u>of Sorrows</u>

Tim Rutten co-wrote Johnnie Cochran's book m. to
Leslie Abramson
def. atty.

Victoria Tensing   m.
to Joe di Genova (?)
Jay Monahan
m. to Katie Couric

CHARLIE ROSE: On the other hand, I've seen one story after another saying that there was a different reaction and that even—if not cheering the acquittal of Mr. Simpson, cheering the indictment of the police, and some people will suggest to you that in this trial the defense was successful in putting the police on trial, the LAPD, rather than Mr. Simpson, and that was in fact what they were able to do, and people were cheering the fact that someone beat that corrupt—

GLORIA STEINEM: But there were a lot of white people cheering the fact that the LAPD was—not cheering, that's a bad word, but you know—approving of, understanding of—I mean, the sexism in the LAPD was underplayed by the press, but actually Fuhrman was being interviewed for a film called *Men Against Women,* which is a group within the LAPD. I mean, you know, what happened here is the racial element got reported much more, and I also question the way the questions were asked. You know, I'd like to really look at the way the questions were asked, because it's—quite possible to believe that some of the evidence was doctored, and O. J. Simpson was guilty and if you've had much more experience with the police force that's biased, you know, then that seems the greater punishment. The only person I've seen on television so far who actually reflected a lot of what I felt was a kid interviewed—a black kid with his hat on backwards in the street, you know, who was saying "I think he's guilty, but, you know, white men since time immemorial have been getting off and—on reasonable doubt—

CHARLIE ROSE: Sure.

GLORIA STEINEM: —and he got off on reasonable doubt. I have no sympathy for, for him whatsoever, you know—domestic violence, beating up women is terrible." I mean, you know, the kid was fine.

PATRICIA WILLIAMS: I also think it's sort of dangerous to talk about the issue of police. I mean, certainly in the media, in the trial, in the movie, O.J., the movie—as it played out in the place of soap operas, what was on trial was at least Mark Fuhrman and much more. But it is also important to remember that the jury was sequestered in this case. They got a piece of the Mark Fuhrman tape. What we, as the audience got, was the Mark Fuhrman tape played over and over and over again.

CHARLIE ROSE: We got unabridged Mark Fuhrman.

PATRICIA WILLIAMS: Yes. And we got the history of the L.A. Police Department, we got news about the Philadelphia Police Department, and it seems to me that the people who were cheering in the streets, they were cheering in this very much larger theater, football game of what the media made in terms of its slow reenactment and replaying of things that the jury never saw. So on some symbolic level, yes, when people danced, they were dancing at something that went far, far beyond this verdict, I think.

 I'm very suspicious of this blacks are over here and whites are over here. The media coverage, the spectacle that this trial was turned into, really transformed O. J. Simpson from the beginning of this trial, from the white, black man into the penultimate black suspect. And I think the thing that reinforces that is if you recall—

CHARLIE ROSE: Johnnie Cochran did that for him, rather than the media.

PATRICIA WILLIAMS: Well, Johnnie Cochran did his job for him as a defense attorney, which is to scratch sand in the face of the prosecution, put the prosecution to its test. To the extent that what Johnnie Cochran did was broadcast to the world, he can't do two things at once, and certainly what he did—if he were arguing policy, if he were arguing domestic violence, if he were arguing police—was probably not appropriate, but that was not his job. His job was to represent, zealously, the interests of his client and to throw sand in the face of the prosecution. But if you recall in the very beginning, there was that slow sort of chase—running of the bulls around the city of Los Angeles, in which it was white people who were gathered saying, "Go, O.J., go."

GLORIA STEINEM: Yeah, that's true.

PATRICIA WILLIAMS: The pictures—it's almost a mirror image of what happened at the end, in which there were black people cheering, saying, "Go, O.J., go." And that seems to me the extent to which what happened was really a symbolic reversal and not what was going on in the courtroom.

CHARLIE ROSE: Are you saying that there was no racial divide?

PATRICIA WILLIAMS: Oh, absolutely. But I don't think that the trial undraped it. I think that what you had in this trial, on the symbolic level—not necessarily what went on in the courtroom, but on the symbolic level—was a meeting of Grade B movie out of

Hollywood, sporting event, and miscegenation, which has always pushed America's hot buttons.

CHARLIE ROSE: But that's what made it such a media frenzy, and that's what made it so attractive to an American audience?

PATRICIA WILLIAMS: But it is also what has always represented our deepest divides. It is precisely the aspect of theater that has made blacks most resentful of this kind of display. And again, I'm not surprised that in terms of the theatrical what was played out on that larger theater, the court of passionate public opinion, that when the police lost, so to speak—but again, symbolically rather than actually in the courtroom—that there would be theatrical response.

GLORIA STEINEM: —I mean, in a personal—you know, I don't know where you were and where I was when we heard the verdict.

CHARLIE ROSE: But you do know where you were. Where were you?

GLORIA STEINEM: Well, I was at home, and then I had to go out and travel, and I kept telling myself, "I'm not going to let this take over my life," and so I was trying to work—nonetheless, I felt, and I can feel it now, kind of tears, you know, behind my eyes because it just seemed so unfair, and, and I kept thinking of the kids and Rosie Greer, to whom he apparently confessed or at least said he did it in an argument—you know I couldn't stop thinking about it. And when I finally got out to Milwaukee or wherever it was that I was going, an older black man stopped me in the airport, and he said, "I'm so sorry. I just want you to know that not all of us feel this way." And I think we have to trust our human encounters as well as what the numbers are with some questions.

CHARLIE ROSE: Well, let me ask you this, then. Do you think you felt that way because your long and valiant effort against domestic abuse and spousal abuse made this—and you, especially, sensitive on this issue, or was it because there was evidence here of a brutal crime, period?

GLORIA STEINEM: Well, I, I identify with the powerless person, especially women, but anybody who's—and, you know, I absolutely, totally identified. I also understand, though, that there are women of every race who don't identify. And if the juror who said it wasn't a matter of domestic violence—I mean, maybe she is saying that because she doesn't—she's experienced—I don't know what's in her heart. I'm not trying to say that, but maybe she experienced domestic violence and she doesn't want to believe she could be killed. Or maybe she sees it in her neighborhood, and she doesn't want to believe it can escalate. I don't know. But it's more complicated.

PATRICIA WILLIAMS: I—again, I think the media recounting of what was presented in trial played two aspects over and over again that became, I think, the contest in a larger court of public opinion. One was the police lying, Mark Fuhrman—and the other was the feature of domestic violence. As to the jury, the sequestered jury, these were introduced as pieces of evidence having to do with motive, motive of O. J. Simpson as to the domestic violence, and motive as to the police officer. They were part of the evidence. When that juror said that—again, she has not been subject to the entire context of the violence.

GLORIA STEINEM: Right. That's important because she only saw one instance [of abuse]—because only one instance was reported to the police.

PATRICIA WILLIAMS: And so the question that was posed to her is, you know, is literally the extent to which domestic violence was on trial, and she said, "Domestic violence wasn't on trial. It was a murder trial."

CHARLIE ROSE: This was—the juror's name was Moran.

PATRICIA WILLIAMS: Moran. Yes. And again, you'd probably have to do a more complete interview with her than that particular question—but I think that a more reasonable interpretation of that comment was that domestic violence was, in fact, not on trial in this any more than police brutality in some general sense. Domestic violence, generally, was not. It specifically had to do with motive.

GLORIA STEINEM: And also, they did only see this one instance. I think it's important to say, perhaps because [Simpson's defense attorney] Peter Neufeld was sitting at this table saying the contrary, which is not true—that domestic violence in his view was not relevant because he had never seen a case in which it failed to escalate, and this had just been one instance long ago. That's not true. It did escalate. Just because it didn't turn up in the police blotter or, you know—and also there was stalking and so on, that showed the intensity of obsession of O. J. Simpson, whether he committed the murder or not, did in fact escalate. So I really resent these lawyers.

I mean, they—okay, they tossed sand in people's faces and they won, but let them stop with the sand now and start telling the truth.

PATRICIA WILLIAMS: That's—they have a fiduciary responsibility to their client. I mean I think that—

GLORIA STEINEM: Even forever? Even when he stops paying?

PATRICIA WILLIAMS: This trial may go on forever. I'm sorry. Whether we like it or not, it may go on forever. But I do think that it would be, it would be an astonishing sort of turnaround if a defense attorney—and I think that it's unfair to ask the defense attorneys to continue to represent the entire cause of domestic violence.

GLORIA STEINEM: No, but just to—all I'm asking—he could have said [the other instances where O.J. abused Nicole were not] admissible evidence. I would have accepted that. But to say [they] didn't exist, I think, is beyond—

PATRICIA WILLIAMS: These are not the people who should be framing our arguments about this.

GLORIA STEINEM: No. That's certainly true.

PATRICIA WILLIAMS: I mean, it's bizarre that we even expect somebody in [the Simpson defense attorney's] position to be coming out saying the right thing [about domestic violence]. I mean, let me also put this in perspective. I have a reasonable doubt about O. J. Simpson's innocence. And that's the prosecution's burden. That's the way the system works. I have always passionate suspicions about O. J. Simpson, but that's very different from saying that the prosecution proved its burden beyond a reasonable doubt—

GLORIA STEINEM: Yes, and I wonder—

PATRICIA WILLIAMS: —particularly where you had the chief prosecution witnesses lying.

GLORIA STEINEM: Right, and I wonder if—

PATRICIA WILLIAMS: It's an exceptional case in that regard.

GLORIA STEINEM: —if the questions in the public opinion polls reflected this—what I find is, so far, is the opinion of most people, which is both that the LAPD lied in some way and therefore there was reasonable doubt, and that he was not innocent. I mean, you know, as I travel around, that seems to me to be the biggest piece of public opinion.

CHARLIE ROSE: Do you share that—I run into a lot of people who believe that the LAPD had an opportunity to contaminate, and they had in at least one case an acknowledged liar on trial, testifying as a principal prosecution witness.

PATRICIA WILLIAMS: And police who had access to the evidence rooms.

CHARLIE ROSE: Is there anything, do you think, in your experience—because you're black and I'm white, Gloria's white—that would have led you, in a sense, to have that evidence, that fact be a more penetrating fact for you, do you think?

PATRICIA WILLIAMS: I'm sorry. Which [evidence]?

CHARLIE ROSE: The notion of the LAPD being corrupt and the police being—having the capacity to contaminate evidence and planting evidence.

PATRICIA WILLIAMS: I resisted the question because I think that every black person is asked to speak for all other black people, which is precisely what people sort of read into this jury opinion that, that every black juror there is all black people and therefore—

CHARLIE ROSE: But I don't ask you to speak for everybody. I asked you specifically.

PATRICIA WILLIAMS: In my experience, I specifically actually worked for the L.A. City Attorney's office for a while. I was a prosecutor for a while and perhaps I speak as a lawyer rather than as a black person. There are very few people who have done any kind of criminal case, either prosecution or defense, who [don't] know that witnesses, both police and other kinds of witnesses, are human. You find witnesses who lie. You know, you read a report. It looks good. You get them on the stand, and suddenly—or you overhear a conversation in the—back in the office, you realize that somebody has lied. Again, I'm somebody who follows these statistics, so I know that while it's endemic, that is not to say it's universal. But there's this contradictory statistic where black people want more police protection but at the same time represent those most distrustful. And I think that the contradiction gets resolved in the fact that, that black communities are poor communities. They're underserved, they're frequently misserved by police departments. But there's still a yearning within the black community for good police officers and a great respect for the police officers.

CHARLIE ROSE: Gloria said that she thought that the first reaction on hearing [the verdicts] was a sense of it's unfair. Did you feel that?

PATRICIA WILLIAMS: Yes. I think that any time there's an acquittal and there's a violent crime, there's a sense of lack of resolution that is to some extent inconsolable, and there's a way in which we attach to the outcomes, and particularly of criminal verdicts in violent crimes, horrible crimes such as this—I was very moved, too, at the end of that trial when the family was sobbing. We want some sort of theological resolution. You want vengeance, and a verdict comes closer to that. An acquittal, even where it can be said that the system works, or you can say that the prosecution didn't meet its burden, leaves one with a terrible sense of lack of closure. I have that feeling about this case, too. You know, either you have to believe a conspiracy theory, which I'm not sure I'm—you know, it would have to be a complicated conspiracy for me to buy into that, or you have to say that the prosecution failed its burden, and it failed by virtue of a variety of institutional failings in my opinion, principally the police department, but you know, I would be more afraid if you could convict even with corrupt evidence.

GLORIA STEINEM: Well, I sort of came around—I'm just speaking personally now, because I was thinking about Nicole, and thinking, well, she has two children, whom she loved, and these children are going to be hounded by society as people of color and if she were here and she thought that her death was going to contribute to less possibility that those children would suffer, because of bias within the society and law enforcement in particular, maybe that would be okay, providing that we continue with an understanding of how universal domestic violence is and trying to really use the lessons of this case.

CHARLIE ROSE: Because of this verdict, do you think it has implications in terms of domestic violence and in terms of the response of men and women? There have been some reports that men have said, you know, because of the Simpson verdict, I now have the freedom to do more than I ever thought I could, that kind of thing.

GLORIA STEINEM: Well, that was happening long before the verdict. I mean, you know, as I went around doing benefits for battered women shelters and so on over the months, what you saw was that women would come in and say, "My husband or my boyfriend cut out the O. J. Simpson clipping and put it on the refrigerator door, and said, 'See, I can do anything I want to you.'" Now, sometimes that was a plus, in the sense that it got the woman to come in to the shelter, and—but of course, I don't know the end of the story. I don't know what happened to her. I think it's somewhat analogous to the Anita Hill situation where there was one verdict at the end of a process and then a special process went forward with people talking about a set of experiences, whatever the merits of the case might have been—it brought discussion—

CHARLIE ROSE: There was a positive, there was a positive reaction to that.

GLORIA STEINEM: It brought discussion, it brought revealing—and so it really changed the country for the better. It's possible if we work on it, that this could have that effect, too.

CHARLIE ROSE: But do you think that's where it's leaning now, based on the anecdotal evidence that you have, i.e., people that you talk to, that there is a sense of we really—because of this, we have to really focus on the question of spousal abuse?

GLORIA STEINEM: Well, I can only tell you my real experiences, which I have more faith in than the numbers. I was in Minneapolis, and I was in the PBS station there, and they have a very diverse staff. They said that they had been feeling quite a lot of tension because of—I don't know whether their own response to the verdict or what they saw on television—but they were feeling tension between the black and white members of the staff, and so they had come together and really talked about it for hours, and now they felt they'd come to some better understandings.

PATRICIA WILLIAMS: I think it's a disaster. I think this was bread and circus, and one of the functions of spectacles and bread and circus is to divert from real issues. I think that's all this trial has done. And it substitutes O. J. Simpson for all black defendants, and then gives policy discussions an excuse, using the figure of O. J. Simpson, to say that this is a typical black defendant. O. J. Simpson had sixteen attorneys on his team, and the idea that you're going to make it harder for defendants to win completely belies the empirical evidence about how easy it is to convict a black defendant who walks into court.

If Nicole Brown Simpson had been black, this case would never have been heard from. I would love to see as much—just half, a quarter, a sixteenth of the media attention that this trial received going into real battered women's shelters—

GLORIA STEINEM: Right.

PATRICIA WILLIAMS: —relating welfare and poverty to the large numbers of women who are there: 50 percent of women on welfare supposedly battered, 60 percent of homeless.

GLORIA STEINEM: We ought to get Geraldo Rivera and everybody to continue their shows—just like *Nightline* continued, you know, after the hostage crisis or whatever it was, and cover ordinary cases—

PATRICIA WILLIAMS: Ordinary cases.

GLORIA STEINEM: —so we see what's really happening.

PATRICIA WILLIAMS: If TV would sort of randomly go into courtrooms to see the ordinary plight of a black defendant, they would not see justice overdone, as it was in this case; they would see it tremendously, tremendously underdone. If they would just go into battered homes and battered shelters—it would be a completely different—

GLORIA STEINEM: And if we could get them—the media to stop romanticizing—sexualizing violence and murder, which is what they do. I mean, there is no such thing as a crime of passion. There's a crime of possession. Right at the same time as the verdict, there was a big headline in a New York paper that said, "Love Rage." All right, now what was this love rage? It was a man who had blown up his children and his wife in a car with such force that body parts were found hundreds of yards away. Had he killed anyone else but his wife and children, they—it would not have been called "Love Rage." Even his own parents, it wouldn't have been called that.

PATRICIA WILLIAMS: And Nicole Brown Simpson was eroticized relentlessly in this. Nobody's talking about that, but she was this sexy blond bombshell who, again, I think that if she'd been a plain black woman, nobody would have cared.

GLORIA STEINEM: No, if he'd killed his first wife, it would have been very different.

PATRICIA WILLIAMS: Exactly. Yes, I mean, we have to stop eroticizing because it does no service to the human being Nicole Brown Simpson was, and it makes invisible the plain brown bodies who are also the victims of this, and it puts a dividing line between black and white in terms of the pervasiveness which domestic violence actually represents.

CHARLIE ROSE: I thank you both. Thank you very much.

PART III

Lawyers

---

*Their Strategies and
Their Ethics*

O.J. v. DNA

What the DNA Really Showed

HARLAN LEVY

The most formidable challenge facing O. J. Simpson's defense lawyers at his double murder trial was the trail of blood evidence implicating the former football star in the murders of his ex-wife Nicole Brown and her friend Ronald Goldman. Even before DNA testing became available, any defendant in such a spot would have been hard-pressed to explain the presence of blood in his car and at his home immediately following the crime. DNA technology took Simpson's problem to a new level; it was now possible to establish to a scientific certainty that the blood was that of the victims.

When the results of the DNA testing were reported, the defense team had to face the worst. Blood with DNA that matched Simpson's was found at Nicole Brown's home. Blood spots in Simpson's car contained DNA matching Brown's, Ronald Goldman's, and Simpson's. Blood at Simpson's home contained DNA that matched Nicole Brown's and Ronald Goldman's.

To those familiar with the capabilities of this new technology, the case against Simpson seemed airtight, and to many observers the matter ended right there. DNA had sealed Simpson's fate; his guilt had been proven conclusively. He would be sent to prison for the rest of his life. What the DNA evidence showed, how Simpson's lawyers contested that powerful evidence, and how genuine were the issues raised, is one of the major untold stories of the trial. Here is that story.

BLOOD NEAR THE MURDER VICTIMS

There were five blood drops at Nicole Brown's home containing DNA that matched Simpson's. Four were located on the walkway; a fifth blood drop was found in the driveway. The blood drops on the walkway began near the murder victims, to the left of bloody footprints leading away from Nicole Brown's home, and continued past the rear gate and into the driveway. Their location indicated that they were shed by the killer, bleeding drops to the ground as he left the scene of the crime, heading from the walkway, to the rear gate and then the driveway.

DNA analysis on the blood drops was conducted by three different laboratories: the LAPD lab, a private lab in Maryland called Cellmark, and the California Department of Justice lab. All three labs independently found that the DNA in the blood drops matched Simpson's DNA. The blood drop in the driveway was large enough to be tested by the classic DNA procedure known as Restriction Fragment Length Polymorphism Analysis (RFLP). This test produced a 1 in 170 million match of Simpson's DNA to the DNA in the driveway. Other blood drops were subjected to a second kind of DNA testing capable of examining even tiny amounts of blood—the Polymerase Chain Reaction (PCR) Test. There was a 1 in 240,000 PCR match to Simpson on four of the blood drops, and a 1 in 5,200 match on a fifth.

These five blood drops were among the most powerful evidence against Simpson because they represented the DNA evidence least persuasively contested by the defense. They were collected by criminalists on June 13, prior to the time later the same day when the police first obtained a sample of Simpson's own blood. This means that any police tampering would have involved not simply planting the evidence but substituting the evidence, and it would have had to have taken place while the drops were in the custody of police criminalists. Just as significant, this substitution would most likely have had to have taken place between the collection of the blood drops on June 13 and DNA analysis of the blood drops on June 14 at the LAPD lab, since that analysis already showed a match to Simpson.

To meet this evidence, the defense offered testimony designed to show that tampering may indeed have taken place, and within that brief window. Their main witness offered to support this point was Dr. Henry Lee, chief criminalist of the state of Connecticut, a man frequently described as the "world's foremost criminalist."

Dr. Lee testified that there were blood smudges on the packaging of one of the five blood drops. This, said Dr. Lee, indicated that the swatches (the pieces of cotton) on which the blood drop had been collected were wet when placed inside their packaging. The swatches, left to dry on June 13, had more than adequate time to dry before they were placed in the packaging on June 14, so a stain from wet material, when the material should have been dry, raised a question. "Who did it, what happened, I don't know," testified Lee. Asked his opinion of the significance of the existence of these stains, Lee said that the "only opinion I can give under this circumstance" is that there is "something wrong." Lee then rejected several potentially innocent explanations for the presence of these smudges.

Defense lawyer Barry Scheck, never shy, took up Lee's implication that the swatches may have been switched. As usual, he provided facts purporting to support his claim. A criminalist had given testimony that she had placed her initials on the packaging containing the swatches, but no initials were found. Besides, claimed Scheck, swatches like those on which the blood was collected are distributed to detectives for purposes of evidence collection, so that a detective intent on switching swatches would have had material to work with, swatches to wet with blood.

There were significant problems with this argument that swatches had been switched, even beyond the audacity of the conduct alleged. The DNA found in the blood drops was heavily degraded, and there was no reason why swatches dabbed in O. J. Simpson's pristine blood sample with a preservative in it would have been degraded. And why would rogue police officers, who according to the defense's own theory truly believed that Simpson was guilty, have removed evidence that they would have thought would point directly to him? Besides, switching swatches would have required not simply substituting five planted swatches for the five blood drops collected, but many more than five swatches, since some of the blood drops were sufficiently large that they were collected not just on one but on several swatches, later tested by DNA analysis. The jump from the statement that there was "something wrong" to the conclusion that multiple swatches had been switched between June 13 and June 14 was a great leap with little basis in logic, reason, or evidence.

But the defense relied not just on the insinuation that evidence had been deliberately removed and replaced; it also argued that laboratory procedures had so thoroughly contaminated blood evidence that any DNA analysis of the blood was unreliable. A defense microbiologist, Dr. John Gerdes, testified that he had found an "extremely serious" pattern of contamination in the LAPD's PCR analysis in other tests. Gerdes also criticized the testing practices in the Simpson case itself, and even claimed that the RFLP result matching Simpson from the driveway might have been contaminated, although that test is much less vulnerable to contamination than PCR. The defense took particular aim at Collin Yamauchi, the DNA analyst for the LAPD. According to the defense, Yamauchi had contaminated the blood drops found at the scene of the crime while preparing them for DNA analysis on June 14 after getting blood from Simpson's voluntarily given sample on his laboratory gloves. There were various weaknesses with this argument, but the most important one lay in the strength of the DNA that would have been in the underlying blood drops themselves.

Had the blood drops from the walkway and driveway been infected with Simpson's own DNA by laboratory error, they would have shown not just his DNA profile but also that of the real killer. But there was only one DNA profile, and that was Simpson's.

So the defense constructed a scenario to explain the absence of a second DNA profile, that of the real killer. And the defense skillfully offered facts to support their theory. They began with genuine scientific evidence that the DNA from the blood drops was heavily degraded—that it had broken down into smaller pieces of DNA.

It was hardly surprising that the blood drops had degraded. These particular blood drops had been stored in plastic bags in a hot truck for seven hours, an environment conducive to degradation. But degradation itself does not change a person's DNA type; it remains the same. So the defense had to go one better than heavy degradation, and argue that the DNA in all five blood drops had totally degraded, totally broken down to the point where it had literally disappeared for purposes of DNA analysis.

This scenario required a highly unlikely series of events. Degradation would have had to have been so severe that the DNA disappeared entirely in each of five separate blood drops. Next, a transfer would have had to have taken place in which the blood present in Simpson's blood sample made its way into each of the blood drops themselves. Finally, there would have had to have been a failure in five separate controls, each designed to determine whether contamination had taken place. In each instance, for each blood drop, contamination would have had to have jumped onto the blood drop being tested, but declined to jump onto a control that would have revealed its presence. In an alternative explanation for this third eventuality, Barry Scheck argued to the jury that there was no reason to assume that the controls were handled properly in a laboratory that was a "cesspool of contamination," although Yamauchi testified in detail to his proper use of the controls.

No one of these three events—total degradation, a transfer of DNA, and failure of five controls—was a strong possibility. The defense had built factual support for its own case by bringing out statements from the prosecution's own witnesses establishing that each of these occurrences was a theoretical possibility. It was unlikely that any one of these possibilities had occurred; there was less than a chance that all three had coincided. Besides, traditional blood tests that are not susceptible to contamination also typed to Simpson on one of the blood drops, reflecting a 1 in 200 person match to the former football player, indicating that contamination had not in fact taken place. This was powerful but subtle proof that there had been no contamination, but it could easily have been missed or discounted by a jury overwhelmed and troubled by extensive and complex scientific testimony about contamination.

BLOOD ON THE GATE
AT NICOLE BROWN'S HOME

Simpson was next implicated in the double homicide by three separate bloodstains on the rear gate of Nicole Brown's home. The largest stain produced a 1 in 57 billion RFLP match to Simpson. Two smaller stains matched Simpson using PCR analysis, each producing a 1 in 520 person match. These stains were analyzed by the California Department of Justice.

In challenging the significance of these bloodstains, the defense abandoned its double-barreled approach about planted *and* contaminated evidence, and relied solely on a claim that the bloodstains had been planted.

There was, first of all, the matter of opportunity. The bloodstains on the gate were not collected by police criminalists until July 3, three weeks after the murders. The innocent view of such late collection recognizes limited resources and the human tendency to miss certain things initially and then find them later. Still, the delay allowed the defense to pose a devastating question: Who knows what rogue police officers might have visited the crime scene in the interim between the crime and collection, and what they might have done?

But the defense's proof of planting went beyond opportunity. A defense expert testified that the blood recovered from the back gate included a preservative, thereby suggesting that it had come from O. J. Simpson's "missing blood." The nurse who drew blood from Simpson on June 13 testified before trial that he had drawn between 7.9 and 8.1 milliliters of blood. However, after allowing for the 1 milliliter of Simpson's blood used for DNA testing at the LAPD lab on June 14, only 5.5 milliliters remained. This means that 1.5 milliliters were missing—although the nurse, in an unsworn statement, later took back his testimony about the amount of blood he had taken from Simpson, stating that he had overstated it. The defense also focused on the condition of the bloodstains on the gate relative to that of the stains on the walkway, noting that those that had supposedly been on the rear gate, exposed to the elements for weeks, were in better condition and contained more DNA than the stains that had been collected immediately.

The prosecution sharply challenged the defense expert who asserted that the blood on the rear gate contained a preservative, and an FBI expert said that he had found no preservative. The prosecution also offered explanations for the relative condition of the blood on the rear gate. The painted surface of the gate was less absorbent than that upon which the other stains had been deposited, and there was no testimony that the rear gate stains had been placed in a hot truck for seven hours, as had the other, more degraded stains.

Most compelling, though, was the testimony by two police officers that they had seen bloodstains on the rear gate on the night of the murders. But here, too, the defense lawyers had an argument to make. The gate was rusty, argued the defense, and had various imperfections and discolorations. The defense did not question the veracity of these officers, but claimed that they were mistaken, and thought that they saw blood when they in fact saw rust or berry stains. That, argued the defense, was the reason that the LAPD criminalists had not collected blood from the rear gate on June 13. It was not yet there.

BLOOD IN O. J. SIMPSON'S CAR

The trail of DNA continued into Simpson's car, the Bronco. A first set of bloodstains was collected on June 14, and they were all analyzed with the PCR technique. Bloodstains containing Simpson's DNA had been found at five locations: the instrument panel, the driver's side carpet fiber, the steering wheel, the center console, and the driver's side wall. Nicole Brown's DNA was found in a partial bloody footprint on the driver's side. A stain containing a mixture of Simpson's and Ronald Goldman's DNA was found on the center console.

But that was not the end of the DNA evidence against Simpson from the Bronco. Collected at a later date, August 26, 1994, were bloodstains containing a mixture of the DNA of Simpson, Nicole Brown, and Ronald Goldman. Most of the stains, both those collected on June 14 and August 26, were analyzed by the California Department of Justice.

Here again, the double-barreled defense was back in full force, though with some twists. For example, as to Simpson's own blood in the Bronco, there was the innocent explanation that he claimed to have cut himself while in the car on June 12. As to the potentially damning bloody footprint in the Bronco containing the blood of Nicole Brown, the defense argued that it was made by Detective Mark Fuhrman, not Simpson. Fuhrman, they offered in explanation, had stepped in the blood at the crime scene and then later had stepped in the Bronco after arriving at Simpson's home and walking in the morning dew. Fuhrman denied having been in the Bronco at all, but the defense claimed that he was lying.

As the trial proceeded, the prosecution developed more DNA proof against Simpson relating to the Bronco. Before the trial began, in the second evidence collection on August 26, 1994, the criminalists had gathered three more bloodstains from the Bronco console. PCR analysis showed that the blood from the console contained DNA matching that of Simpson, Nicole Brown, and Ronald Goldman, but initially, there was only PCR analysis from the Bronco. The defense had generally challenged the reliability of the PCR testing, claiming such testing is too easily contaminated to rely upon. So, as the trial proceeded, the California Department of Justice laboratory combined the three stains, producing enough blood to analyze using RFLP analysis. That brew also showed a match to Simpson, Brown, and Goldman.

These stains, however, were subjected to the frame defense. They had, after all, not been collected by the police until August 26, more than two months after the murders. A theft from the Bronco during the time it was in police custody reinforced the view that the Bronco would hardly have been secure from LAPD detectives who chose to plant evidence. And a detective investigating the theft had not noticed any blood in the Bronco, although, she said, she had not specifically been looking for blood.

BLOOD AT O. J. SIMPSON'S HOME

O. J. Simpson's blood was also found at his own estate, in his driveway, foyer, and master bathroom. A blood drop in his foyer produced a 1 in 170 million RFLP match and a 1 in 5,200 PCR match. Two blood drops in the driveway each produced a PCR match to Simpson. The bathroom blood drop from the master bathroom also produced a PCR match to Simpson. The tests on the bloodstains were conducted variously by Cellmark and the California Department of Justice.

But Simpson's claim that he had cut himself while retrieving his cell phone from the Bronco before leaving for Chicago was before the jury, and was essentially uncontested. There was certainly room for skepticism about this claim; after all, Simpson also claimed to have cut himself more seriously in a Chicago hotel room later the next morning upon hearing of Nicole Brown's murder. As prosecutor Christopher Darden asked on his summation, how many times can one man cut himself in one night in how many states? Still, especially given Simpson's claim that he had cut himself in an innocent manner at his own home just before the murders, it was difficult for the government to prove its case through the presence of Simpson's own blood in his own home.

BLOODY SOCKS AT O. J. SIMPSONS'S HOME

Much more damning was the presence of Nicole Brown's and O. J. Simpson's blood on the socks allegedly found at the foot of Simpson's bed. DNA testing produced a 1 in 57 billion RFLP match to Simpson, and a 1 in 7.7 billion match to Nicole Brown. The socks were analyzed by both Cellmark and the California state DNA laboratory.

The defense did not attack the accuracy of the DNA results on the socks. Instead, it relied on a claim that the socks had been planted at the foot of Simpson's bed and that blood had later been planted on the socks.

To establish the first part of its claim, the defense relied on a police department videotape showing the foot of Simpson's bed and no socks. The timer on the videotape indicated that it was taken at 4:13 P.M., and the socks were collected between 4:30 and 4:40 P.M. on June

13. However, the police department employee who took the video-tape said that he had been told to take the videotape of the room only after it had been searched.

The evidence that blood had been planted on the socks was more compelling. The socks had been collected on June 13, but no one had noticed the bloodstains on the socks and arranged for their analysis until August 4, 1994. An LAPD criminalist, Dennis Fung, had not noticed stains on the socks when he collected them on June 13. Defense experts had not noticed any blood when they looked at the socks on June 22. On June 29, an LAPD criminalist had conducted an inventory review of the evidence and noted that no blood was obvious on the socks.

In addition, the defense expert who testified to the presence of a preservative in the blood on the rear gate also testified that there was preservative present in the blood on the socks. Another defense expert testified to his conclusion that one of the stains on a sock came from the other side of the sock when wet, and that such a stain could not have been transferred that way if there had been a foot in the sock at the time that the stain was applied, indicating that the stain must have been placed on the sock when empty.

The prosecution countered these claims with an argument that in substance asserted that it made no sense that a rogue police officer would have planted socks without any blood on them. After all, why plant socks, and then plant blood at a later time? In a world of con-spiracy and intrigue, however, anything becomes possible.

The prosecution explained that the stains were not noticed earlier because they were dark stains on dark socks, not readily visible with-out high-intensity lighting. They asserted that the June 29 review of the socks had simply been an "inventory" review, not a detailed examination of the evidence. The FBI agent who said that there was no preservative in the blood on the rear gate also found no preserva-tive in the blood on the socks. Lead prosecutor Marcia Clark offered the jury several possible explanations on her summation to account for the transfer of the stain from one side of the sock to another, including the way that the socks lay on the floor. However, most of her explanations had been anticipated by the defense, posed to Dr. Henry Lee during his testimony, and rejected as highly unlikely.

The socks were among the prosecution's most powerful evidence. But, at the same time, they aided the defense contention that some-thing was rotten in Denmark. After all, even if the jury were inclined to credit other items of evidence, how many such troubling issues could the prosecution explain away? On his summation, Barry Scheck argued that the jury could not trust any other evidence in the case if the police had manufactured evidence on the socks. That is reasonable doubt, said Scheck, and the end of the case.

THE BLOODY GLOVE AT O. J. SIMPSON'S HOME

Besides the socks, there was a bloody glove allegedly found at O. J. Simpson's home, on his grounds, the glove that Simpson tried on at the trial, the glove that purportedly "did not fit." It was a right-handed glove, the mate to a bloody glove found at Nicole Brown's home, which had contained only the blood of the murder victims. The glove was packed with bloodstains and DNA. These were analyzed by the LAPD laboratory and Cellmark. Fifteen bloodstains were identified on the glove. Most contained the DNA of more than one person, and those people, in various combinations, were O. J. Simpson, Nicole Brown, and Ronald Goldman. DNA consistent with Simpson's was found at four areas on the glove through PCR analysis.

But the person who claimed that he had found this glove at Simpson's home was Detective Mark Fuhrman. Besides its generalized critique of Fuhrman, the defense also argued that there were facts to support its contention that Fuhrman had planted the glove. Most of all, Fuhrman had described the glove as "moist and sticky" when he found it, although, said the defense, it should have already dried if he had in fact found it at Simpson's home. Moreover, the judge had told the jury that it could choose to conclude that a person who had perjured himself in one respect had perjured himself in all respects, and the jury knew that Fuhrman had lied on the stand about his racial animus.

By the end of the trial, some commentators criticized the prosecution for even arguing the significance of the glove to the jury during its summation. This was, however, hard evidence to let go. Most of all, there was the power of the DNA evidence on the glove. But beyond that, there was evidence, separate and apart from Fuhrman's testimony, which seemed to show that the glove had not been planted. The defense theory was that Fuhrman had picked up the bloody glove at Nicole Brown's home and then planted it at Simpson's home. But several police officers had responded to Nicole

Brown's home before Fuhrman, and they had seen only one glove. Besides, there were blue-black fibers on the glove matching fibers found on the socks and on Ron Goldman's shirt. The implication argued by the prosecution was that these fibers had all rubbed off the dark sweatsuit that Simpson was seen wearing earlier that evening, before the murders. There was more evidence linking Simpson to the gloves; the jury could even see photographs that seemed to show Simpson wearing both gloves, or at least very similar gloves.

And there was still another indication that the glove had not been planted. If Fuhrman had taken the glove from the murder scene, and planted it at Simpson's home while he was still in Chicago, why would Simpson's DNA have been on the glove? The presence of Simpson's DNA on the glove not only implicated him in the crime but also undercut the claim that the glove had been planted.

The defense's principal answer to this argument once again lay in the interplay of the frame defense and the contamination defense. In the defense scenario, the glove was "found" at Simpson's home because it was planted there. Then, they claimed, the glove was contaminated by Collin Yamauchi when he worked with the glove in the evidence processing room on June 14. This would have necessitated the introduction by Yamauchi of spots of Simpson's blood sufficient to contaminate four PCR results from the glove. In this version of reality, it was not that the evidence was planted *or* contaminated, but that it was both planted *and* contaminated.

The defense also suggested another scenario to account for the presence of Simpson's DNA on the glove. What if Fuhrman had the glove in the Bronco, and the glove had come into contact with the side of the console, where Simpson had earlier left blood when he retrieved his cell phone? That, the defense argued, could account for the small transfer of blood to the glove—although it was hard to understand how it could have explained four results implicating Simpson both inside and outside the glove. It was not a realistic scenario, but it was one more argument for the jury to consider, one more defense claim of doubt.

DNA AND THE VERDICT

When the jury received the case for deliberation, they had been told by the judge that their decision must be governed by the law applicable in a "circumstantial evidence" case. After all, there were no eyewitnesses who saw Simpson commit murder, no knife found in his pocket, no confession of guilt. The prosecution argued that guilt could be inferred from all the circumstances, including the blood and DNA evidence.

Circumstantial evidence cases are governed by special legal rules that can be extremely exacting. In these cases, juries may not simply consider all of the evidence and derive from it a cumulative sense that the prosecution has proven the defendant's guilt beyond a reasonable doubt. In circumstantial evidence cases, juries are told that each essential fact must be proved beyond a reasonable doubt. Where two reasonable inferences are possible from a circumstantial fact, the jury must provide the defendant the inference consistent with innocence. To convict, the jury had to take into account only those items of circumstantial evidence that could not be reconciled with any rational conclusion but guilt.

As a legal matter, it was an issue not of whether the prosecution's or the defense's inferences were more reasonable, but of whether the interpretations urged by the defense were reasonable at all. The defense team had provided the jury with inferences that it argued were consistent with innocence for virtually every piece of blood evidence implicating Simpson.

By this route, the defense was able to neutralize the impact of the six sets of stains that all pointed to Simpson, and even the two sets of stains—the blood drops at Nicole Brown's home and the bloody glove—for which the defense's explanations were least convincing. Those two sets of stains (and most of all the blood drops at Nicole Brown's home) formed an irreducible core of evidence that strongly indicated Simpson's guilt. Although the defense challenged those results vigorously and elaborately, its arguments regarding those stains, when carefully scrutinized, finally had little support in logic or reason. Still, in a case where the government was on trial, its conduct so strongly questioned, so many doubts raised, and the evidence so complex, even the compelling impact of those two sets of stains was blunted. On October 3, 1995, Simpson was acquitted, despite some DNA results that were, on their face and at their core, as strongly indicative of guilt as the prosecution could have wished.

Johnnie Cochran and Marcia Clark

Role Models?

CHARLES J. OGLETREE, JR.

On an otherwise quiet and uneventful day in June 1994, tragedy struck in Los Angeles, California. The exclusive and prosperous community of Brentwood was the site of a triple tragedy that will long be remembered as one of the most significant events in American history.

Nicole Brown Simpson, a young, attractive, vibrant woman admired by all who came in contact with her, was viciously murdered on the steps of her home. Her killer took her life mercilessly. She was not only stabbed multiple times, but was nearly decapitated, according to the testimony of the medical examiner. Ronald Goldman, an aspiring actor and waiter at an upscale restaurant in the same community, was clearly an innocent victim of this vicious attack. Unlike Nicole Brown Simpson, Ronald Goldman violently fought with his attacker or attackers, only to be mortally wounded. The event which made this case so significant was not so much the lives of the victims, but of the person accused of the crime. Within hours, law enforcement officials in southern California identified

O. J. Simpson, a Heisman trophy winner, professional football hall of fame member, actor, and sports commentator as the primary suspect.

Two people, from very different walks of life, played an important role in this case. One, Marcia Clark, an Assistant District Attorney in Los Angeles County, was assigned to be the primary prosecutor. As such, she would be responsible for identifying, charging, and convicting the person or persons responsible for Nicole Brown Simpson and Ronald Goldman's deaths. The second person, Johnnie L. Cochran, Jr., a Louisiana native who had handled many significant cases in his lifetime in southern California, was chosen as the lead attorney to defend O. J. Simpson once he was charged with the crime. The lives of Clark and Cochran would never be the same after the O. J. Simpson case.

Now that much time has passed since the trial, one question that remains is whether each of them serves as role model for a wider public audience. Their roles are significant because of the manner in which public debate about the case has developed. In many respects, women's groups saw the Simpson case, particularly in light of what was reported as a substantial history of domestic violence by O. J. Simpson against Nicole Brown Simpson, as a referendum on domestic violence. On the other hand, African Americans saw the case as a referendum on the ability of African Americans to receive a fair trial in our criminal justice system. These two diametrically opposed issues were highlighted in other respects. For the prosecution, there was evidence that Nicole Brown Simpson kept a diary, and documented numerous instances of domestic abuse at the hands of O. J. Simpson. On the other hand, many African Americans, including those in southern California, knew how police had a reputation for use of excessive force and brutality and saw this as a referendum on police practices against black citizens. The stage was thus set: Marcia Clark would vindicate the rights of women who are victims of abuse, and Johnnie Cochran would vindicate the rights of African Americans who were victims of police brutality.

It is interesting that very little attention was given to the fact that a number of people, including many African Americans and women, were conflicted on the Simpson case. While many found domestic violence intolerable and inexcusable, they were also concerned about the propensity of the Los Angeles Police Department to use excessive force and engage in brutal conduct that ignored the rights of African-American citizens. Moreover, very little discussion was given to the special role of African-American women, who could identify with Nicole Brown Simpson's abuse, but also were aware of the all-too-frequent episodes of police violating the rights of blacks. Thus, gender and race intersected in this case, and made the trial even more complicated.

With the stage set, it is hard to imagine two more appropriate people to vindicate the communities of interest than Marcia Clark and Johnnie Cochran. While there have been many prominent trials in our history, it is hard to imagine another one where a woman and an African American were selected as lead counsel on opposite sides of the case.

PRAISE OF COCHRAN AND CLARK

Both national media and members of the black community applauded the addition of Johnnie Cochran to the Simpson defense team. Cochran, who has always worked in Los Angeles, was already a local hero for representing blacks in several high-profile cases beginning in the 1960s. Today, the bulk of his firm's work consists of representing citizens in lawsuits against local police agencies. Cochran's colleagues hold his courtroom ability in high esteem. Even District Attorney Gil Garcetti, who headed the prosecution against Simpson, marveled, "The smartest thing O. J. Simpson ever did was hire Johnnie Cochran."

African Americans around the United States embraced Johnnie Cochran as he gained national prominence. One praised Cochran as "a role model our children have been needing for a long time. He ... spoke eloquently and presented an image not seen enough of—a successful, educated and intelligent African-American male." By the trial's conclusion, Cochran had so impressed black Americans that he had firmly established himself as someone that the black community admired, a "silky smooth attorney secure within himself, super-competent and aggressively at ease with the world around him."

It is not just the fact that Cochran is a black man who operates with aplomb and skill in a position of influence that endears him to most of the country's blacks. It is also their view that he is an advocate for racial justice. Said a *Boston Globe* columnist: "During the trial, Cochran became many black observers' champion against an oppressive judicial system and a corrupt police department... Cochran... best articulated their feelings about the system and made them proud to be African Americans." Former Los Angeles mayor Tom Bradley took notice of the rising black sentiment: "He is a national hero, especially among African Americans. He has taken on a new mantle because they regard his victory in trial as a victory over some racist actions by some members of the Police Department."

Marcia Clark has also received high praise for her abilities. Barry Levin, a defense attorney who opposed Clark in a trial about ten years ago, said, "She's tenacious, she's ethical, she's highly competent. ... She was born to be a trial prosecutor." He called her the "best choice" Los Angeles District Attorney Gil Garcetti could have made to head the Simpson prosecuting team.

Women both young and old throughout the country saw Clark as a role model soon after she gained prominence in the Simpson trial. A grandmother in Oklahoma proclaimed that her "fourteen-year-old granddaughter's ambition is to become a prosecuting attorney. I can't think of a better role model than Marcia Clark."

Even in defeat, women held Clark in high esteem. One reporter noted that "Simpson's arrest, prosecution and acquittal... chronicled Clark's ascension as a role model for professional women. [To the] college-aged women who waited to get Clark's autograph outside Judge Lance Ito's courtroom, she's a national hero who showed herself as better than an equal in the once male-dominated field of law." Rosemary Agonito, an expert on women in the workplace, thought that "Clark's greatest accomplishment was getting the media and much of the public to focus on her as a woman lawyer, not just a woman." After the trial, Clark made her first public remarks at Governor Pete Wilson's Conference for Women in Long Beach, California. There she drew a standing ovation from a mostly female audience of more than 6,800. She "became a symbol for working mothers during the trial."

Clark's ability to serve as a role model for those concerned about domestic violence became evident, in an unusual manner, during the course of the Simpson trial. During the course of the government's case in chief, Ms. Clark wore a pin to court that was being worn by supporters of the victims. When the defense objected to this display of sympathy being presented before the jury, Ms. Clark's response reinforced her purpose, stating that the pin was a "very small show of support, very tasteful."

CRITICISM OF COCHRAN AND CLARK

Certainly, Cochran and Clark did not receive unqualified praise. The crux of Cochran's defense alleged a racist police conspiracy against Simpson. However, many people took offense to what they viewed as his hyperbolic comparison of former LAPD detective Mark Fuhrman to Adolf Hitler in his closing argument:

"There was another man, not too long ago in the world, who had those same . . . racist views. . . . This man, this scourge, . . . Adolf Hitler, because people didn't care or didn't try to stop him . . . had the power over his racism and his anti-religion. . . . Fuhrman wants to take all black people now and burn them or bomb them. That is genocidal racism. . . . There is something in your background, in your character, that helps you understand this is wrong."

Cochran was heavily criticized by some for making race a "central and misleading issue" in the trial. Civil rights activist Robert Woodson wrote that "[W]e cannot allow the rich legacy of the quest for racial equality to be squandered for opportunist use of the 'race card' strategy. . . . [W]e cannot allow the issue of race to eclipse the necessity of personal responsibility. [Those who use the race card] are exploiting African Americans as well." Fellow defense attorney Roy Black, in an interview on CNN, was less vehement in his criticism: "[R]ace was a legitimate issue in this case . . . [though] it went a little bit far, and . . . Johnnie Cochran probably went overboard in his summation."

Some also pointed out a certain hollowness in Cochran's newfound national role. A prominent L.A. businessman and fund-raiser for Jesse Jackson and other Democratic political candidates opined, "I wouldn't deny [Cochran] anything. But . . . he stepped into a vacuum."

Marcia Clark received critical comments on many trivial issues during the trial. Commentators seemed as interested in her makeup, hemline, and facial expressions as they were in her courtroom skills. Despite her impressive advocacy skills, some commentators found reason to question whether she could appropriately be considered a role model.

THEIR OWN WORDS: COCHRAN'S AND CLARK'S
APPEAL TO AFRICAN AMERICANS AND WOMEN

During a televised hearing about whether the jury should hear of Mark Fuhrman's use of "nigger," prosecutor Christopher Darden passionately contended that the slur was the "dirtiest, filthiest, nastiest word in the English language," and would only inflame the mostly black jurors against the prosecution and cloud their judgment. Cochran responded by apologizing "to blacks throughout the United States" for what he described as Darden's attack on their "ability to judge fairly." Whether fair or not, this exchange shows Cochran's awareness in midtrial of his newfound role beyond Los Angeles.

Cochran made statements both while evidence was being introduced at trial and in his closing arguments which were intended to demonstrate to blacks in America that he identified with them. During his closing argument, Cochran emphasized to the predominantly black jury that he, like them, endured daily the pain of living in a country divided by racism: "I live in America. I understand. I know about slights every day of my life." Cochran allied himself with the mostly black jury, claiming that they were all united in a struggle to combat discrimination and preserve democracy. He urged the jury that "you and I, fighting for freedom and ideals and for justice for all, must continue to fight to expose hate and genocidal racism and these tendencies. We then become the guardians of the Constitution."

Cochran also urged the jury to send a message to the LAPD, evoking still-powerful images of Rodney King: "Who, then, polices the police. . . ? You police them by your verdict. You are the ones to send the message. Nobody else is going to do it in this society. They don't have the courage."

Cochran made references to popular black culture when he constantly extolled the jury to "do the right thing," the title of a well-known Spike Lee film.

Cochran seems to be more than comfortable with his new status as a national role model. He has spoken at numerous engagements since the end of the trial, both in the U.S. and abroad. In November, he was one among many lawyers who traveled to Bogalusa, Louisiana. Cochran put together a legal team to represent residents harmed by a toxic gas leak at a local chemical plant and to look into claims that white neighborhoods near the plant were evacuated more quickly than black neighborhoods. Speaking to an audience at a local

Baptist church, Cochran said, "I'm an outsider. I'm not here to be a leader on this team. . . . I'm just a soldier for justice. That's all I've ever been."

In her closing argument, Clark showed why so many women find her a compelling role model. She herself referred to her toughness during the trial, even admitting that she "could have been nicer to" some of the witnesses. She frequently steamrolled over the defense's objections—at one point, Judge Lance Ito admonished her to stop speaking when there was an objection by the defense (which she claimed she hadn't heard).

Her pleas for the jury to "hear" Nicole Brown Simpson's cries for justice surely were well-received by women sensitive to the issue of domestic abuse.

THEIR SIGNIFICANCE AS PUBLIC FIGURES/ROLE MODELS

The importance of Johnnie Cochran's rise to national prominence stems from the fact that he is a black man in a position of esteem who previously enjoyed local respect and fame and now enjoys them at the national level. Why? Not because he is a good athlete, movie star, or musician, but because he is a tremendously skilled courtroom lawyer, a black man who has risen on his intellect and savvy. (A sampling of what some southern California lawyers and judges say about his courtroom skills: "Cochran has an approach with the jury that is unbeatable, . . . an ability that is phenomenal. . . . He has a sixth sense. . . . The trick is to break down a case to very simple concepts so that a jury can understand [that] your client is the good guy and that the other side is the bad guy. Johnnie knows how to do that.")

In this way, he busts stereotypes just as Colin Powell and the late Boston Celtic basketball star Reginald Lewis (though with less fanfare) did, making him a valuable source of inspiration/role model to the black community.

He is also seen by many throughout the country—including himself—as a "soldier for racial justice." Cochran's efforts have inspired the black community at a time when distrust of the criminal justice system and police establishment is high, and the supply of visible black leaders is low.

However, as has been discussed, some have argued that he used the race issue in the Simpson trial in a mercenary way. If one sub-scribes to this belief, it is only fair also to note that "racial justice" has been the predominant theme of his three decades of law practice. Some may see it as ironic that the Simpson trial gained him national recognition as a good race man, considering that his previous work measures up much better in this regard.

As with Cochran, the fact that Marcia Clark was in the position she was—lead prosecutor in the most publicized trial in American history—is an important symbol for women. Her work as a skilled and strong-willed prosecutor undermines any notion that such work is a man's job.

She has special appeal for groups concerned with domestic bat-tery, as she showed herself to be a passionate advocate for a battered woman whose murder, the prosecution believed, was the culmination of a cycle of abuse. This is why a reporter for the *Chicago Tribune* could note that "for many women the professional defeat of [Clark] was a defeat for all battered women." Despite Clark's success in showing what women can achieve today in America, her role also showed the challenges they still face. While she was substantively scrutinized throughout the trial, her hairstyle and clothing also received undue attention. This focus on their appearance is a cross that women still bear. (It must be noted that Cochran's style of dress was also examined, though probably not to the same degree.)

Marcia Clark experienced less praise and criticism during the trial, with legal criticism frequently directed at issues of judgment rather than talent; some criticized her style of courtroom tactics and her abrasive manner in the courtroom.

It is interesting to note the nearly parallel roles of Cochran and Clark. As noted, both Cochran and Clark are figures whose very pres-ence in their vital positions in the Simpson trial meant a lot to blacks and women respectively. Further, their respective images as a seeker of justice for blacks and a fighter for downtrodden women are a fur-ther parallel between the two.

Contributing to their appeal is the fact that they are both people that their "constituent groups" can identify with. Cochran does not talk like an ivory tower intellectual. In fact, his closing arguments echo with the style of black preachers—his use of rhyme ("If it doesn't fit, you must acquit") and repetition in his closing statement is the clearest example of this. Marcia Clark, taking on the enormous task of being the lead attorney in the trial of the century while also assuming the primary responsibility of raising two young children alone (with the added burden of defending a lawsuit by her ex-husband during the Simpson trial), was a shining example of someone doing two important jobs, and doing them well.

Cochran and Clark shared something else. As lead defense attorney and lead prosecutor in an adversarial courtroom, their jobs forced them to present only one side of any issue. For any trial lawyer there is always tension between aspiring to be an intellectual role model and the fact that trial advocacy not only does not permit lawyers to weigh and present both sides of an issue in a reasoned way but requires that they *not* do so.

For example, in his opening statement Cochran portrayed Simpson as a good family man. As advocate, he was forced to downplay and minimize Simpson's history of spousal abuse. An ideal role model would condemn spousal abuse or battery rather than downplay it. But Cochran's duty as a zealous advocate left him no choice but to take the position that he did.

Both Johnnie Cochran and Marcia Clark found themselves in the national spotlight under banners they had not chosen and pursuing agendas driven by public opinion. Whether we approve or disapprove of their conduct during the Simpson trial, we do well to understand their lingering appeal as role models.

The Dream Team's Dream Resources

LORRAINE ADAMS AND

SERGE F. KOVALESKI

They were called the Dream Team and, a critic once added, the Scheme Team. But in the story of how O. J. Simpson's defense attorneys won what was arguably the "trial of the century," prestige and guile counted for less than far more powerful tools: money, speed, detailed legal work, and the inexact science of jury consulting.

"Money meant everything in this case," said Alan M. Dershowitz, the Harvard law professor who was part of the team. "If this were a poor defendant without resources, there is no chance he could have challenged the forensic evidence in this case."

Added his colleague, Gerald Uelmen: "I think the resources made the difference. . . . And it haunts me because we should ask how many people's lives are put in jeopardy because we don't give them the resources to defend themselves."

Money meant that by the day after Simpson was first questioned by police, defense attorney Robert L. Shapiro had hired the nation's two best forensic scientists, criminalist Henry Lee and pathologist Michael Baden, men who usually testify for the prosecution. Insisting on a speedy trial in the first weeks left the prosecution playing catch-up. Winning the dismissal of the grand jury and forcing a preliminary hearing instead allowed the defense to cross-examine and lock in the stories of prosecution witnesses—testimony that came back to haunt some of those witnesses later.

Less visible but no less important, in the view of the lawyers involved, was the woman who largely chose, watched, and analyzed the jury—Jo-Ellan Dimitrius. Squeezed on a bench in the second row behind a bank of video consoles, she spent more than a year trying to codify and predict human behavior.

Before the trial even began, she knew which demographic groups would be predisposed to hear the defense's side. During the case, she coached the attorneys on how their direct and cross-examinations, even their opening and closing arguments, were playing to the only audience that really mattered: the jury.

So it was no surprise that after the jury acquitted Simpson in the murders of Nicole Brown Simpson and Ronald L. Goldman, the first person Cochran thanked at his victory news conference was Dimitrius.

Simpson's defense began as a disaster. By the time Shapiro became involved in the case on Monday evening, June 13, 1994, the night after the murders, when businessman Roger King, a close friend of Simpson's called to plead for his help, police were in the process of gathering what prosecutors later called a "mountain of evidence" against the celebrity suspect.

The worst for the defense included the bloody glove said to have been found on the walkway behind Simpson's house and, in what in retrospect seemed a huge blunder, the police interrogation that the defendant's previous lawyer, Howard Weitzman, had allowed him to submit to.

Shapiro agreed to take the case after talking to Simpson the next morning. Within twenty-four hours, he had hired Lee and Baden and had them on flights to Los Angeles. He also had contacted Simpson house guest Brian "Kato" Kaelin and limousine driver Allan Park and had interviewed them both.

Shapiro made another canny early decision, according to members of the team. He arranged for Simpson to be photographed stripped, showing no bruises, a fact that juror Brenda Moran later identified as important to her view of the case.

Uelmen credited Dershowitz with the decision to look into Detective Mark Fuhrman's past. It was Dershowitz, Uelmen said, who had a hunch the bloody glove might have been planted, even before he knew of Fuhrman's history.

Baden and Lee were meticulous in their investigation, photographing the crime scene and carefully examining evidence.

"Contrast that with what the prosecution did," Dershowitz said. "The blood on the sock, they had to wait a month to discover it. The blood on the gate, they missed it. [Detective Philip] Vannatter, they allowed him to walk around with blood in his pocket. They were never able to establish presence of blood around the glove. It was the contrast between the defense handling the investigation very professionally, and the prosecution handling it utterly unprofessionally in the first two weeks."

Uelmen said another strategic move was the decision not to waive the deadline for a speedy trial. He noted that conventional wisdom dictates that defendants waive such a right to give them more time to build their cases. "It was a gutsy move, and a move you would not make unless you had the resources in terms of lawyers available to roll up their sleeves and go to work," he said. "It put the prosecution in such a bind to put their case together. They thought they would have an extra month or so as their scientific gurus were coming in. But they were playing catch-up the whole time."

Simpson defense lawyer Peter Neufeld said that he thought another critical move was "the decision to take on the Los Angeles Police Department and the criminal lab and dismantle it bit by bit." Many attribute that decision to Cochran, who joined the defense team a month after the murders and was officially named its leader January 1995. "If you have a common source of the evidence, you have one target," Neufeld said. "It is much more difficult to cut off tentacles. It is easier to cut off the head and kill the beast. In this case, the beast was the LAPD crime laboratory."

Here too money played a role, enabling the team to chase down hundreds of tips and leads on many issues, but particularly relating to Fuhrman. Patrick McKenna, the defense's lead investigator, said the defense had from the beginning of the case about six full- and part-time private investigators. McKenna said he got an anonymous tip about the existence of tapes [on which Fuhrman could be heard making racist remarks], which was then reluctantly confirmed to him by North Carolina screenwriting professor Laura Hart McKinny, the tapes' owner.

By the end of July, *The New Yorker* published an article that showed just where the defense, then still under Shapiro's direction, was headed: that Fuhrman was a racist and he had planted the glove.

The hiring of Cochran, a prominent black defense lawyer who specialized in high-profile cases involving alleged police misconduct, was the last piece of the puzzle. Team members said Cochran helped refine the themes of the case and the attack strategy that put the prosecution on the defensive from the moment the trial began. He also appealed to the majority black jury on an emotional level, with a style designed to engage their sympathies. If Barry Scheck and Neufeld's detailed demolition of the evidence was aimed at jurors' heads, Cochran's rhetoric and manner was aimed at their hearts.

Shortly after joining the team, Cochran suggested in an interview that he had not ruled out the possibility of Simpson testifying in his own behalf. It would have been a tremendous gamble—and it never happened. A mock cross-examination of Simpson did take place, but on this subject the voluble defense team refuses to comment. While confirming that the questioning took place, team members would not talk about reports that they decided not to put Simpson on the witness stand because he faltered badly when interrogated about his history of abusing his ex-wife.

When Leroy "Skip" Taft, Simpson's business attorney, called Dimitrius, who had served as a jury consultant to the police officers accused of beating black motorist Rodney G. King in both the state and federal trials, and asked her to make a presentation, she was in New York interviewing to be a "color commentator" for CBS News. Three weeks later, Shapiro hired her.

Trial consulting is a service so expensive it is often reserved for corporate clients in civil cases. Here, applied to a criminal case, the results were striking, said several members of the defense team. Dimitrius's Forensic Technologies International conducted community attitude surveys and focus groups before and during the trial. It helped devise a 300-item questionnaire for jury selection.

It was crucial that the jury be receptive to the defense's theories of police misconduct. And while Dimitrius says her research indicated mistrust of police is at an all-time high among all demographic groups because of high-profile misconduct cases such as King, she also acknowledges that African Americans are special.

"In the life experience of an African American, I don't think any of us understand the problems they face on a daily basis," she said. "So are they predisposed to distrust law enforcement? You bet they are. There are a lot of other groups that have that—maybe not to that extent."

Dimitrius said she did not really "select" a jury, she "de-selected" the members of the panel who were "foreclosed from hearing the defense's side of the case." There were no white males on the final jury partly because the only one who had been selected to the final twenty-four-person pool, Tracy Kennedy, was dismissed, but Dimitrius insisted this was not because the defense automatically rejected them.

"White males were not detrimental to the defense's side of the case," she said. "It's much more complex than that. You have to look at the characteristics by sub-category—domestic violence; the racial element, a black man being married to a white woman; the law enforcement aspect of the case. The whole purpose of the questionnaires was to evaluate people's opinions about a variety of subjects integral to either side's theory of the case."

As to the educational level of the jury, Dimitrius said the final configuration resulted in only two members who had college degrees because the length of the trial ruled out people whose employers would not pay their salaries: the county would reimburse them only $5 a day. Panels in protracted trials tend to consist mainly of government workers—local, state, and federal agencies pay their salaries during jury service.

Donald Vinson's trial-consulting company Decision Quest worked pro bono for the prosecution—which he said ignored his advice during jury selection.

Vinson's research showed that the majority of African-American women felt protective toward Simpson, and saw him as a symbol of black male success. Although jurors who have spoken out dispute that, saying they relied on the evidence, Vinson said he believes what really happened is that the defense gave jurors who were looking to acquit Simpson reasons and evidence to do so.

"Are they lying? Are they being dishonest? Not at all. From their perspective, they sifted through and understood Johnnie Cochran's case. Marcia Clark's just didn't register."

Neufeld and Scheck, two New York attorneys whose knowledge of DNA and scientific evidence dwarfed anyone else's on the team, became more pivotal as the case wore on, and Shapiro examined fewer and fewer witnesses. And they too began to work more closely with Dimitrius.

"Jo-Ellan became very key because we had so many issues come up in regard to juror conduct," Uelmen said. "When it came up, Jo-Ellan was right there to give us her own assessment on what impact it would have to lose a particular juror."

Uelmen said that in some instances, Dimitrius recommended that defense attorneys cut short their cross-examinations because they were starting to lose the attention of jurors.

"She was watching the jurors very closely and getting back to us on what we could read into about how the jurors were reacting to evidence, and the risks we were facing in terms of jurors shutting down and turning off," Uelmen said.

Dimitrius recommended that Scheck go with such phrases as "contaminated, compromised, and corrupted" in the beginning of the trial. And during closing arguments, Dimitrius wrote him a note saying that the pieces of tampered evidence should be described to the jury as being like "a cancer."

For all their careful work on jury selection and on undermining the prosecution's evidence, defense lawyers believe that the Fuhrman saga was still a key element in their victory. When the Fuhrman tapes were played, revealing that the key prosecution witness had lied about using racial slurs, Neufeld said, jurors decided the prosecution had misled them.

In Neufeld's view, the prosecution's case was badly hurt not just by the fact that "Mark Fuhrman was a racist, but that they [prosecutors] tried to package him as a choirboy. When they found out that the prosecution had lied to them, the jury could no longer trust the prosecutors and was no longer listening to their message."

In an interview on CNN's *Larry King Live*, Shapiro also pinpointed the Fuhrman tapes as a critical moment. "When we had the tapes," he said, "at that point in time this case was over."

PART IV

Reforms

Proposals for Juries, Police,
and Prosecutors

PART IV

Reforms

Proposals for Juster Policies and Prosecutions

Our Faltering Jury

ALBERT W. ALSCHULER

Once I was invited to dinner by an elderly gentleman from China. When my host discovered that I was a law student, he talked about the American legal system. "There, in the courtroom," he said, "are two lawyers. They have been to school for many years. They are wise, able, experienced, and greatly respected in their communities. And above them, at the head of the courtroom, is the judge. He is even older, even wiser, even more experienced, and even more respected than the lawyers. But who decides the case? Twelve people brought in from the street!" The old man laughed.

With youthful enthusiasm, I sprang to the defense of the jury system. Law is too important, I said, to be left to the people who do it for a living. I argued that the jury offers an essential check against overzealous prosecutors and against high-handed judges. To my surprise, the more I talked, the more the old man laughed.

Today's newspaper stories, particularly the ones from California, offer good reason to believe that the old man was right. Our jury system often appears to have grown preposterous. Perhaps one should not criticize a particular verdict without undertaking a review of all the evidence before the jury. When viewed in the aggregate, however, the news accounts of jury verdicts in recent high-profile cases seem troublesome.

STRANGE NEWS FROM THE JURY BOX

The Menendez brothers drove an Alfa Romeo, a gift from their father, to San Diego where they purchased a 12-gauge shotgun. Two days later, they used the gun to kill their father and their mother. Ambushing their parents as the couple watched television, the young men fired the gun sixteen times before they were done. Two juries heard their essentially uncorroborated (though tearful) claims of sexual abuse and of a paternal threat to kill them if they made the abuse public. In addition, jurors heard expert testimony concerning scientific research on snails and the "rewiring" of Erik Menendez's brain that occurred as a result of his father's abuse. The jurors were not permitted to hear about a play that Erik Menendez had written twenty months before his crime—a play in which a young man kills his parents with a shotgun for their money. Neither of the juries could agree that the Menendez brothers had committed murder.

When Nicole Brown Simpson and Ronald Goldman were murdered, the manner of their killings suggested a crime of passion. At the crime scene, the police discovered a brown, extra-large Aris Isotoner Light glove, model 70263. This glove's mate was found at the estate of O. J. Simpson, the abusive former husband of Nicole Simpson. Soon after the killings, a limousine driver kept an appointment to pick up Simpson at the estate, but no one appeared to be at home. After the driver repeatedly called the house from his car, he saw a man who looked like Simpson enter the darkened doorway. Simpson then answered the buzzer, saying that he had overslept. DNA testing revealed that stains on the glove found at Simpson's estate matched the blood of Nicole Simpson, Ronald Goldman, and O. J. Simpson. Also on the glove was a hair matching Nicole Simpson's and fibers matching the carpet of O. J. Simpson's Bronco.

Nicole Simpson had purchased two pairs of Aris Isotoner Light gloves, model 70263, just before Christmas in 1990; at most, 240 pairs of these gloves were sold. Photographs and videotapes showed O. J. Simpson wearing similar gloves at football games from shortly after Christmas 1990 through early 1994, the year of the murders. An expert testified that he was "100 percent certain" that the gloves appearing in one photograph were Aris Isotoner Lights, model 70263. The glove found on O. J. Simpson's estate was only one of nearly three dozen blood exhibits connecting Simpson to the murders. Abundant other evidence pointed to his guilt.

Following an eight-month, twenty-three-day trial, a jury deliberated three hours and forty minutes before finding Simpson not guilty of murder. Mark Fuhrman, the detective who testified that he had found the bloody glove at Simpson's estate, had perjured himself before the jury by denying his use of racial epithets. Moreover, when prosecutors required Simpson to try on the Aris Isotoner gloves at the trial, the gloves did not fit. (A pair of the same model and size that had not been soaked in blood or subjected to forensic testing, however, did fit.) The defense theorized that Fuhrman had discovered a bloody glove at the crime scene, although it had gone unnoticed by others; that Fuhrman had concealed this glove in his sock or elsewhere and carried it to Simpson's estate; and that Fuhrman, without knowing whether Simpson had a provable alibi or whether another person could be shown guilty of the crime, had "planted" the glove.

Many observers were stunned by Simpson's acquittal. Many found the failure to convict the Menendez brothers disturbing. Many also raised their eyebrows when juries acquitted John and Lorena Bobbitt of brutalizing one another; acquitted Damian Williams and Henry Watson of the most serious charges against them following their videotaped attack upon truck driver Reginald Denny during the Los Angeles riots; acquitted Jack Kevorkian of aiding suicide after he had placed a mask over the face of a man with a degenerative muscle and nerve disorder and then pumped carbon monoxide into the man's lungs for twenty minutes; and acquitted Oliver North of all charges of lying to Congress, convicting him only of a single count of obstruction and of two other relatively minor crimes.

TAKING TO THE STREETS

Although none of these cases brought protesters to the streets, George Fletcher of the Columbia Law School notes that a number of jury verdicts of the past two decades have. Earlier in our history, Americans marched to protest convictions, such as those of Sacco and Vanzetti; but the recent verdicts sparking outrage and protest have all been full or partial acquittals.

In 1979, a jury tried Dan White for murdering George Moscone, the mayor of San Francisco, and Harvey Milk, a San Francisco Supervisor and prominent gay activist. The jury accepted White's partial defense of diminished capacity, a defense often called "the Twinkie defense" because a defense expert testified that junk food was one of the influences that had deprived White of the capacity to act with malice. Following the verdict, 5,000 gay men marched on city hall, smashed windows, and overturned and burned eight police cars.

In 1991, a Manhattan jury acquitted El-Sayyid Nosair of killing Meir Kahane, the founder of the Jewish Defense League. The judge who presided at the trial declared that the jury's verdict was "against the overwhelming weight of the evidence and devoid of common sense and logic." Jews in New York and Israel took to the streets in protest. In 1992, a Brooklyn jury acquitted Lemrick Nelson Jr. of stabbing to death Yankel Rosenbaum during a violent encounter between blacks and Hasidic Jews. Before his death, Rosenbaum had identified Nelson, a black teenager, as his attacker, and the murder weapon had been found in Nelson's possession. Thousands of Hasidic Jews protested the acquittal.

The worst race riot in American history began on April 29, 1992, the day that a California jury failed to convict any of four Los Angeles police officers accused of misconduct, despite the fact that most of these officers had been videotaped kicking and beating Rodney King as he lay on the ground. The jury's action precipitated two days of violence that claimed fifty-eight lives and cost nearly one billion dollars in property damage.

Americans take to the streets following criminal trials because our justice system, unlike those of other Western democracies, often acquits people whose guilt of violent crime seems obvious. When a jury reaches a verdict inconsistent with our predilections, we should be able to say that the jurors have heard more of the evidence than we have, yet many of us find it increasingly difficult to say, "We must have been wrong." Perhaps our fellow citizens cannot be trusted, or perhaps lawyers, judges, and television broadcasters have corrupted them.

SKEWED JURIES

Juries represent all of us, but the jurors in publicized cases often seem to have been drawn from the less-informed portions of the community. For example, two-thirds of the prospective jurors in the case of Oliver North were dismissed because they had viewed part of North's congressional testimony on television or had read about it. Those who remained eligible included one, the jury's eventual fore-man, who reported that she never followed the news because "it's depressing," one who said that he read only comics and horoscopes, one who recalled that North was "a head of soldiers or something like that," and still another who declared that he "didn't understand whatever I heard about this case."

The jurors who tried Imelda Marcos included one who had never heard of her and who could not say whether she was a woman or a man—and another who had not heard of Ferdinand Marcos either. A man who said that the media had made him think of the Menendez brothers as wealthy, spoiled kids was struck from the Menendez jury for cause while a woman who said that she read only *Cosmopolitan* and *Water Ski* magazine was accepted.

The Simpson jury included only two college graduates. It included no Republicans or independents. Most jurors indicated that they obtained their information primarily from "early evening 'tabloid news' programs." One juror reported that she never read anything "except the horse sheet." Three-quarters answered yes to the ques-tion, "Does the fact that O. J. Simpson excelled at football make it unlikely in your mind that he could commit murder?" When the lead Simpson prosecutor, early in her closing argument, encouraged jurors to take notes, only two did. One juror appeared to doze off repeatedly.

American juries have been especially tolerant of violence when the victims were black and the defendants white. Skin color sometimes has been, for jurors, a good indicator of who needed killing. In 1955, an all-white Mississippi jury took less than one hour to acquit the defendants accused of killing Emmett Till, a fourteen-year-old black visitor from Chicago who had accepted a dare and spoken to a white woman. Southern juries in the 1960s repeatedly failed to convict defendants accused on strong evidence of killing civil-rights activists (notably, Medgar Evers, Viola Liuzzo, and Lemuel Penn). At the same time, all-white juries voted not only in the Scottsboro prosecution but also in many others to impose the death penalty on blacks who had been accused, often on doubtful evidence, of raping white women or of homicide. Incidents like the first Rodney King verdict suggest to many that the jury remains an instrument of racial oppression.

In a reversal of historic roles, whites have begun to fear black jurors. The acquittal of O. J. Simpson by a predominantly black jury and the jubilant response to the verdict of many blacks heightened white concern, as did the acquittals of Lemrick Nelson, Jr., in the murder of Yankel Rosenbaum and the partial acquittal of Damian Williams in the beating of Reginald Denny. In Washington, D.C., a black juror forced a hung jury in the case of a black accused of murdering a white aide to Senator Richard Shelby; the jury's foreman had earlier sent a note to the judge accusing this juror of racism and of refusing to discuss the evidence. In Smith County, Texas, black jurors blocked the conviction of a black accused of sexually assaulting a white woman and then cited as a reason the earlier failure of a grand jury to indict a white police officer for killing a bedridden black woman during a botched drug raid.

Whites have begun to experience a glimmer of the fear of our justice system that blacks and other minorities have experienced throughout our history. Of course, most black and white jurors seriously seek justice, and multiracial juries often reach unanimous verdicts in cases of interracial crime. "Most" and "often" may not inspire confidence, however. In a nation divided by racial sentiment and tolerant of violence, trial by jury increasingly appears to promote lawlessness and self-destruction.

JUSTICE GOES HOLLYWOOD

The perception that racism now cuts both ways is one reason why the mistrust of juries, particularly on the part of whites, may be greater than in the past. More importantly, the American jury now suffers from some of the problems that plague other democratic institutions.

Although in most governmental matters, the framers of the Constitution preferred representative to direct democracy, they trusted citizens, not their elected representatives, to resolve civil and criminal disputes. Lawyers, however, now hire experts to help them maneuver jurors in the same ways that candidates for public office hire experts to tell them how to push voters' hot buttons. The lawyers conduct lengthy voir dire examinations designed partly to determine jury qualifications but mostly to indoctrinate jurors. They sometimes hire shadow juries to observe trials and debrief the lawyers at the end of each court day.

Television may make it easier for trial lawyers with seemingly hopeless cases to confound fantasy and reality—something that the lawyers for O. J. Simpson apparently realized from the outset. As prosecutors at the preliminary hearing in the Simpson case presented a wealth of incriminating evidence, some of which the defendant's attorneys were seeking to suppress, I wondered why the defendant's lawyers had not sought to have the television cameras removed. Broadcasting the preliminary hearing would ensure widespread knowledge of the damaging evidence even if the judge suppressed it.

My first guess was that the lawyers were just grandstanding—seeking publicity for themselves through a broadcast that could only harm their client. After further reflection, however, I decided that the lawyers were better strategists than I. They realized that the more the Simpson case came to be seen as a television drama, the better their client's chance of escaping punishment. "Cinematization" of the case might make more plausible the scenarios that talk-radio callers, defense attorneys, and jurors would later invent: Simpson's older son, whose DNA is much like his father's, killed Nicole Simpson and Ronald Goldman. Or Colombian drug dealers with very bad eyesight committed the crimes to punish Faye Resnick for not paying her debts. Or racist detectives planted bloody evidence to punish Simpson for marrying a white woman. Or the real murderer is the shoe salesman who testified that Simpson always wears size 12 shoes (no one always wears the same size shoe as he shifts from brand to brand). A basic rule of screenwriting is never to write "on the nose." A scene must not be quite what it seems or what the characters say it is, for the writer must leave room for the imaginative participation of the audience.

HOW TO FIX IT

The American jury trial needs reform. The following measures would help:

1. Eliminate or greatly restrict the ability of lawyers to challenge prospective jurors peremptorily. The frequent exercise of peremptory challenges on the basis of group stereotypes is demeaning to the jurors who are dismissed, and peremptory challenges facilitate lawyers' efforts to stack juries. These chal-

lenges also ensure that juries rarely are composed of a defendant's peers and rarely reflect a cross section of the community.

2. Eliminate or greatly restrict the use of lengthy jury questionnaires and voir dire examinations. Both are insulting and invasive of privacy.

3. Eliminate all professional exemptions from jury service. Doctors, firefighters, morticians, and lawyers should be expected to serve.

4. Enforce jury summonses. In some jurisdictions, as many as two-thirds of all jury notices are disregarded, and, despite the warnings printed on the notices, nothing happens.

5. Do not disqualify prospective jurors who have seen news accounts of a case unless they have been exposed to inadmissible evidence or appear unwilling to judge the case on the basis of the evidence admitted in court.

6. Do not sequester juries or order changes of venue simply because a case has been the subject of very intense publicity.

7. Reduce the influence of professional jury consultants—perhaps by making their reports available to both sides. If a lawyer could not gain any partisan advantage by hiring a jury consulting firm, the lawyer probably would not pay the $10,000 to $250,000 per case that these firms charge.

8. Offer jurors instructions on the law at the outset of the trial. As Judge William Schwarzer has observed, the current judicial practice resembles telling jurors to watch a baseball game and to determine who won without telling them the rules until the game is over.

9. Redraft standard jury instructions to enhance their comprehensibility, and permit jurors to take written copies of the court's instructions with them to the jury room. Allow judges to offer further instructions without fear of reversal for imprecise statements of the law unless these statements seem very likely to prove prejudicial.

10. In a lengthy trial, permit and encourage lawyers to present mini-summations and arguments as the trial proceeds.

11. Permit and encourage jurors to take notes. A minority of courts still forbid note taking, even in cases in which the lawyers must carry personal computers to keep track of the evidence. Other courts, without formally prohibiting note taking, fail to supply paper and pencils or to advise jurors that they are welcome to take notes.

12. Permit and encourage jurors to ask questions of witnesses after

submitting these questions in writing for review by the court and counsel.

As helpful as these measures would be, all of them together cannot fix what is fundamentally wrong with the American jury trial. The vices of this institution cannot be corrected simply by improving the care and handling of jurors. Repairing our defective evidentiary rules and trial procedures is much more important.

The opponents of televising trials once argued that viewers would watch only lurid cases such as those in which football heroes were accused of killing their ex-wives. The proponents insisted that broadcasts would educate the public about the workings of the third branch of government. Both were right. Viewers might have watched the Simpson trial for entertainment, but many were appropriately appalled as Judge Lance Ito forced lawyers endlessly to "rephrase the question" for reasons that no one could understand; as he admonished jurors twice a day to perform the astonishing task of forming no opinions while they heard the evidence (they disobeyed); as he excluded obviously significant evidence; as lawyers on both sides forced witnesses to repeat their testimony interminably (How long does it take someone to say that he heard a dog barking at 10:15 P.M.? In an American courtroom, about two hours); as Johnnie Cochran and Marcia Clark played games of legal "gotcha"; as ten of the initially impaneled jurors and alternates were discharged for their sins (mostly avarice and dishonesty); and as witnesses were never permitted to explain their answers.

LEGAL TURNING POINT

Though the Simpson trial was atypical, it tells us a great deal about the legal system. It shows how readily this system can be abused when skillful lawyers have the resources to press it hard. It shows a system in which, in Justice Hugo Black's phrase, the kind of trial a man gets depends upon the amount of money he has.

It also shows a system that can survive only because very few litigants have the resources to invoke the procedures that it offers on paper. Because our legal system cannot deliver on its extravagant promises (Simpson's trial cost the taxpayers more than $8 million), lawyers and judges have effectively repealed the right to jury trial. Ninety-two percent of the defendants convicted of felonies in state courts plead guilty because prosecutors and judges tell them in effect, "You have a right to jury trial, and we have the right to sentence you to fifty years if you exercise it." The criminal justice system's taste for champagne and caviar in the few cases that reach trial seems to be causing its starvation in the many cases that do not, and to judge from the Simpson trial, even the caviar does not taste good.

The Simpson trial will be remembered as a flamboyant media event, but it conceivably could prove to be something more. This trial could mark a turning point in our legal history, the moment when the need for America to reinvent a fair and workable trial procedure became too obvious to deny.

Lessons about Jurors

NANCY J. KING

Three out of every four adults in the United States paused at midday on October 3, 1995, to watch or listen to the live broadcast of the verdict in the trial of O. J. Simpson. Some estimated that as many as 150 million adults in this country tuned in, making the Simpson verdict the most watched television event ever, topping President Kennedy's funeral and the Apollo 11 moon landing. Throughout the preceding months, reports of the trial saturated print and broadcast media, exposing Americans night and day to the criminal proceedings against Simpson. During this year, 1996, fifteen to twenty million of these same adults will receive a summons for jury duty. Those who appear for jury service will bring to the courthouse their reactions to the "trial of the century" along with their other life experiences. Has the trial and its coverage affected potential jurors' expectations about the ways in which jurors, lawyers, witnesses, judges, parties, and the press should behave during criminal jury trials? The answer may be turn out to be "No." The case may have had no more influence on the beliefs and behavior of future jurors than any other popular crime drama on television. Nevertheless, litigants, judges, and legislators seem to be wary about the effect of the trial on post-Simpson jurors. This essay examines some of their concerns, and discusses how those concerns may affect the regulation and conduct of jury trials in the near future.

RACE-BASED VERDICTS

One of the unmistakable implications of public commentary on the O. J. Simpson trial was that the verdict was attributable to the race of the jurors. After the verdict, public opinion polls showed that the belief that verdicts are influenced by race is widespread. *USA Today* reported that 40 percent of whites and 59 percent of African Americans agreed that white jurors are more likely to convict a defendant if he is African-American than if he is white; 36 percent of whites and 18 percent of African Americans agreed that African-American jurors are more likely to convict a defendant if he is white than if he is African-American. After the Simpson verdict, 48 percent of whites and 18 percent of African Americans had less confidence in the ability of jurors to reach a verdict without letting their racial attitudes affect their judgment than they had before the trial. When asked if the Simpson jury based its verdict on the evidence or whether, instead, it was trying to send a message about racism, 47 percent of whites and 17 percent of African Americans in Los Angeles County responded that the jury's verdict was a political message, while 69 percent of African Americans and 41 percent of whites thought it was based on the evidence.

The public was not alone in focusing on race; experts also chimed in. Jury consultants who researched the case for the defense were quoted as having concluded before the Simpson jury was selected that the race of a potential female juror would be a useful predictor of her views on domestic violence. Even the jury consultant who offered his services pro bono to the prosecution, but whose advice was reportedly declined, concluded that "based on race and gender" certain jurors would not be willing to believe Simpson was guilty and that "those kinds of people ultimately found their way onto the jury." The implication of these reports is clear: African-American jurors will vote to acquit some defendants whom whites would vote to convict. It is a proposition that many would just as soon deny, qualify, or delete from the civic curriculum entirely. If embraced by litigants, judges, and legislatures, this alleged link between race and verdicts may affect the ways in which juries are selected, as well as the arguments and instructions that they hear in the courtroom.

JUROR RACE: STACKING THE DECK

Lawyers may interpret the Simpson verdict as proof that they should rely on race when deciding whom to challenge during jury selection, despite the constitutional prohibition against doing so. Some attorneys anticipate that post-Simpson jurors are more likely to act as racial partisans, more likely to convict African-American defendants in retaliation for the Simpson verdict if they are white, and more likely to distrust police evidence and vote to acquit African-American defendants if they are black. If attorneys act on these beliefs and succeed in disguising their race-based peremptory strikes with race-neutral reasons, the legacy of the Simpson trial may be further flouting of the Supreme Court's recent attempts to eliminate race discrimination during voir dire. At the same time, the Simpson case may persuade trial judges, who enforce the Court's prohibition, to recognize race-based strikes, or to be more skeptical of race-neutral explanations.

Renewed focus on the link between juror race and jury outcome during and after the Simpson case may also intensify judicial or legislative efforts to limit or eliminate a trial attorney's ability to manipulate the racial composition of juries through peremptory challenges. Like most of the potential changes to the jury system discussed in this essay, proposals to eliminate peremptory challenges first surfaced many years before O. J. Simpson was charged with murder. Those seeking to abolish peremptory challenges have complained for at least a decade that even with the Court's recent regulation, peremptory strikes still permit prosecutors to secure all-white or disproportionately white juries in criminal cases. Some maintain that the verdicts of these racially skewed juries are inaccurate. Others are concerned about the damage that racial manipulation of juries can inflict upon the public acceptance of verdicts. These arguments have been confined for the most part to books, articles, and scholarly forums. Lawmakers, judges, and attorneys, cautious about tinkering with the much revered institution of the jury, have not rallied behind proposals to eliminate peremptory challenges. For instance, a survey of federal judges conducted by Professor Christopher Smith in 1995 revealed that most considered peremptory challenges to be valuable tools and were not particularly dissatisfied with the ways that litigants were using them.

However, Simpson's acquittal, the most recent of a string of racially charged verdicts delivered by racially skewed juries, might prompt lawmakers and some judges to drop their reluctance to question existing contours of jury selection and to take a more critical look at the mechanisms that allow lawyers to manipulate the composition of juries. One legislator has already reacted to the Simpson case by introducing a bill that would outlaw the use of jury consultants in Illinois. Other bills in Louisiana and New York have proposed reducing the number of peremptory challenges available to litigants. If measures to curtail the peremptory challenge finally succeed because of the Simpson trial, the accompanying irony should not be overlooked: The Simpson verdict, perceived by many incredulous whites as the flawed product of a jury containing a disproportionately *large* number of African Americans, may eventually help to abolish the peremptory challenge—one aspect of selection that helps prosecutors keep the numbers of African Americans on the nation's juries disproportionately *small*.

JUROR RACE: PLAYING THE CARD

The message that "race matters" may also influence the extent to which race-based appeals to jurors are encouraged, tolerated, or prohibited in the courtroom. At least one study has suggested that there is a relationship between the willingness of white subjects to evaluate African-American defendants negatively and the subjects' exposure to ethnic slurs, a relationship prosecutors continue to exploit by appealing to racial prejudice during criminal trials. But the idea that African Americans could use race to their *advantage* in a jury trial has not captured the same kind of academic attention, and seemed to those reporting the Simpson saga a sensational phenomenon worth highlighting. Front pages sported headlines such as "Race-based Verdicts Rising" in the *Miami Herald* and featured stories suggesting an increasing number of cases in which African-American jurors are either finding reasonable doubt about the guilt of African-American defendants where whites found none, or deliberately voting to acquit African-American defendants whom they suspect are guilty. Simpson watchers have also expressed concern that post-Simpson jurors are even less likely than pre-Simpson jurors to believe police testimony. Some Florida prosecutors are already compensating for this possibility by calling additional witnesses to vouch for the integrity of evidence in their cases.

Like many empirical claims about jury behavior, these claims are difficult to verify or refute. A fair reading of jury studies on the correlation between race and verdict reveals that juror race probably does not matter in most cases. Only in certain types of cases does it seem to have an effect, and then only when those cases are based on ambiguous or close evidence. Proof that the influence of African-American jurors on verdicts is *increasing* is much more limited. The hypothesis is plausible. It coincides with the subjective impressions of several criminal trial attorneys and with popular impressions about the motives of the African Americans who have served as jurors in a few widely publicized cases, including the Simpson case or the case against Marion Barry. Also, as a result of constitutional and statutory proscriptions against racial discrimination, the adoption of more inclusive jury pools, and the elimination of certain procedures that disproportionately excluded minority groups, the number of minority jurors in most jurisdictions has increased. The increasing number of African-American jurors at least provides more *opportunities* for race-based decision making to favor African Americans for a change. Yet more conclusive proof remains to be gathered. Some reports of increased race-based verdicts cite higher-than-average acquittal rates in jurisdictions such as the District of Columbia and the Bronx. For example, 39 percent of state jury trials in the Bronx end in acquittal, compared to only 20 percent of jury trials in predominantly white Richmond County, New York. But acquittal statistics are difficult to evaluate without information about the proportion of defendants acquitted who are of different racial backgrounds, and whether defendants of different racial backgrounds elect jury trials at the same rate. Moreover, according to Justice Department statistics, between 1975 and 1994 in federal courts nationwide, when the number of minorities on juries was presumably *increasing,* jury acquittals *declined* from 22 percent to 20 percent or lower. During the same period, the rate at which *judges* acquitted defendants in bench trials rose from 20 percent to 53 percent.

While we await more information about whether race is playing an increased role in jury verdicts, some are advocating that it should.

Among them is Professor Paul Butler, an ex-prosecutor from Washington, D.C. Professor Butler's contribution to this volume proposes that African-American jurors should acquit factually guilty African-American defendants accused of certain drug offenses in order to promote criminal justice reform. In a similar essay in the *Yale Law Journal*, Butler argues, "I hope that there are enough of us out there, fed up with prison as the answer to African-American desperation and white supremacy, to cause retrial after retrial, until, finally, the United States 'retries' its idea of justice." Professor Butler arrived at his position before the Simpson jury delivered its verdict, and specifically rejects race-based nullification for violent crimes such as the one Simpson was accused of committing. Still, as Professor Butler argues, the more exposure this message gets, and it certainly received plenty during and after the Simpson trial, the greater the likelihood that it will be heard, and perhaps even heeded, by jurors.

THE PERILS OF PUBLICITY

During the Simpson trial newspapers reported that the case was creating a new wariness among jurors, judges, and attorneys about the sequestration of juries. Some post-Simpson jurors, apparently expecting to be locked up for weeks like Simpson's jurors, expressed relief when assured by judges that they would not be sequestered. In other courts, parties have asked judges not to sequester jurors, and the judges are listening. Although the timing may only be coincidental, before the Simpson trial had ended legislators in Louisiana and New York considered relaxing rules regarding the sequestration of jurors.

Jury sequestration is not common in most jurisdictions, and very little is known about the effects of sequestration on juror behavior. Indeed, we have only limited information about the effects of the months-long sequestration in the Simpson case. In a forthcoming article in the legal journal *Judicature* surveying the possible drawbacks and benefits of jury sequestration, Professor James P. Levine concludes that its potential for "unnerving and infuriating jurors," its deterrent effect on jury participation, and its capacity to create rather than repair dissent within juries overshadows sequestration's purported benefit—shielding jurors from unwanted information. If judges take Levine's critique to heart after the Simpson trial, there may be even fewer sequestered juries with which to validate or refute his theories.

Television coverage of trials may be another casualty of the Simpson fallout. Television coverage was undoubtedly one of the reasons why jurors were sequestered in the first place, although probably not the sole cause. Many blamed television for jeopardizing the fairness of the verdict itself. Televised coverage of the prosecution may have put added pressure on the Simpson jurors as they considered their verdict, and could have provided prejudicial information to jurors' families that leaked through holes in the jurors' sequestration seal. But whether television, as opposed to other forms of publicity, affected the Simpson jurors in these ways has not been demonstrated. Nor is it at all clear that eliminating the "watchful eye" from other courtrooms would eliminate these and other supposedly negative effects.

Nevertheless, shortly after the Simpson verdict, the California Judicial Council decided to consider a ban on cameras in the court. Judge Gilbert S. Merritt, chairman of the executive committee of the Judicial Conference of the United States, stated that "lawyers, judges and the public have been influenced by the perception that cameras are not good for a trial because of the Simpson case." The Conference deferred making any recommendation regarding televising trials to the spring of 1996. Judges in other cases have reacted to the Simpson case by banning cameras, including the second Menendez trial, the trial of Susan Smith for the murder of her two young sons, and the California trial of Richard Davis, who was accused of kidnapping and murdering Polly Klass.

Television's coverage of the Simpson trial meant that its jurors could claim celebrity status, and California's legislature feared the jurors would exploit that status to the detriment of the fairness of the proceeding. A statute that would have prevented Simpson's jurors from cashing in on book deals was rushed through the legislature and signed into law. It was not long after the bill became law before a federal judge agreed with lawyers for dismissed Simpson juror Michael Knox that enforcing the statute to bar Mr. Knox from publishing his life-as-a-Simpson-juror story would violate his rights under the First Amendment. In his order, the judge noted the absence of any evidence that "the prospect of financial gain at the conclusion of a juror's service as a result of his or her supplying information in relation to an action or proceeding has ever affected a . . . juror in the carrying out of his or her duties." Professor Marcy Strauss, who recently wrote an article about concerns over "juror journalism," agrees. Empirical proof or not, as ex-juror Knox's book climbed to the *New York Times* best-seller list and remained there for four weeks, statutes barring jurors from reaping profits from their service in criminal trials were introduced or considered in two other states, Georgia and Pennsylvania. Proof of the supposedly dangerous influence of the expectation of book royalties upon a juror's impartiality is not likely to appear anytime soon. Jurors who can realistically hope to profit from their stories are even scarcer than sequestered jurors.

The intense media attention paid to the jurors in the Simpson case may accelerate the passage of legislation designed to protect jurors from intrusions and scrutiny of the press and from harassment or retaliation by parties or the public. Juror names and addresses in every jurisdiction are now presumptively public—available for any reason or no reason to parties, witnesses, court personnel, trial voyeurs, and the press. A new statute in California requiring judges to seal juror names after trial was signed into law shortly after the Simpson jurors delivered their verdict. Measures that would go even farther and guarantee that from the beginning of trial all jurors in criminal cases are numbered and not named are under consideration in California and Florida. These proposals reflect concerns that jurors' safety and privacy is compromised by their public status, and that the apprehensions of jurors about being approached by the press, parties, or the public may deter eligible citizens from responding to jury summonses, or may temper jurors' candor during voir dire and deliberations.

MORE EFFICIENCY, PLEASE

Proposals to seal the names and addresses of jurors, to abolish sequestration, and to limit trial publicity may be prompted by more than seat-of-the-pants juror psychology. To the extent that these reforms reduce the need for expensive protective measures to protect sitting jurors from tampering or temptation and don't cost much to implement, they might reduce the amount of tax dollars spent on jury trials. The cost of the Simpson circus, as some have affectionately termed it, was extraordinarily high. Even though each of the Simpson jurors took home only $5 a day in juror fees, the bill to the taxpayers for feeding, housing, and guarding the jury totaled $3 million, more than one-quarter of the price of the trial. Widespread disgust with the amount of resources devoted to the case has apparently translated into general impatience with some traditional features of jury trials.

Impatience like this may explain why the Simpson case, in which all twelve jurors agreed on a unanimous verdict in four hours (lightning speed compared to the trial), has paradoxically boosted support for an initiative in California that would allow nonunanimous verdicts in criminal cases. Fred Goldman is leading the crusade against unanimity in California, an effort that began well before a unanimous verdict in the Simpson trial freed the man accused of murdering his son. Similar bills allowing nonunanimous criminal verdicts were introduced during the Simpson trial in several other states, including New Jersey, New Mexico, and New York. Once again, little empirical information is available to support or refute the claims made in favor and against such proposals. In their classic study of the American jury, Professors Harry Kalven and Hans Zeisel estimated that about 5.5 percent of criminal trials in the United States in the early 1960s resulted in a hung jury. A study of the ten most populated California counties in the early 1970s reported a much higher rate, about 12.2 percent. The California District Attorneys Association claims the same higher rate persists today in that state. Hung juries in federal criminal trials nationwide average under 3 percent; in Manhattan and some other jurisdictions the rate has been just as low. Other than these few statistics little is known about how often juries deadlock, how many mistrials result from hung juries, how many of those cases are retried, how many deadlocks are caused by a lone holdout, how many deadlocks are broken after "dynamite charges" by the judge, and so forth. Without more data, projections of salvaged convictions and tax dollars saved by a rule allowing verdicts of 10–2 or 11–1 are guesswork. This has not stopped the initiative in California from gaining widespread support. Polls of Californians reveal that the overwhelming majority of respondents favored nonunanimous verdicts.

The quick verdict in the Simpson case may also have sparked efforts to abandon instructions warning jurors not to discuss the case before the end of trial, which now are used in most jurisdictions. After the Simpson verdict one poll of Los Angeles residents revealed a widespread assumption that the Simpson jurors had discussed the evidence among themselves before the end of the trial. In a report prepared in 1994, prior to the Simpson trial, judges in Arizona agreed with behavioral researchers who concluded that the rule forbidding discussions is "anti-educational" and "not necessary to ensure a fair trial." As a result, Arizona civil jurors are now allowed to discuss evidence freely throughout the case, but are instructed to reserve judgment until they begin deliberations. The Simpson case may prompt more judges to reconsider the utility of instructions to jurors not to talk about the evidence before deliberations.

LESSONS WORTH LEARNING ABOUT JURORS

It is hazardous to overhaul the jury system on the basis of one case, particularly a case that involved such aberrational levels of expense and exposure. If rash reaction is the legacy of the Simpson trial, it will prove to be an unfortunate event indeed. Yet the case has its silver lining for jury reform. It could help to provide a greater understanding of how jurors behave and prompt reasoned debate about seemingly petrified features of our jury system. Many of the questions it has pushed into the open will recur, even if the experiences of the nearly two dozen people who served as jurors throughout the Simpson case are not repeated. We should welcome the scrutiny of the jury system that the case has prompted as an opportunity, a challenge to generate better answers to these enduring controversies about the American criminal jury.

Jury Dismissed

MICHAEL LIND

In the months following O. J. Simpson's acquittal, a small army of eminent jurists, politicians, and journalists responded with soothing assurances to popular outrage over the jury's verdict. They told us that, though fallible individuals sometimes make mistakes, the contemporary American jury system remains the best arrangement ever devised for ascertaining guilt and innocence. The jury system works.

Don't believe a word of it. The American jury system does not work to free the innocent and punish the guilty in an efficient and humane manner. It never has. Juries have always abused the institution, sacrificing impartial justice to political or ethnic goals. In colonial America, the jury gave colonists a way to subvert local overlords appointed by London. From independence until the civil rights revolution, the jury was a means by which white bigots legally lynched Indians, blacks, and Asians (or acquitted their white murderers). Today urban black juries all too often put race above justice in the same manner.

Even in a society less racially polarized than ours, the Anglo-

American jury system would be a bad idea. The progress of civilization can be measured by the distance between the idea of crime as a matter between the criminal and his victim's relatives (the feud, *wergild*), and the idea of crime as an offense against the impersonal, constitutional state. The twelve-person jury, which the Vikings bequeathed to Anglo-Saxon England, lies on the barbaric end of the spectrum. For all the refinements of the past millennium, the jury system bears the marks of its primitive origins. There's the magical number twelve (about which irrational debates occasionally erupt when the idea of ten- or eleven-member panels is suggested). And there's the competition between attorneys and the ritual of cross-examination, which resemble, respectively, trial by combat and torture (both of which, come to think of it, were also jurisprudential approaches of the ancient Teutons).

Though the news may come as a surprise, juries as we know them are limited to the English-speaking, common-law world. Most other Western democracies have inherited their system of criminal justice from the continental European civil-law (Roman law) tradition. The contemporary civil-law tradition is not, as Anglo-American propaganda would have it, one of authoritarian, "inquisitorial" justice, with all-powerful judges railroading helpless innocents. On the contrary, all civil-law democracies today provide for some form of trial by jury. In civil-law countries, however, the jury is typically made up of a small number of professional and lay judges. The professional judges bring their experience to bear in sifting the evidence; the lay judges prevent the professionals from acting on the basis of prejudice or politics. Yet another professional judge presides over the trial (in some countries, impartiality is further assured by three-judge tribunals).

The differences between the common-law and the civil-law approaches to criminal justice do not end with the composition of the jury. Grotesque battles over the admissibility of evidence like the Fuhrman tapes just do not occur in the civil-law world, where the trial is usually preceded by a relatively calm investigation and examination under the direction of the public prosecutor and an examining judge. The defendant is treated more fairly, in these early phases, than in the United States. According to Stanford Law Professor John Henry Merryman in his study *The Civil Law Tradition*, "The dossier compiled by the examining magistrate is open to inspection by the defense, routinely providing information about the prosecution's case that in an American proceeding would be unavailable to the defense until its production was compelled by a motion for discovery or it was revealed at the trial." No surprise witnesses, no sealed evidence envelopes, no sleazy tricks during discovery.

Suppose that the United States, like France and Germany, had adopted its own national version of the civil-law system in the eighteenth or nineteenth century, in place of the British common-law inheritance—an American Civil Code, like the Code Napoleon or the Prussian Code. Suppose, furthermore, that O. J. Simpson had been tried for murder under civil-law rules. How likely is it that the Simpson trial, in those circumstances, would have degenerated into an appalling spectacle of dirty tricks and bizarre legal hairsplitting? How likely is it that Johnnie Cochran would have played the race card and asked the jury to send a message to the L.A. police, if the jury had consisted of, say, Judge Ito and several other professional magistrates, as well as a few laymen? And the outcome of the Simpson case in a civil-law America? According to Professor Merryman, "a statement made by an eminent comparative scholar after long and careful study is instructive: he said that if he were innocent, he would prefer to be tried by a civil-law court, but that if he were guilty, he would prefer to be tried by a common-law court."

I realize, of course, that by suggesting that we Americans might actually learn something from other countries I am questioning the dogma that the political and legal system of the United States has been perfect since its immaculate conception in an act of collective parthenogenesis by the Founding Fathers. The rules of American public discourse hold that no innovation in government or jurisprudence unknown to Americans before 1800, no matter how potentially beneficial, can be suggested for adoption; the opportunity for fundamental political and juridical thought in the U.S. came to an end with the close of the Founding era, rather as divine revelation is thought by Christians to have ceased at the close of the Apostolic Age.

While an intellectual tariff prevents the import of institutional improvements from abroad, Americans are free to export our superior system to the rest of the world. Indeed, doing so is something of a patriotic duty. Otherwise-educated Americans who happen to be completely unaware that our legal tradition is an eccentric deviation from the main tradition of Western jurisprudence do not hesitate to evangelize on behalf of the American Way in matters like criminal justice. In the first few years after the revolutions of 1989 in Europe, when post-Communist states in Eastern Europe and Eurasia were debating different models of democratic constitutionalism (and usually concluding that the West German model is preferable to ours), a great number of representatives of the American bar flew into Eastern Europe to sing the praises of our malfunctioning separation-of-powers system and our even more disastrous jury system. My God, I remember thinking at the time, haven't the Eastern Europeans suffered enough?

We put up with an electoral system and a constitution in wigs and buckled shoes; why not tolerate a criminal justice system that wears a horned helmet and a bear skin? Here's why we should be concerned: the defects of our particular inherited structures of democratic and constitutional government may be mistakenly interpreted by an alienated public as failures of democracy and constitutionalism as such. The result of such unwarranted but understandable pessimism might be support for plebiscitary rule in politics and, perhaps, vigilantism in law enforcement. Huey Long will clean out the crooked statehouse; Charles Bronson or Clint Eastwood will punish the murderers who get off on technicalities. Legality cannot exist for long in the absence of legitimacy. In a contest between a law that seems to regularly produce unjust outcomes and extra-legal justice, rough justice in some form will sooner or later prevail. (How many people have *you* heard say, in response to news of Simpson's acquittal, "Maybe somebody will give him what he deserves?")

To make the American system of criminal justice work will require intelligent reform, which in turn requires honest criticism and debate. Unfortunately, ever since Pearl Harbor, debate about fundamental institutional reform in this country has been deterred by the implication that critics of American political and legal institutions are traitors, with either "brown" or "red" sympathies. It is worth recalling that from the Civil War to Pearl Harbor we Americans progressed by junking large parts of the obsolete Anglo-American colonial heritage and eclectically importing institutional innovations from abroad: the research university, the polytechnic and the kindergarten from Germany, the secret ballot from Australia, workmen's compensation from New Zealand, the public museum from France. As Japan has done recently, we shamelessly copied other nations and frequently improved on what we copied. During that era of American flexibility and progress, Oliver Wendell Holmes, Jr., nobody's idea of a flaming radical, observed in connection with the common-law tradition that the mere fact that a statute goes back to the time of Henry VIII is not an argument in its favor.

In the spirit of the enlightened conservatism of Justice Holmes, we need to audit our inherited institutions, rescuing what is vital by carving away the deadwood. We can begin by admitting that some of the foreigners who look aghast at spectacles like the Simpson trial actually may have something to teach us about devising a criminal justice system capable of telling right from wrong.

In Defense of the Criminal Jury

BARBARA ALLEN BABCOCK

> I personally would have a reasonable doubt, but it's
> true there is overwhelming evidence that he is possibly
> guilty.
>
> *African-American man interviewed on* TV
> *shortly before the verdict in* People v. Simpson

These words reveal the tension in our jury system: "Overwhelming evidence" may lead only to the "possibility" of guilt; in its face, the jury may still entertain a reasonable doubt.

Even without a reasonable doubt, a jury may decide that a defendant deserves freedom. This is the doctrine of nullification—an unspoken possibility in every case. The law itself is nullified, not for all time but as it applies to a single individual. A father who steals to feed his children is the classic example.

In modern times, protestors against government policy, accused of destroying property or of trespassing, have asked the jury to nullify in order to make a political statement. Some have suggested that the mostly African-American jury in the Simpson case was nullifying the law in order to send a message about the racism of the police, and the alienation of black America.

Without nullifying, juries may simply make mistakes, may be swayed by passion, prejudice, or sympathy to acquit a guilty person, may misread the evidence, or misconstrue their duty. The first Simpson jurors to speak out seemed to say that they took quite literally the judge's instruction that they might discount altogether the evidence of anybody who lied to them in some respects. Thus, disbelieving the police who swore they failed to obtain a search warrant because Simpson was not a suspect, or who made a sweeping denial about using racial epithets, the jury may have mistrusted everything else these officers said. In effect, the lay people may have enforced the exclusionary rules that many judges no longer follow.

Another reading of the Simpson verdict is that the jurors misunderstood reasonable doubt and demanded that every piece of evidence meet that standard. Correctly applied, reasonable doubt requires only that, looking at the case as a whole, its central elements must be proved to the ultimate level.

Even as individual jurors come forward, however, and as books on the trial accumulate, we will not fully understand the dynamics that led to acquittal in this case. In the ancient parlance, the verdict is "inscrutable." Like the ballot, it is the people's announcement of a result, not a set of findings of fact and conclusions of law such as we ideally require from judges when they decide cases.

While acknowledging its inscrutability, many people (I am one) believe that the Simpson verdict was not true or accurate. Yet it would be a mistake to turn our frustration and anger upon the criminal jury itself. Far worse than letting a guilty man go would be losing faith in, or working fundamental changes on, this most American of institutions.

Before the Simpson verdict was in, partly in response to other notorious cases involving unpopular jury results (the acquittal in the first Rodney King beating case, the hung jury in the Menendez parricide), legislative moves were afoot to abolish the unanimity requirement, to reduce the number of jurors, and to eliminate the peremptory challenge. The basic problem with these proposals is twofold: they wrongly assume that the jury system is broken; they could profoundly change its operation in unpredictable ways.

Behind the bold proposals for jury reform is the bald desire for more convictions. Yet proponents of change do not recite the current conviction rates, which have remained constant—in the 60 to 70 percent range—over the last fifty years. These are the conviction rates in jury trials—most cases (as high as 90 percent in many places) end in conviction on a guilty plea.

Always attending these high conviction rates have been startling acquittals in a few spectacular cases, defined by the horror of the crime, the celebrity of the accused, or a combination of both, as in the Simpson case. Sometimes the lawyers are famous too and almost always, those who win in the face of overwhelming evidence have money to pay for the best defense.

At the turn of the *nineteenth* century, Lizzie Borden of Fall River, Massachusetts, was accused of killing her parents with an axe. Her case had these now familiar ingredients: powerful circumstantial evidence, first-rate defense lawyers, press from all over the world, a sequestered (though all-male jury), who acquitted after twenty minutes of deliberation. No one wanted to believe that a woman of good family would be capable of such brutality. Her lawyer might have been taxed with playing the "lady" card.

Another example, this one from California more than a hundred years ago is the case of Issach Kalloch, who shot an unarmed man in full view of his fellow workers, and of people on the street who saw the killing framed in a large window. His victim was the editor of the *San Francisco Chronicle*. A jury acquitted Kalloch on a sort of justification/temporary insanity theory because the paper had printed scurrilous stories about his father.

These are but two of the historical instances of notorious mistaken verdicts, or verdicts that express community sentiment that is, at best, extra-legal. We have always, from the foundation of the Republic, been willing to sustain the risk that the jury will be wrong. Nothing in the Simpson verdict should change that. For every jury that goes awry, there are a hundred that do the right thing. Lawyers on both sides of the criminal system, former jurors, and most academics who have studied juries, attest to this fact. While the Simpson case was in its long progress, for instance, a South Carolina jury convened for several weeks and returned a verdict of life imprisonment rather than death for a young woman who killed her two little children. It was fitting that a jury should decide this case because no judge has the same power to speak with the voice of the people—to forgive and to redeem.

I myself believe in juries based on my experience as a young lawyer when I tried many cases, losing some and winning others, representing mostly African-American men before mostly African-American juries in the District of Columbia. Though losing a verdict is one of life's crushing blows, I felt in virtually all the cases I saw close up that the jury made a correct, and wise, decision. More than occasionally, I found that jurors who started with one predisposition changed their minds through the deliberative process.

My trials did not make the papers, nor were there cameras in the courtroom. Nor was any jury in my experience so mistreated as the Simpson jury—indeed I suspect that the mismanagement of the jury helped to produce the acquittal. This brings me to the second point about why this case should not occasion sweeping changes in the jury system: the point of unintended consequences. We do not know what makes juries work well most of the time, which of its features are necessary to its proper functioning.

The jury comes to us with certain historical attributes: the mystical number twelve; the absolute power to acquit without accountability; the judicial filtering of the evidence heard; the requirement that jurors come from the geographical community where the crime occurred; and that they engage each other to the point of total agreement. No one knows which, if any, of these attributes is essential to the integrity of the institution.

We do know, however, that a jury should be assembled once for a single purpose, that it should be composed of strangers who know each other only through their deliberations. This fundamental feature of a jury was violated in the Simpson case by a starstruck judge who lost control of the situation. He caused the jury to spend many hours waiting while he heard and reheard lawyers' arguments, took time off to engage celebrities, and through it all, patronized the jurors, conveying by his tone and manner that their time was not important. He should have taken drastic measures to move the trial along, for instance, by hearing motions in the evenings or holding court on Saturdays. Instead, by his leisurely approach, he violated the very premises of the jury system and opened up the possibility that this jury would become a little band with its own agenda.

Judge Ito, like most judges, was largely on his own in deciding how to deal with this jury. In virtually all jurisdictions, the statutes and common law on the selection, care, and instruction of juries are a hodgepodge of rules adopted piecemeal, often in reaction to unpopular verdicts, without concern for how the system as a whole will be affected. A recent voter's initiative in California, for instance, removed the right of lawyers to question potential jurors. By the report of both prosecutors and defenders this law hampers efforts to identify and remove erratic, unstable jurors who can prevent effective deliberation, and may even cause the jury to hang.

The opportunity for lawyers to question prospective jurors (and to follow up troubling answers with more questions) may help select jurors who can return unanimous verdicts. In a similar role, the peremptory challenge allows each side to eliminate the extremes against its position, leaving jurors with middling attitudes who can reach consensus. Yet a move is on, which I will discuss, to abolish these challenges. This is another instance in which reformers neglect the central point that the jury is a collection of interconnected practices and conventions.

Another of the piecemeal jury "reforms" urged in the wake of the Simpson case and other recent unpopular verdicts is to allow non-unanimous jury decisions. As it turned out, of course, the Simpson case is not particularly apt as an example for the reformers, because the jury was unanimous for acquittal. Even had it hung along racial lines, as many pundits predicted it would, the result of permitting nonunanimous verdicts would still have been to acquit Simpson.

But those who are seizing this moment—in which a famous athlete may get away with murder—to push for majority verdicts risk changing the very nature of the institution. First and most important, a group that must bring along those who see the world differently is more likely to deliberate and discuss the evidence thoroughly. This point is crucial because we have entered a period in which white women and minorities are finally being summoned to jury service in new numbers. In some places, our juries are as diverse as our communities. This is the wrong time to provide for simply outvoting the newcomers. In other words, if there are two or three minority members on a jury of twelve, a system that required that they be convinced to join the verdict, which is our system, seems far better than one in which they serve only to be outvoted.

Finally, a unanimous verdict is a major accomplishment, and carries with it moral authority that a split decision lacks. This point is easily understood when we talk about multijudge appellate courts, and applies even more forcefully to a judgment from the people. Of course, the Simpson verdict shows that unanimity does not guarantee popularity or credibility, yet surely a 10–2 result with the jury divided along racial lines would have been worse.

My devotion to the unanimity requirement began many years ago when one juror in a case I defended held out for three days against the other eleven and finally convinced them to return a not guilty verdict. Oddly enough, this was the only time in which I put the first twelve people in the box, i.e., I did not use any of my peremptory challenges.

That experience does not, however, lead me to think that we should abolish peremptory challenges—another current suggestion for "fixing" the jury. The move has gathered currency because the use of the challenge to strike off white women and minorities has led the Supreme Court to create a sort of modified peremptory. Neither side may challenge a juror on the basis of race or gender. In effect, the Court has created a juror's right to serve. The difficulties of administering jury selection with this modified peremptory challenge as well as the time it can take has roused a call to abolish peremptories altogether.

To reiterate, the parts of the jury fit together, and lopping off one part may cripple it in unforeseeable ways. The function of the parties in striking off biased extremes is interconnected with the unanimity requirement. A second reason for preserving the peremptory is its importance to defendants: they should not face juries that contain people they fear or hate, even for irrational reasons. This is especially true now when long prison sentences are the norm.

Rather than reactive legislation undermining unanimity or the peremptory challenge, a comprehensive statute that preserves the jury's fundamental attributes would be a good outcome of the Simpson verdict. Such a statute should include, for example, provisions regularizing selection practices, including a requirement of juror questionnaires tailored to the facts of the individual case, provision for expedited procedures in cases of sequestration, and for more reasonable compensation and treatment of jurors than we have now. It might also reduce the number of peremptories on both sides, or even eliminate them altogether for the prosecutor, who with a broad general interest in justice should be willing to abide the verdict of the people.

While improvements such as these would be welcome, the mechanics of juries are not at the fault line of the criminal justice system. Especially in the cases that most need community understanding—where defendants are poor people, often racial minorities, charged with horrendous crimes—most juries never have a fair shot at deciding because the defense lawyer is inadequate. When this is the case, the arguments about unanimity, and its connection with peremptory challenges, and whether peremptory challenges are necessary, are all beside the point. Many years ago, Supreme Court Justice Hugo Black wrote that there can be no equal justice when the kind of trial a man gets depends on the amount of money he has. But Black's admonition still only states a hope.

When we think about the Simpson case, we should consider as well *People v. Mayfield,* tried a few years ago in another Los Angeles court. The state's highest court upheld the conviction. Like Orenthal J. Simpson, Demetrie L. Mayfield was a black defendant accused of killing a woman he knew well and a man who appears to have been in the wrong place at the wrong time.

That is about where the similarity ends. Simpson had a team of a dozen lawyers plus forensic pathologists, criminal investigators, and an army of paralegals to defend him. When reporters asked the price tag for all these people, the knowledgeable answer was another question: "How much does he have?" Whatever the final dollar amount, perhaps discounted for the free on-camera advertising, the verdict shows the results of hundreds of hours in preparation and translates into millions of dollars.

Mayfield's attorney, by contrast, practiced alone. According to court records, his entire preparation for the case took forty hours. The attorney conducted only one substantive interview with his client—on the morning the trial began.

Lawyers who appealed Mayfield's conviction argued, as is common in capital cases, that the low level of representation violated his right under the Constitution's Sixth Amendment to the "effective assistance of counsel." Because a series of Supreme Court decisions has lowered the standard for what effective assistance means, those claims are increasingly difficult to make. In Mayfield's case, appellate judges conceded that the defense was less than zealous but concluded that no harm had been done. The evidence was so overwhelming that no defense would have helped much anyway, the courts ruled. Mayfield now sits on Death Row.

His case is not necessarily the most disturbing—no obvious lawyer errors mar the record. There are many worse cases, some in which appellate courts are forced even to overturn convictions. Indeed, our entire system, with its understaffed prosecutors, overcrowded court dockets and harried public defenders, survives only because of a seldom acknowledged bargain: we provide extensive rights to criminal defendants in theory, but do so in a system that allows mostly the affluent to employ those rights in practice.

If every accused defended himself as Simpson did, the criminal justice system would rapidly collapse. I am not suggesting that every defendant should be provided the resources to press as far as Simpson did. But there is, or should be, something in between the rich man's defense and hardly any defense at all.

When the Simpson case started, I thought that it would provide a popular primer on our American criminal justice system. But as it turned out, the case was no good as a prototype, nor does where it went wrong tell us anything about the changes we should make. It would only compound the errors if this freakish episode led us to transform the way that juries operate.

The criminal jury, right or wrong, is still one of our most precious and characteristically American institutions. Like universal suffrage, with its vote for every citizen regardless of class, race, or gender, the interposition of a jury drawn from the community between the accused and the state is fundamental to our kind of democracy.

The Jury System

KENNETH JOST

Police and prosecutors in Prince Georges County, Maryland, thought they had a solid case against Kareem Brooks when he was tried on three drug counts and a firearms charge. Eleven of the twelve jurors who deliberated on the case in October 1995 agreed. But not Walter Charles Boyd.

"Remember the O. J. Simpson case," Boyd told his fellow jurors. The forty-one-year-old medical supply salesman had watched much of the Simpson murder trial. And the trial taught him something about the jury system.

The police in the predominantly black suburban county outside Washington, D.C., said they arrested Brooks after seeing him drop a handgun and a vial of cocaine. But Boyd, who grew up in south central Los Angeles, agreed with the public defender's argument that police should have examined the gun for Brooks's fingerprints to corroborate their testimony.

The other members of the racially mixed panel insisted the officers' testimony was strong enough. At one point, they prevailed on

Boyd to vote to convict. But he changed his mind on the way to the courtroom and told the clerk who polled the jurors that the verdict did not reflect his views.

Circuit Court Judge William B. Spellbring ordered the panel to resume deliberations, but it was no use. Boyd stuck to his position. Two hours later, the foreman reported the jury was hopelessly dead-locked.

For many Americans, Boyd had drawn the right lessons from the Simpson case: the need for jurors to be skeptical of law enforcement. But for many others, the Simpson case represents what is wrong with the jury system: protracted trials, manipulative lawyers, and erratic verdicts based more on emotion than on evidence.

Whatever one's opinion of the stunning acquittal in the Simpson case, the nine-month trial focused attention on the United States jury system in a way that no previous case had ever done. Critics of the jury system say that attention may be a boon to efforts to make some changes. "The jury system is so complex, so expensive, so time-consuming that we cannot afford to give it to more than a handful of people," says John Langbein, a professor at Yale Law School. Langbein favors replacing the adversary procedures used in the United States with a system of judicially supervised investigations and trials like those in most European countries.

Many other experts, however, caution against using the Simpson case to draw any lessons about the jury system. "The Simpson case is such an anomaly that we cannot generalize from it," says Lois Heaney, a jury consultant with the defense-oriented National Jury Project in Oakland, California.

Debates over the jury system are nothing new, of course. As Brandeis University Professor Jeffrey Abramson notes in his study of the jury, Mark Twain satirized the American system of jury selection in an 1871 account of a murder trial. After reputable townsfolk were all excluded from the jury because they had read accounts of the case, Twain concluded: "Ignoramuses alone could mete out unsullied justice." Nearly a century later, Erwin Griswold, dean of Harvard Law School, echoed that sentiment by describing the jury system in a 1962 article as "the apotheosis of the amateur."

What follows are some of the major questions being debated about the jury today.

SHOULD JURY SELECTION PROCEDURES BE CHANGED BY LIMITING OR ELIMINATING PEREMPTORY CHALLENGES?

The jury system came to America from England three centuries ago, but today jury procedures in the two countries are strikingly different. Jury selection in England is short and sweet. Lawyers cannot question the potential jurors and cannot excuse anyone from service except for a specific legal ground. In the United States, on the other hand, jury selection can last days or even weeks and is often contentious. Lawyers and the judge often question jurors extensively about their knowledge of a case, their backgrounds, and their views on legal and social issues. And both the court and the opposing attorneys excuse people from serving in almost any major case.

Many potential jurors are disqualified for some legal reason. These so-called for cause challenges may be based on a juror's knowledge of the case or a professed inability to follow applicable law. But lawyers also have the right to use so-called peremptory challenges to exclude a certain number of potential jurors for any reason—or for no reason at all.

Trial lawyers cherish the peremptory challenge. "Peremptories offer an opportunity to eliminate people who are unwilling or unable to listen to one or both sides of the case," says Marc Whitehead, a Minneapolis attorney who chairs the American Bar Association's task force on juries.

A growing number of jury reformers, however, favor limiting or eliminating peremptory challenges. They say the arbitrary exclusion of potential jurors insults the people who are called to jury duty and contributes to lessening public confidence in the overall fairness of the jury system.

"Obviously, [peremptories] are great things for lawyers," says Albert Alschuler, a law professor at the University of Chicago. "They let the meter run longer. They play great strategic games. Every lawyer believes he or she is a master of the art of jury selection. But there is no empirical evidence to suggest that it makes any difference in the art of jury selection."

"Many of those who are currently removed via lawyers' challenges appear to be more alert and unbiased than many who are seated," writes Stephen Adler in his book on the jury. "And many peremptory challenges continue to be rooted in racial, ethnic, and sex discrimination."

The Supreme Court has acted in the past decade to limit some discriminatory uses of peremptory challenges. In 1986, the Court ruled in a case called *Batson v. Kentucky* that prosecutors cannot use peremptory challenges to exclude potential jurors on the basis of race. The justices later extended the ruling to bar race-based peremptory challenges in civil cases and by defense lawyers in criminal cases too. Then in 1994, the Court also prohibited lawyers from excluding jurors on account of their gender.

The decisions stoked speculation that the justices might abolish peremptories altogether. On each occasion, however, the court insisted that lawyers could continue to use peremptory challenges for other reasons. And in 1995, the court gave lawyers added leeway in justifying peremptory challenges that are challenged as discriminatory. In a little noticed, unsigned decision, *Purkett v. Elem,* the Court said that a lawyer's reason for excusing a juror can pass muster if it is race-neutral even if it is not reasonable. The decision upheld a prosecutor's use of peremptory challenges to remove two black jurors, ostensibly because they had mustaches or beards.

Lawyers on both sides of the table continue to defend peremptory challenges. Elizabeth Semel, a defense lawyer in San Diego, says peremptory challenges are often needed to excuse jurors who cannot accept that a defendant is presumed innocent. "Sometimes the only way you can excuse them from a jury is through a peremptory challenge," she says.

Greg Totten, executive director of the California District Attorneys Association, says prosecutors also want to retain the peremptory challenge. "I think most prosecutors think there is value to peremptory challenges and would not want to see them eliminated," he says.

Critics acknowledge that lawyers' unified stance on peremptory challenges makes any change difficult, if not impossible. Typically, state law establishes the right to peremptory challenges and prescribes the number—ranging from as low as two or three per side in civil cases to as many as twenty-five in capital cases. Prosecutors, defense attorneys, and civil trial lawyers on both sides would be likely to resist any legislation to reduce the number or abolish peremptories altogether.

Still, critics say public discontent with jury selection procedures has increased because of high-publicity trials like the O. J. Simpson case. "The distress that people have about the O.J. verdict and other verdicts has people concerned about lawyers stacking juries through the use of jury consultants," Alschuler says. "One way to reduce that concern is to eliminate peremptory challenges."

SHOULD NONUNANIMOUS VERDICTS BE PERMITTED IN CRIMINAL CASES?

The very first juries—the ancient Greek assemblages of up to 500 or more persons called dicasteries—decided disputes by majority vote. English courts, however, adopted a rule by the fourteenth century requiring jury verdicts to be unanimous. The unanimity requirement moved to America and became a central element of the U.S. jury system.

The Supreme Court in 1972, however, upheld laws in two states, Oregon and Louisiana, permitting criminal verdicts by 10–2 or 9–3 votes, respectively. Several states have since decided to allow nonunanimous verdicts in civil cases. Now, prosecutors in California, the nation's largest state, hope the state's voters will approve an initiative to permit 10–2 verdicts in all criminal trials except death penalty cases.

The proposal is part of a ballot initiative called the Public Safety Protection Act of 1996. "The unanimity requirement is like a cloud hanging over the criminal justice system," Totten says. In addition to forcing retrials in cases of jury deadlocks, he says the rule also affects plea bargaining by forcing prosecutors and courts to agree to less serious charges.

Defense lawyers and many jury experts, however, strongly support unanimous verdicts. They say that the proposal not only would give prosecutors a big advantage over the current system but also would result in less deliberation among jurors. "One of the chief advantages of a jury over an individual decisionmaker is the notion of deliberation," says Stephen Adler. "The problem with going to 10–2 or 9–3 is it encourages juries to vote, not to deliberate."

Jury expert Valerie Hans of the University of Delaware says that retaining the unanimity requirement has become more important because of the focus on the impact of race in juries. "Race does make a difference" in the jury room, Hans says. But retaining the unanimity requirement, she says, "means that you won't allow the verdict to reflect the racial breakdown. That would be a real disservice to the jury system."

For their part, prosecutors insist that permitting a verdict on a 10–2 vote would eliminate the danger that one or two "aberrant" jurors can prevent a panel from reaching a decision. Although statistics on hung juries are imprecise, California seemingly has a higher rate than other states. The state district attorneys' group says, for example, that Los Angeles County has had a hung jury rate of about 14 percent over the past three years, compared to 5 percent in Oregon, with its 10–2 verdict requirement.

The prosecutors group also cites potential cost savings from avoiding the need for retrials in cases that end in deadlock. "It costs the taxpayers approximately $10,000 per day to have a jury trial conducted," Totten says. "And many of these cases that result in hung juries need to be retried, at tremendous cost."

Totten notes that California prosecutors were urging nonunanimous verdicts long before the Simpson case. He says that both Louisiana and Oregon appear to be satisfied with their systems. And he adds that England, the source of the U.S. jury system, moved to allow nonunanimous verdicts in 1967. However, jury expert Abramson notes that English juries must deliberate for at least two hours before they may return a 10–2 or 11–1 verdict.

SHOULD JURORS BE GIVEN A MORE ACTIVE ROLE DURING TRIAL?

Jurors today have a largely passive role in trials. They listen silently to testimony, pass in and out of the courtroom when told, and, if they follow instructions, avoid any discussion of the case until the trial has ended.

Judge Michael Dann, an Arizona judge who has become a leading advocate of jury reform, argues for giving jurors a more active role during the trial. Dann headed a committee appointed by the Arizona Supreme Court that fashioned a set of jury reforms that went into effect in December 1995. The proposals are aimed at helping jurors understand a trial while in progress by encouraging note-taking, permitting jurors to ask questions, and having lawyers and the judge give interim summations and instructions. Most controversially, the new rules permit jurors in civil cases to discuss evidence among themselves during the trial.

Many of the proposals find broad support among judges and lawyers, even though they differ with trial practices used in most places until recently. Juror note-taking, for example, has traditionally been viewed with suspicion. Judges and lawyers feared that a juror's notes might taint or unduly influence the deliberations. But note-taking has become common today, and few lawyers, judges, or experts object to the practice any longer.

Allowing jurors to ask questions raises greater concerns. The Arizona plan allows jurors in civil cases to submit unsigned written questions to the judge, who then asks the questions after giving lawyers an opportunity to object outside the presence of the jury. Supporters believe that jurors will have a better opportunity to understand complex testimony if they can use questions to clarify their confusions.

Still, some lawyers doubt that jurors will ask many useful questions and warn that they may ask improper ones. "It's important to remember who's trying the lawsuit: the lawyers and the judge," says defense attorney Elizabeth Semel. "Sometimes a juror asks a question about an item of evidence that has been properly excluded. But there may be a time when a question has been well founded and is appropriate."

Dann concedes that the practice requires careful judicial supervision. "The judge is going to have to ride herd on that process," he says. "It can get out of hand. But that's no different from controlling other aspects of the trial."

The new provision for jurors to discuss evidence while the trial is still in progress provokes more divided opinions. Dann and others say that jurors will benefit from talking about a case with the evidence fresh in their minds. "Real-time discussions will aid comprehension, aid in formulating the questions that they ask, and assist in reducing stress because they are able to talk to each other aside from small talk," Dann says.

In any event, Dann and other supporters of the idea say that many jurors ignore the admonition not to talk about a case during the trial. In its report on jury reform, Dann's committee noted research suggesting that anywhere from 11 percent to 40 percent of jurors discuss evidence among themselves before deliberations.

Some law professors agree that it is unrealistic to expect jurors to avoid talking about a case until the end of a trial. "It's a bad dynamic to tell them something that may not be realistic," says Columbia's Gerard Lynch.

Trial lawyers, however, voiced nearly uniform opposition to the plan. Marc Whitehead, head of the ABA's task force on juries, says he bases his opposition on studies by social scientists that indicate people tend to hold to an opinion after once publicly expressing it. He is concerned "that interim discussions solidify thinking prior to hearing all the evidence, [and] that interim discussions foreclose debate because the discussions do not necessarily happen with the whole group present."

Defense lawyer Semel maintains that interim discussions would be particularly dangerous in criminal cases. "The presumption of innocence is supposed to apply literally through the entire trial," Semel says. "The idea of interim deliberations is a way of undermining that presumption prematurely."

For the time being, Arizona is limiting these interim discussions to civil cases. Dann favors extending the idea to criminal cases, but acknowledges a reason for caution. "There are some legitimate concerns and weightier concerns on criminal than on civil," he says. "We should wait and see how it works."

Nonetheless, Dann says that jurors in cases where the idea has been tested have told him they did not form hard opinions before the trial ended. "They scold me for even thinking that they would rush to judgment before they hear all the evidence," Dann says.

Today, Americans have decidedly ambivalent views about the jury system. "We love the idea of the jury but hate the way it works," Stephen Adler writes. Jurors themselves approach their jobs with the same ambivalence along with some natural resentment about the personal hardships imposed. Yet, as shown by a National Law Journal poll in 1993, most jurors come away with confidence in the system. Three-fourths of the 800 or so jurors surveyed said that if they had a case of their own in the courts, they would want it decided by a jury instead of by a judge.

Some of the reforms being discussed in the aftermath of the Simpson trial are aimed at easing the burdens on jurors by shortening jury selection procedures, controlling the length of the trial, and reconsidering the need for sequestration of jurors—which happens only rarely in any event. But many of the other problems of the criminal justice system highlighted by the trial have nothing to do with juries—such as the need for better police procedures or the disparity in legal representation for well-off and indigent defendants.

While criticism of the jury system has increased in recent years, juries are such an ingrained part of our system that major changes limiting the role or power of the jury seem unlikely. And many experts say that on close examination, the system works better than the public recognizes. "It was only after studying it for a long time that I came to the conclusion that it works well, amazingly well," says Shari Seidman Diamond, a researcher at the American Bar Foundation. "Jury service is really the only opportunity that most of us have to participate in true democracy, where individual citizens are making decisions on behalf of the government," says Frances Zemans, executive director of the American Judicature Society, a court reform group. "This is direct democracy."

Inside the Jury Room

ANDREW HACKER

About the case of *People v. Simpson,* one thing is certain: it was in no way typical, representative, even illustrative, of criminal trials in general. In addition to the defendant's celebrity, there was the huge cast of attorneys, the length and intricacy of testimony, and the obvious impact of television on the proceedings.

But despite its status as a spectacle, legally speaking, the jury was the only audience. Even as millions were watching, the evidence and exhibits all aimed at swaying the dozen citizens who would be voting on a verdict. So for the rest of us, much of the drama consisted of trying to guess how members of the panel were reacting to witnesses, reenactments, even the composure of the man accused of a double murder. To this end, Court TV and CNN called in lawyers as commentators, since they were presumed to know how jurors respond to what happens in a courtroom. However, lawyers may not be the best judges of how jurors and juries behave. What goes on within those closed rooms, where citizens are essentially on their own, often seems to elude even the shrewdest of legal experts.

In describing members of the Simpson jury, commentators tended to focus on external attributes: mainly race and gender, plus age and occupation, with the last a surrogate for income and social class. Since the defendant was himself black, the premise was that jurors of his race would be more likely to accord him a presumption of innocence. We do know that for generations, Southern prosecutors habitually ensured that blacks charged with crimes would be judged by all-white juries, and by so doing they gained many convictions. Over the last two decades, since its 1975 decision in the case of *Taylor v. Louisiana,* the Supreme Court has held that jury pools must be drawn from a "cross section" of the community. While that requirement does not ensure that persons of any one race will be selected in all cases, in practice it has brought more racially diverse juries.

Clearly, race remains relevant. Both during and after the Simpson trial, polls found most whites who had opinions saying they felt he was guilty, whereas most black respondents supported an acquittal. Hence the widespread view on the part of whites that the black jurors would have biases related to their race.

Similarly, both genders must be fairly represented on jury lists. Thus far, rulings on cross-sectional juries have not been extended to age and social standing. Yet as with race and gender, it could be argued that these attributes affect not only the ways we evaluate evidence, but our overall assessment of the person on trial. Lawyers, sometimes with the aid of consultants, factor in what they think may be other indicators like loquacity or rigidity, even hairstyle and style of dress. In the Simpson trial, they had considerable grist for this mill, since prospective jurors had to write out answers to 294 questions on their experiences and preferences. Because counsel are allowed so many challenges, even unpublicized trials can run through upward of a hundred citizens before finally settling on a panel. As a result, most Americans' exposure to the system has consisted of showing up and being rejected, largely on the basis of lawyers' intuitions.

Of course, the real question is what twelve well-screened individuals will do when they sit down together. Jury scholar Jeffrey Abramson, after reviewing the research in this area, feels compelled to conclude that "there is no scientific way to predict whether an individual juror will conform, in any one case, to the general attitudes of his or her group." Michael Knox's memoir of his service as a Simpson juror substantiates this view. He was sequestered with that panel for almost eight weeks, sufficient time to get to know everyone in the group. What impressed him was not the salience of race or sex or age or class, but friendships and antagonisms that cut across those lines. As it turned out, the most serious tensions were between two black women, both of whom eventually left the jury. Indeed, given the confined quarters, personal quirks mattered more than sociological categories.

Except when biases are blatantly apparent, elaborate efforts by lawyers and consultants to predict how people will behave if placed on a jury are usually futile. (Indeed, if both sides retain "experts," one set will end up with egg on its face.) As Abramson points out, how members ultimately vote will turn mainly on "the fluid group dynamics that influence jury deliberations."

In 1955, a group of University of Chicago professors were allowed to make recordings of deliberations, without the jurors' knowledge, in several Kansas civil cases. Word of this got out, an uproar ensued, and Congress and over half the states proceeded to outlaw any kind of taping. Since that time, both research projects and real-life litigants have had to depend largely on simulations. Abramson relates how practice juries have been assembled by lawyers for companies like MCI and General Motors. Various kinds of arguments are tried before these paid panels, whose deliberations were then observed. These exercises, we are told, help in shaping trial strategies. Academic experiments also pay students to watch films of fictional trials, after which the researchers study simulated deliberations. Thus one such project found that requiring unanimity took an average of 138 minutes to come to a verdict, whereas allowing a 10–2 vote cut the time to 103 minutes. Yet my suspicions remain, if only because few real juries reach consensus in such brief time spans.

As it happens, during the past twenty years, I have served on five juries, all of them criminal cases, including two involving murders. I look forward to being summoned, not as a civic duty, but because I find it an exhilarating experience. So I know what Stephen Adler, author of a recent book on juries, means when he says that speaking with former jurors

> was like having a conversation with someone who was just back from Nepal or who'd just had sex for the first time. They betrayed the same sense of wonder at having been to a new place and having seen life differently.

When before has a citizen been given so grave a responsibility? Freedom or imprisonment; the triumph of truth or a tragic error; adherence to law or malice and caprice—all this and more rests on your shoulders. Nor will it do to say that the onus is shared with eleven others. In all of my juries, I could see each member acting as if the verdict was his alone. Needless to say, no simulation can carry this moral weight.

As part of this process, something akin to bonding begins, starting once the last member has been chosen. As anyone who has served can report, jurors find themselves spending a lot of unsupervised time together, even in proceedings that may last only a week. In the Simpson trial, observers were struck by how often the jurors were told to leave the courtroom, sometimes for quite prolonged periods. In my own trials, we were usually kept waiting in the morning or after lunch, because the judge had to deal with motions from other cases. Confined to a small anteroom, one finds bus drivers and bond traders soon chatting on first name terms. Indeed, I have found it rare for anyone to hide behind a newspaper or a book. In one case, while the trial was still in progress, we all agreed to lunch together at a nearby restaurant. Adding an air of mystery is that during all this socializing, you cannot talk about the trial, the one thing that is uppermost in your minds. Therefore, while "together" in the courtroom, each juror absorbs the testimony in isolation, almost as if you were at home watching the proceedings by yourself on television.

What certainly cannot be replicated by researchers is the process we call deliberation. Like others, I have served on bodies charged with difficult decisions. But none of these match the bearing and demeanor I have observed in jury rooms. In even a car-theft case, reaching a verdict took six hours. Perhaps what impresses me most is that no one, at least in my experience, tried to dominate the discussions. After the first half hour, the foreman becomes just another juror.

In my first murder trial, the initial balloting—which we decided to take before starting talking—came out 6–6. Nor did this surprise me, since while in the jury box we had been watching different trials. We then sought to move from twelve versions to one, or at least to sufficient consensus for a unanimous verdict. By the fourth hour, three of us had changed our votes, now making it 9–3. As one who shifted, I did so because I had been reminded of certain facts I had ignored or felt were unimportant. Or that testimony could be given other interpretations. Jean-Jacques Rousseau once said that for democracy to work, citizens must be willing to say, "I was mistaken." This is not something most of us are prone to do. Yet it must happen if juries are to function, and I have watched fellow New Yorkers make just that admission. About two hours later, we were down to 10–2, and it took another four to arrive at 12–0. At no point were the divisions along racial or other social lines.

And as we moved toward unanimity, it became evident that each of us was gaining a broader perspective than we had brought in as individuals. That twelve minds, twelve sets of eyes and ears, can take in more than one is the epistemological rationale for the jury system. But it only works when bond traders are willing to listen and learn from bus drivers, and thus far the only place I have found that happening is inside jury rooms.

In theory, juries attend to the facts, leaving the judge to settle matters of law. If only the distinction were that simple. In her account of serving as a juror in the Menendez trials, Hazel Thornton shows that the "facts" her jury had to find were actually legal constructions. As I trust needs no detailing, Erik and Lyle Menendez did not deny that they had killed their parents. Rather, they pleaded that there were exonerating circumstances, ranging from preemptive self-defense against further sexual abuse to impaired mental capacity. So while they admitted having done the killings, they stressed that they were not confessing to a crime. For its part, the prosecution argued that some felony had been committed, and the brothers must be punished.

So while the jury was relieved from finding whether the sons had caused their parents' deaths, they were given what turned out to be an even more formidable task: deciding what class of offense—if any—had been committed. As will be recalled, two juries sat in the courtroom, one for each brother (Thornton was on the jury for Erik). To complicate matters further, each jury would have to decide whether its defendant had committed the same order of crime when killing the two parents or if the two deaths represented two types of slayings.

Nor would things get simpler. The prosecution gave each jury the same set of choices. Each brother was charged with having committed all four of the following crimes against each of his parents: first degree murder; second degree murder; voluntary manslaughter; involuntary manslaughter. For its part, the defense emphasized, there was a fifth alternative. By voting "not guilty" on all four counts, the juries could find that the brothers had committed no crime at all.

After almost five months of testimony, the panels retired to deliberate. Assuming for the moment that an identifiable crime had been committed, which of the four it was depended on several combinations of conditions. Thus one of the "facts" each jury had to ferret out was whether their brother had "intended" to kill either or both of his parents. (Needless to say, each jury also spent a lot of time speculating about the brothers' relationship, since either one's intention could turn on how they influenced each other.) At issue too was whether "intent" to kill, which requires a clear aim to bring about death, might have been accompanied by "premeditation," i.e., a previously planned scheme to kill, although the distinction between the two is often murky. In first degree murder, both states of mind must be present, and they must also be combined with "express malice," i.e., a clearly indicated desire to harm which, again, is all too easily confused with the other legally required states of mind. Second degree murder also needed intent, but did not require premeditation; the jury would only have to find "implied malice."

The two different manslaughter charges contained similarly puzzling distinctions, hinging on how far the accused were in control of themselves; and to what degree, if any, they had been threatened or had suffered psychologically from sexual abuse.

Not surprisingly, Thornton tells us that her jury kept going back to the judge for clarifications on definitions, and each time he read them abstract legal paragraphs that offered no assistance. After 106 hours of deliberations, she and the others on Erik's jury declared it could not reach a unanimous decision; and 33 hours later, Lyle's did the same. What most of us recall is that the trial ended with a "hung jury." Yet as Thornton's book makes very clear, this does not adequately describe what happened. All twenty-four of the jurors felt that the brothers had committed a crime when they killed both of their parents. But each panel divided sharply over which of the charges best described what had occurred. Only one of the twenty-four felt that the least severe charge, involuntary manslaughter, was an appropriate verdict, and that juror applied it only to Lyle's slaying of his mother.

As matters currently stand, jurors are not forewarned that they may have to deduce mental and emotional conditions like "premeditation" and "intent" and "malice." Nor should they be asked to. The table on this page shows how what was being asked of the juries was virtually impossible: to come to four different 12–0 decisions on a tangled web of words far removed from palpable realities.

Final Voting in the Menendez Trials

Erik's Killing of His			Lyle's Killing of His	
Father	Mother	Votes For	Father	Mother
5	5	First degree murder	3	3
1	3	Second degree murder	3	3
6	4	Voluntary manslaughter	6	5
0	0	Involuntary manslaughter	0	1
0	0	No crimes committed	0	0
12	12		12	12

What happened in the Menendez case supports Adler's view that we can ask too much of jurors. Why not let them decide whether the defendant has committed a simply defined criminal act—instructions on that can be given—and then allow the judge the broader scope to determine the class and severity of the offense? In fact, something much like this happens when, after hearing the jury's verdict, the judge sets the length of the sentence.

While I continue to have misgivings about presenting jurors several charges for a single offense, I should add in fairness that such options sometimes serve a practical purpose: graded alternatives give the jurors room to maneuver. This was plainly the prosecution's hope in the Simpson case, when it asked—and the judge agreed—to make second degree murder a possible verdict. In one of my trials, a young woman plying her profession was being harassed by a drug dealer. She called out for her protector, who dashed gun in hand from a nearby bar, and proceeded to fire at the man she identified. As it happened, he missed and the bullet killed a bystander. We all managed to agree that a slaying had been "intended"—even if he did not hit his intended target—which made it some kind of murder. But two jurors were not persuaded that it had also been "premeditated," as it had not been previously planned, which was necessary for a first degree conviction. So the rest of us offered to vote for second degree murder to get a unanimous verdict. Since we knew that a lesser charge would bring a lighter sentence, we were in fact engaging in a variant of plea-bargaining. Legally, this should not happen, and judges warn against it, since sentencing is supposed to be outside the jury's purview. Still, everyone knows there would be many fewer 12–0 votes if juries adhered to this aspect of the law.

Michael Knox devotes most of his book to describing how being sequestered affected the Simpson jurors. It is a dispiriting story. While each had a single room on a special hotel floor, they were not allowed to visit one another, even to exchange a few words. The only choices were to be alone in your own room or to be thrown in with all the others, where the main activities were watching television, or chatting warily in everyone's hearing. Not to mention the sheriff department's uniformed deputies always on hand. Nor were these adults allowed to have anything alcoholic, even a glass of wine at dinner. Entirely out of the question was for a couple of jurors to have dinner together in one of their rooms. All these restrictions were based on the premise that if jurors were left alone outside the sight of a deputy, they would start discussing the trial. The assumption held for visitors, who could be seen only in the common room. (Exceptions were made for spouses, who could make conjugal visits between 7 P.M. and midnight.)

In short, it amounted to collective solitary confinement. "When you're sequestered," Knox noted, "you can't avoid anyone." And, as in all confined settings, "minor incidents became major blow-ups." I can vouch from my own experience that personal antagonisms often prolong deliberations, since rankled feelings must be soothed, if they are not to derail the jury altogether. Yet this did not seem to be so with the Simpson jury. The speed with which they came to a unanimous verdict suggests an absence of tensions.

Still, the question remains whether sequestration is truly necessary, even in high-profile cases. My original view was that if jurors were allowed to go home, they might have to fend off friends or strangers who wanted to discuss the case. Not to mention intimidating mail or telephone calls, since there would be no assurance that their identities would remain secret. But even if none of this happened, they might turn on televised accounts of the trial, where they could hear arguments or testimony meant to be outside their hearing.

I had these and other worries until I learned from Hazel Thornton's book that Menendez jurors were permitted to return to their homes every evening, not only while testimony was being heard but also during deliberations. In terms of publicity and popular feeling, theirs was a close counterpart to the Simpson case, yet apparently jurors were not molested. Nor, so far as is known, did they read or look at reports of the trial.

And what of critics who challenge the competence of juries? With complex civil trials, they have a strong case. In matters like patent infringement, securities fraud, even product liability, decisions could well be left to a judge. However, cases like libel and employment discrimination, where facts are more readily grasped, deserve a panel drawn from the public. On the criminal side, it has yet to be shown that judges acting alone are more able to render valid verdicts. How many of us would have given the decision in *People v. Simpson* solely to Lance Ito?

Abandon the
Military Model of Policing

JOSEPH D. McNAMARA

It would be a profound mistake to believe that the acquittal of O. J. Simpson of double murder was simply the jury's response to the Los Angeles Police Department's sloppy investigation, faulty handling and analysis of the evidence, or to the racism of Mark Fuhrman. It certainly was that. But it was also much more—a vote of no confidence in the LAPD.

Once, when I was on foot patrol in Harlem, an African-American woman with a head wound approached me. "Officer," she apologized, "I know you're very busy, but I've just been robbed." I wasn't at all busy, but I wondered what we white cops were doing that caused a victim to apologize for reporting an armed robbery.

The LAPD should view the Simpson verdict as a similar call for self-scrutiny. If the Police Department were a private business, it would long ago have gone bankrupt because significant numbers of its customers have no faith in its product. Unfortunately, the LAPD, like the Postal Service, does not have to worry about customers taking their business elsewhere. Yet, effective policing requires that the department understand why it is distrusted, why it is losing credibility and try to stop it.

When I was hired to run the San Jose, California, Police Department, it was known as a little LAPD—a reference to a military style of policing that alienates minorities. There was no communication between rank-and-file police and the neighborhoods they patrolled.

Then, for a number of years, beat officers were directed to leave their patrol cars and attend school and neighborhood meetings and to hear what the people thought of them. At times, it was painful. But in the end, mutual respect developed; the public began to participate more in police issues.

Officers learned what services were needed. At the same time, procedures were improved for receiving and investigating citizen complaints. A number of cops who refused to get the message ended up in other occupations. Most important, officers began to realize that unless people reported crimes, provided evidence, served as witnesses, and—when on juries—believed police testimony, criminals would not be convicted.

Training was provided for the police to learn about the diverse cultures that made up San Jose. This helped eliminate some of the negative stereotypes that can all too easily flourish in departments. Interestingly enough, the police made more arrests than ever, and crime decreased to the point that San Jose became one of the safest large cities in America, a city of minorities.

There are no panaceas to prevent crime, but the military model of policing, which is supposed to scare criminals into obeying the law, is a failure. What the LAPD must realize is that it is, above all, a service agency obligated to provide communities with the kind of lawful policing they desire and deserve. Community condemnation of crime is a stronger deterrent than police-state methods, which create sympathy for criminals.

In addition to establishing real communication with neighborhoods and a sense of partnership, the police should abandon drug-war tactics and strongly support campaigns to treat and educate drug users. Criminologist Alfred A. Blumstein has described the drug war as an assault on the African-American community that would not be tolerated by whites. A study released by the Washington, D.C.–based Sentencing Project bears this out. African Americans and Latinos, the study concludes, constitute nearly 90 percent of offenders sentenced to state prison for drug possession. Ending the drug war would eliminate many of the racial inequities in the criminal justice system and would be a step toward rehabilitating the image of officers in minority communities.

The police did not create America's race problems and will not solve them. Nonetheless, denying that the police and law enforcement need to be improved only aggravates an open sore. Disclosure of police abuses during the civil rights movement forced a healthy self-scrutiny in law enforcement and led to increased community efforts to improve policing. The result was a steady improvement in police relations with minorities.

It is time to acknowledge that much of that progress has eroded. The minority community, which has the highest crime rates, must come to realize that it suffers the most when law enforcement fails to punish violent criminals. It is not enough merely to criticize the police and celebrate police failures. Minorities must work with the police to reduce racial polarization by establishing trust in justice and better safety in neighborhoods.

Policing the Police

The D.A.'s Job

SCOTT TUROW

The problem was not only the way the police went about gathering evidence at Mr. Simpson's home the morning after the murders, but more important the way the Los Angeles District Attorney's Office subsequently defended those arrogant blunders.

At the preliminary hearings, Detectives Philip Vannatter and Mark Fuhrman testified that they and two other detectives traveled to Mr. Simpson's home on Rockingham Avenue to inform him of the murder so he could make arrangements for his children.

The detectives testified that after getting no response to the buzzer at the gate, and following their discovery of a small spot of blood on Mr. Simpson's Bronco, which was on the street, they jumped the wall because they feared for Mr. Simpson's safety. It was after this adventure in low-rent rappelling—which was not only a violation of the Fourth Amendment but also criminal trespass—that Detective Fuhrman says he found the famous bloody glove.

The trouble with this testimony, in my view, is that the detectives' explanation as to why they were at the house is hard to believe. At the time of the preliminary hearing, before the DNA results had come in, the bloody glove, which matched one found at the crime scene, was the foremost evidence against Mr. Simpson. So the police were under tremendous pressure to explain their actions in a way that would legally excuse them for violating Mr. Simpson's rights and allow the glove to be introduced as evidence.

Thus the dubious claim about fearing for Mr. Simpson's safety. Four police detectives were not needed to carry a message about Nicole Simpson's death. These officers undoubtedly knew what Justice Department statistics indicate: that half of the women murdered in the United States are killed by their husbands or boyfriends. Simple probabilities made Mr. Simpson a suspect.

Also, Mark Fuhrman had been called to the Simpson residence years earlier when Mr. Simpson was abusing his wife. Thus Mr. Simpson was more than the usual suspect husband; he had a known propensity to do violence to his wife. Of course, he is also one of the most exceptional physical talents of his generation, a member of the relatively small class of human beings capable of murdering two persons at once and of wielding a knife with sufficient power to virtually decapitate someone.

If veteran police detectives did not arrive at the gate of Mr. Simpson's home thinking he might have committed these murders, then they should have been fired.

The detectives went to Rockingham for one reason: they wanted to question Mr. Simpson before he had a chance to lawyer up. Perhaps he would explain himself, offer an alibi. But it's more likely they were hoping he would confess or tell one of the stupid little lies that so often become a defendant's undoing.

The detectives did not need a spot of blood on the Bronco to have powerful reasons to question Mr. Simpson. But assuming they did see the blood, why were they fly-specking the car if they had come only to deliver tragic news? The cops went over the wall to find Mr. Simpson, not to save him, and anyone who has spent time as a player in the criminal justice system had to recognize that.

The fact that the District Attorney's Office put these officers on the witness stand to tell this story and that the municipal judge at the pretrial hearing, Kathleen Kennedy-Powell, accepted it is scandalous. It is also routine.

Everybody hates the Fourth Amendment, of course. What a lamentable concept: the constable blundered so the evidence is lost. But the Fourth Amendment was not added to the Constitution to make most of us happy. It was intended to protect individuals from the state and to insure that political minorities would not be the object of random searches engineered by the political majority.

And when the Fourth Amendment and the other constitutional rules restricting police behavior are violated, it necessarily carries with it a strong message to our political minorities—including members of racial minorities, who are more likely to have contact with the police than are whites—that the legal system is a two-faced joker, one which says: We make the rules and we'll follow the ones we like.

I was an Assistant United States Attorney for eight years, and I never had a piece of evidence suppressed in a case I handled. This is not because I am such a great lawyer or mastered any special legal legerdemain. It was because the federal agents I worked with understood the Fourth Amendment and didn't violate it.

Assistant United States Attorneys were available to answer federal investigators' legal questions twenty-four hours a day. The agents were forbidden to make an arrest or enter a residence without our approval. They made it their business to follow the law, because they knew we would not put them on the witness stand to play make-believe. We couldn't even if we wanted to because the district court judges turned aside all such efforts with fury and scorn.

A legal system, like any moral system, is a complex and interdependent social arrangement. No one does good on his own. It requires the constant support, reinforcement, and allegiance of all players for each to resist the ever-present temptations to let ends justify means. And that system appears to have broken down in Los Angeles.

To lambaste only Detectives Fuhrman and Vannatter misses the point. It was the Los Angeles District Attorney's Office that put them on the stand. It was Judge Kennedy-Powell who took their testimony at face value rather than stir controversy by suppressing the most damning evidence in the case of the century. And it was Judge Lance A. Ito who refused to reverse her decision.

Because the prosecutors routinely accepted even the most unlikely stories from police officers, they were unable to recognize Mr. Fuhrman as a genuinely bad character. By the time news of Mr. Fuhrman's background began to emerge, prosecutors were hip-joined to him, their star witness—a foul-mouthed racist cop, the latest poster boy of the Los Angeles Police Department, his image hanging on the wall of the public mind next to those of the officers who beat Rodney King.

The jury made them pay. The jurors were impaneled knowing from the start that this was business as usual in Los Angeles. Nothing the prosecutors could do could convince them that this case was not corrupted by the Police Department's world-renowned racial hostility.

It is worth thinking about how this case would have developed had the authorities played it straight from the start. If Judge Kennedy-Powell had said: "I know these police officers want to believe what they've said, but that defies the realities of the work they do. This evidence is suppressed." If the District Attorney's Office had conceded that the police had violated Mr. Simpson's rights, but tried to have the evidence admitted on the "inevitable discovery" theory, which allows evidence that would have surely been found had the police gotten a search warrant.

Yes, suppressing the glove would have made headlines. It would have been another black eye for the Police Department. But it would have been a clarion announcement to the world—and to Los Angeles's black community—that the criminal justice system had mended its ways and was committed to treating all citizens fairly.

Paradoxically, it would also have given the District Attorney's Office its best chance to win this case. It would have relieved the jurors, all but two of whom were black or Hispanic, of the troubling choice they ultimately faced—between convicting Mr. Simpson or vindicating their own rights, which no one else in the legal system seemed to have bothered to protect.

PART V

Cameras in the Courtroom?

The Pros and Cons of Televising Trials

JEFFREY ABRAMSON

The debate over cameras in the courtroom dates back to the 1935 Lindbergh case, when Bruno Richard Hauptmann went on trial in Flemington, New Jersey, for kidnaping and murdering Charles Lindbergh's infant son. Apparently without the trial judge's permission, newsreel companies managed to film the trial from a courtroom balcony. Even before the trial's end, those reels found their way into theaters and were shown to moviegoers everywhere. Outraged, the American Bar Association recommended a ban on cameras in court, which effectively kept trials film- and television-free for the next thirty years.

However, by the time the O. J. Simpson trial began, forty-seven states (all but Indiana, Mississippi, and South Dakota) had lifted the ban on televised trials and permitted cameras in court at the presiding judge's discretion. In the federal system, the Judicial Conference of the United States, the policymaking body for federal courts, approved a three-year experiment with television coverage of civil cases in six trial courts and two appellate circuits.

Even before it was over, the Simpson trial ushered in a backlash against televised trials. Writing in the *New York Times*, law professor Susan Estrich echoed the sentiments of many when she blamed the interminable length and the theatrical antics of the trial on the distraction of cameras. Governor Pete Wilson of California began urging the state Judicial Council, which sets policy for California courts, to reconsider its position in favor of cameras. A task force is currently holding hearings on the issue. A Los Angeles Superior Court judge urged the task force to ban cameras, saying, "It is time for the judiciary to declare that we are not part of the entertainment industry."

In September 1994, the Judicial Conference temporarily ended its three-year experiment with televised federal civil cases. Across the nation, a number of trial judges also used their discretion to ban the televising of particular cases, most notably the Los Angeles retrial of the Menendez brothers (convicted of first-degree murder on March 20, 1996), the South Carolina murder trial of Susan Smith for drowning her two children (convicted of first-degree murder on July 22, 1995), and the Massachusetts murder trial of John Salvi (convicted on March 18, 1996, of first-degree murder of two receptionists at Boston-area abortion clinics). All of these trials had the potential to become mega–media events. But in the absence of television coverage, public interest clearly waned. Some commentators connect the decline of media attention to these trials with an increase in the speed and decorum with which the cases were conducted. Others bemoan the fact that important opportunities for civic education (for instance, about the insanity defense in John Salvi's trial) were lost.

The backlash against televised trials is by no means complete. According to *Broadcasting and Cable* magazine, Court TV received permission to televise forty-seven of the fifty trials it sought to cover during 1995. The magazine quotes Court TV founder Steven Brill as saying "that's a higher rate than at any other time." Court TV has televised approximately four hundred trials over the past four years and has about 24 million subscribers.

Most recently, on March 14, 1996, the Judicial Conference of the United States voted by a 14–12 margin to give federal appellate courts the option to televise oral arguments on appeal. It is unclear whether this permission extends to criminal appeals, since rule 53 of the Federal Rules of Criminal Procedure bars "photographic and electronic coverage of judicial proceedings from the courtroom."

At the same time, the Conference continued to disapprove of televising actual trials, a position that will keep cameras out of the upcoming Oklahoma City bombing trial. However, in March 1996, a federal judge sitting in Manhattan relied on local rules to permit Court TV to televise a civil lawsuit seeking to place New York City's child welfare agency in receivership. Fourteen of the ninety-four federal districts have similar local rules permitting cameras in trial courts.

Arguments in favor of televised trials stress the democracy of the technology: people should be able to see and judge for themselves what is going on in court, unfiltered by the spins or selections of journalists. Of course, public judgment can be skewed if only atypical cases such as the Simpson trial are broadcast. But Court TV and CNN have said they are committed to offering live coverage of a broad and representative sample of trials. Moreover, supporters of cameras in court say that we should not lambaste the messenger for delivering messages we do not want to receive—messages about a judicial process that needs fixing. It is a basic First Amendment principle that information is good for a democracy and that citizens discharge their civic duties more intelligently when the affairs of the government, including the judiciary, are subject to publicity. The practical question is whether that publicity should be delivered secondhand, through the eyes of professional journalists and the relatively few spectators present in court, or whether the people should be permitted to "attend" trials themselves. In this regard, defenders of televising the Simpson trial point out that the unseemly coverage came from the tabloids and entertainment shows; gavel-to-gavel coverage permitted attentive citizens to know the difference between what actually occurred in court and what these lurid and titillating sideshows made of it.

Arguments in favor of cameras in the courtroom assume that cameras are essentially a neutral conduit, recording only what would go inside the court in the absence of television. Critics dispute this starting assumption and claim the mere presence of cameras changes courtroom behavior for the worse. They claim that fearful witnesses may be intimidated from testifying, that jurors will start thinking of Oprah appearances, that lawyers will play to the cameras, and that judges will lose control of their courts out of fear of coming across as dictatorial. In her contribution to this volume, Diana Trilling contrasts the mouthing offs of the lawyers in the Simpson trial with the civility with which all participants in the 1981 trial of Jean Harris, charged with killing her lover, a famous Scarsdale diet doctor, treated one another. The trial had Simpsonesque details: rich and celebrity defendant and victim, high-priced lawyers, sexual scandal. But the trial stayed away from sexual innuendo, with lawyers showing the kind of respect for the trial process that becomes less likely, critics allege, when the cameras are turned on.

To date, there is almost no reliable empirical research on whether televised trials have these feared, deleterious effects. Anecdotedly, the relative quickness of the Susan Smith and John Salvi trials lends support to the intuitively plausible claim that trials become more efficient and focused when cameras are absent. But more study is needed to verify even this limited claim. Moreover, the question remains whether one side or the other benefits when trial presentations are streamlined and the public loses interest in the case.

In a rough sense, critics of cameras in the courtroom are correct when they point out that television is an entertainment medium, not an educational one, and that entertainment values are inconsistent with the civility, decorum, and slow pace we need inside court. But the question remains whether television is condemned for all time to titillate viewers rather than to educate us. The Simpson trial gave us both—the endless parade of out-of-court video clips of the Simpsons in swimsuits, on golf courses, in nightclubs. But the 631 hours of coverage CNN alone devoted to the trial were television of a different sort, coverage that permitted an average 2.2 million viewers tuned in at any given moment to have a remarkably unvarnished look at the American trial process. Surely, some if not most of those viewers understood that O. J. Simpson was not a typical defendant and that they needed a context within which to understand and to judge what they were seeing. If and when television goes on to provide this context, by attracting similar-sized audiences for the trials of ordinary, indigent defendants, then it will have turned the corner from entertainment toward education.

The Failure (and Promise) of Legal Journalism

LINCOLN CAPLAN

The impulse to keep the overkill of the O. J. Simpson trial from happening again rekindled the debate about whether cameras should be allowed in courtrooms. Momentum shifted sharply to the con. But in fixing on trials and TV, the debate missed a larger insight from Simpson coverage about legal journalism. With or without the cameras, it's foundering badly.

At first blush, this notion must seem silly. Legal coverage has expanded enormously: from gavel-to-gavel TV presentation of O.J.'s trial and many others, to talk shows that concentrate on sensational legal events, to print and radio showcases for glamorous, highly paid lawyers.

Because of the Simpson case, legal journalism appears to have moved from a specialized niche into a central place in the media. Virtually all the major media provided constant coverage of the trial. The major news magazines ran ten cover stories about it between June 1994 and April 1995. CNN's ratings increased fivefold when it televised the trial. For cable television watchers, it was possible to catch perspectives on the trial from ex-judges, ex-prosecutors, ex-U.S. Justice Department officials, and ex- and current defense lawyers. There were so many it was hard to keep count.

The new legal journalism is different from the old. It's more comprehensive, more direct, and more accessible. One of its premises is that, with the opportunity to witness legal proceedings entirely, viewers are better able to take or leave the opinions of reporters and experts, to "judge for themselves." It prides itself on substituting technology for judgment, however, and that isn't really journalism.

It is information delivered without knowledge, often escorted by opinion without explanation and soothsaying without heed of consequences. It treats the law as a game of stratagems—a tendency exemplified by the televised coverage at the end of the Simpson trial especially, when virtually everyone in the pack of predictors (How long did you say the O.J. jury would take to reach a guilty verdict?) was proven wrong.

While legal journalism appears to be booming, the dominant version offers coverage that isolates the law from the world it reflects and shapes. It turns America's paradoxical feelings about lawyers—Americans cannot get enough of lawyers, yet detest them—into a self-fulfilling prophecy: the more people learn, they less they like, because the coverage is so narrow.

Followers of the new legal journalism pick up lawyerly lingo, but they get little help in understanding the significance of the events reported or even in following their narratives. As coverage of the Simpson trial underscored, the new legal journalism has ghettoized legal coverage, providing an unprecedented amount but of a blindered, ingrown kind.

It does not have to be this way. The best legal affairs reporting— whether on television, in legal or news magazines, or newspapers— has its roots in a generation-old Supreme Court case as detailed in the 1964 classic, *Gideon's Trumpet* by Anthony Lewis. It tells, in 238 pages, how Clarence Gideon, a poor, fifty-one-year-old white man, induced the U.S. Supreme Court to find a new right to counsel for indigents in the Constitution.

As Lewis practiced legal journalism, the genre combined storytelling, legal analysis, portraiture, history, and social commentary. Relating American choices, his reporting was a form of civics: in a rule-of-law country, it illumined the country by concentrating on a distinguished part of the nation.

Lewis's work begins in the once-upon-a-time manner of a fairy tale: "In the morning mail of January 8, 1962, the Supreme Court of the United States received a large envelope from Clarence Earl Gideon, prisoner No. 003826, Florida State Prison, P.O. Box 221, Raiford, Florida." It ends like one, too, with a final comment from Gideon: "'Do you feel like you accomplished something?' a newspaper reporter asked. 'Well, I did.'"

In between, it tells the stories of Gideon's quest, the Supreme Court's dealings with his case, and the stuff of the legal dispute. *Gideon's Trumpet* was first serialized in *The New Yorker* in 1964, was a best-seller as a hardcover book, and remains in print as a paperback. Lewis conveys the right proportions of each story, in prose that is engaging, open, and surprisingly light.

Gideon's Trumpet is Lewis's grand work of journalism, but not his most celebrated. In 1955, he won a Pulitzer Prize for his investigation in the *Washington Daily News* of the U.S. Navy's unjustified dismissal of an employee on grounds that he was a security risk. In 1962, Lewis won a second Pulitzer for his reporting about the Supreme Court for the *New York Times,* especially his coverage of the decision in *Baker v. Carr* (1962) about the reapportionment of state legislatures.

Lewis's *Trumpet* appeared as the legal profession began to grow exponentially—in the next twenty-five years, four times faster than the population—and just before legal journalism began to burgeon as a specialized field within the trade. He started and seeded it, the Supreme Court intervened, and the market took over: in 1976, with a push from Lewis, Yale Law School inaugurated a one-year masters program for journalists; in 1977, the Supreme Court ruled that the legal profession could no longer prohibit advertising by lawyers; in 1978, *The American Lawyer* was launched as the first in a chain of publications about lawyers that thrived because of advertising from lawyers, palpable interest among lawyers expressed through the purchase by law firms of expensive subscriptions, and cooperation from lawyers that ranged from wary through calculated to eager.

The magazine became the flagship of a media company that grew to include nine local law-based newspapers, a computer service called Lexis Counsel Connect, and Court TV, which began to broadcast in 1991. By 1995, cable carried Court TV to 22 million households, with a fraction of that number watching it to see the Simpson trial. Steven Brill is the co-founder and editor-in-chief. Other outlets provide similar coverage of legal affairs, but the Brill empire is the epitome.

In the beginning, *The American Lawyer* presented itself as performing a public service by exposing the hidden workings of law firms and other legal institutions—the business of law. It sometimes lived up to its own billing. It presented data about law firms that previously had not been regularly compiled and published, exposed how juries decide verdicts, and, with a tone of iconoclasm, put the legal establishment on notice that it had a watchdog.

But the magazine also became a shaper of a sharp-edged picture of reality that established a new order of status. The monthly ran big headlines and looming photographs that made their subjects appear larger than life, and was printed as an oversized tabloid. *The American Lawyer* zeroed in on a blunt, tantalizing measure of ultimate success—how much money lawyers make. While it went through various incarnations (muckraking, celebrating, predicting the future), it set the character of the new legal journalism.

Its hallmarks are:

- highlighting the machinations of the legal process and the lawyers who move it along, rather than the substance and the drama of ideas;
- treating the legal world primarily as a self-contained, isolated universe;
- maintaining a focus on the present scene of some proceeding and excluding the kind of instructive sense of history that characterized classics of legal journalism like *Gideon's Trumpet*;
- offering, in place of a narrative whose explanatory power derives partly from its wholeness—its ability to line up events, characters, legal ideas, and their consequences in a meaningful order—a collection of isolated fragments.

Despite its small circulation (at its highest, 21,000 copies), *The American Lawyer* and its sister outlets have had a tremendous impact on how other media present the legal profession. The general-interest press now relies on the magazine's bestowals of status in the profession, especially its rankings of law firms. The elite general media have followed its lead in deciding whose expertise to highlight. Metro newspapers imitated *The American Lawyer* by starting legal gossip columns that focused on big verdicts and lawyers' comings and goings. Former staffers from *The American Lawyer*'s empire have turned up as high-profile legal reporters for the general media—NBC's Jack Ford and ABC's Cynthia McFadden, to name two.

A position paper from Court TV describes what it tries to offer: "[T]elevision coverage of trials tells the whole, real, true story about a complicated, often misunderstood and underreported subject. It allows the participants in a democracy to judge for themselves how well the government institution that makes the most fundamental decision that any government makes—liberty or prison—is working." As Court TV explains it, its coverage is a supplement to (and sometimes a check on) traditional journalism.

That frames the major issue about contemporary legal journalism and points up the basic problem with it: in theory, the new and the old liberate each other to do what each does best and provide complementary coverage. In reality, the new is driving out the old.

Court TV has set the broadcast standard; in consequence, legal journalism has become increasingly like sports and political reporting, a form of play-by-play. It is preoccupied with topicality, narrowly defined. Its main criterion is who's winning and losing, and—as the who's-hot-who's-not coverage of both legal teams in the O.J. trial showed all too clearly—without much regard for why it matters.

Why it matters is reinforced by the lack of any other accessible medium to answer that question. The most influential writing about law was once published in academic law reviews. Today, instead of reviews feeding ideas to trade journals and the latter feeding ideas to the general media—how the media chain might work—law reviews have become arcane and insulated, trade journals, dominant.

To the extent that the new legal journalism deals with ideas, its approach is vocational—news you can use. Its contents are much more understandable to lawyers than other readers. For its original audience—lawyers—the new legal journalism could get away with this approach. It could assume familiarity with the law and legal affairs.

But using the trade approach, the general media have magnified its defects. Even the best practitioners do pieces that presume their readers are informed about the events they cover and mostly require analysis. This presumption is a disservice to all consumers of legal news, even in the trades. With the law, every major factor warrants inquiry. Even if an element of a story is as well known as *Brown v.*

Board of Education, the 1954 landmark decision outlawing segregation in public schools, its meaning in fresh circumstances has to be examined.

Of course, the turn in legal journalism matches the turn in journalism, generally. Narrowcasting has replaced broadcasting, segmentation has succeeded where sweeping coverage has declined in favor, rankings (who's-hot, etc.) supplant explanatory reporting. Editorial decisions are dictated by economics. With fewer reporters and editors staffing newsrooms, the talking heads prevail, as the notion of taking the long view, of devoting weeks to research, often seems impractical.

For a more expansive vision of law and society—and to see what money can buy—you must turn not to news coverage but to television dramas like *Picket Fences* (about the family of the sheriff in the fictional Rome, Wisconsin), *Chicago Hope* (about the staff of a large, city hospital), and *Murder One* (about the saga of a murder case).

David Kelley is executive producer of the first two shows. He's a former Boston lawyer who jumped to TV as a writer for *L.A. Law.* Steven Bochco is the executive producer of the third. He created *L.A. Law* and the cop shows *Hill Street Blues* and *N.Y.P.D. Blue.* According to the *New York Times,* he is "perhaps the most powerful and innovative writer and producer in prime-time television."

The essence of a Bochco-Kelley show is a narrative conflict about a legal issue with the drama supplied by a twist in conventional wisdom. In a *Murder One* subplot, it is the protagonist, a white trial lawyer, giving a black client acutely good advice. The young teacher has been acquitted of criminal charges in a car accident but thrown in jail for contempt of court, after challenging a white judge who is blind to his own racism; the lawyer tells the teacher that he should swallow his pride, cop an apology to the judge, and go back to the corner of the world where he is in control and can make a difference.

In a *Picket Fences* episode about court-ordered school integration, it is the liberal mayor (she happens to be the sheriff's wife) who questions the wisdom of busing black children from the city into the foreign territory of suburban Rome. In a *Chicago Hope* episode about treating Parkinson's disease with tissue from a fetus through an abortion, a pregnant wife and her ill husband are willing to sacrifice their future baby (they have other children) to keep the husband alive. They have a court order for the procedure, but the head of the hospital opposes it on moral grounds.

To educate Americans about the real legal system—"to substitute real law for *L.A. Law*"—is an ambition of Court TV, according to its own position paper. Bochco ecstatically agrees with this ambition. He told the *New York Times* that Court TV is "the best show on TV." For a self-proclaimed "junkie," it provides almost endless matter to ingest: to Bochco, the power of the network resides in "the camera" in the courtroom, which "reveals so much more than what we've ever revealed before."

To most people, however, what the camera shows is cloaked in legal code. With their presentation of narratives and ideas, Bochco and Kelley dramas decode the law. They are more effective in framing important legal choices than most of what Court TV broadcasts.

In an era when "reality" TV blurs the line between nonfiction and fiction by re-creating events, what people see on *Picket Fences, Chicago Hope,* and *Murder One* gets closer to the truth—especially since the events they stage are often taken from the news. They are not the only TV dramas that meet this standard. *Law & Order,* for example, has explored the idea of the so-called abuse excuse (the Menendez brothers used a history of child abuse as an excuse for killing their parents) more affectingly than any journalism. Despite their theatrical license, those dramas do a basic job of journalism, as Lewis did in his best reporting.

They tell a story by framing its major points rather than treating each small part as equally significant—they explain what is important and why. They are psychologically attuned, especially about how the biases of anyone in the legal system sway his or her judgment on how it should work and push lawyers to the emotional edge. They are also packed with details: the stuff on a lawyer's desk, the casual talk between cops and prosecutors.

How can legal journalism be as revealing?

First, it should reintegrate the elements of narrative and analysis that Lewis did effectively, that the best of the television series do in their dramas, and that, in other types of news besides legal, are now viewed as the essential way to hold a time-deprived audience and inform it better.

Second, it should re-emphasize the importance of ideas—by lengthening the frame of reference for even topically oriented television programs and increasing the drama by showing how legal ideas and their uses change over time. This is not a proposal just for print outlets that have a lot of space. Television can get at what print does by asking different questions. It can draw on the inherent tension in a shift of ideas to supply a sense of conflict.

Third, if legal-trained journalists or lawyers are going to be asked to comment on issues and events, they should go outside their experiences as a basis for observations and offer something besides perishable predictions they are glad that people will forget.

But the style of the new legal journalism reflects a deeper problem: it is often delivered in a tone of ironic knowingness that is meant to convey a command of the subject but is itself a barrier for the audience. At its high end, legal journalism sometimes gives the impression that reporters with a law degree believe that, but for a shift of fate, they could be doing the job of the lawyer (or judge) they're criticizing—and better.

The tone of *Gideon's Trumpet,* by contrast, is respectful of its main characters, of the Supreme Court, and of the law, as if all possessed an integrity that were above serious doubt. In Lewis's reporting, there is no confusion about the boundaries of his role or about the line between his journalistic observations and the decisions of officials on whom he reports.

This is remarkable because, behind the scenes when he was a legal reporter, according to Victor Navasky in *Kennedy Justice,* Lewis acted as if he knew the best way for a brief to be argued in a landmark case. Lewis lobbied Attorney General Robert Kennedy and Solicitor General Archibald Cox that the Justice Department should argue that the Supreme Court had the power to consider the reapportionment of state legislatures in *Baker v. Carr,* as the justices ultimately decided.

By current standards, "kibbitzing" like Lewis's (Navasky's word) would be considered wrong for a reporter—it would call into question his impartiality on a topic he was covering and had editorialized about. (Lewis had written the "definitive analysis" [Navasky] of reapportionment for the *Harvard Law Review.*) But to Navasky, Lewis "did his best not to overstep the boundaries of propriety": he did not express his bent in his reporting, which won him his second Pulitzer.

Today, neither the law nor the Court holds the same level of confidence among Americans as it did thirty years ago. Journalism has plummeted even further in its standing. And the focus of the new legal journalism on the process and the players of the law enables it to skirt the prevailing doubt about what matters most: the integrity of the law. Its tone begs the issue of confidence in journalism, by accepting the current wisdom that the best means for dealing with journalism's inherent lack of objectivity is to flaunt it.

But the guiding belief of Lewis's work is one that the new legal journalism claims as its reason for being: that the law is a vital element of public affairs. *Gideon's Trumpet* conveys that belief in its author's voice. The new legal journalism often conveys the opposite. Lewis's voice may be uncool compared to the ironic tone of journalism in the last decade, but the new legal journalism must find something to replace that voice possessing at least a thread of respect, if only for the impact of the law. Otherwise it will choke itself to death.

To find its voice, however, legal journalism must have editors and producers in the general media who believe in it. The notion of legal journalism as a form of civics is fading fast—just when you might expect the opposite, with law and lawyers having moved beyond their post at the heart of American society to quicken the very pulse of the culture.

PART VI

The Trial in Historical Perspective

The Rights of the Accused in a "Crime Crisis"

YALE KAMISAR

I grieve for my country to say that the administration of the criminal law in all the states in the Union (there may be one or two exceptions) is a disgrace to our civilization. . . . The institution of trial by jury has come to be regarded as such a fetish in our country that state legislatures have exalted the power of the jury and diminished the power of the court. . . . The counsel for the defense, relying on the diminished power of the court, creates, by dramatic art and by harping on the importance of unimportant details, a false atmosphere in the courtroom which the

---

I have relied on the following: Anthony Amsterdam, *Perspectives on the Fourth Amendment*, 58 Minn. L. Rev. 349 (1974); Thomas Davies, *A Hard Look at What We Know (and Still Need to Learn) about the "Costs" of the Exclusionary Rule*, Am. Bar Found. Res. J. 611 (1983); Milton Loewenthal, *Evaluating the Exclusionary Rule in Search and Siezure*, 49 UMKC L. Rev. 24 (1980); Harvey Silvergate, *Simpson Jury Sends a Subtle Message on Race*, The National L. J., Oct. 16, 1995, p. A21; Gerald Uelmen, *Legends and Landmarks, Criminal Defense*, Sept./Oct. 1982; Gerald Uelmen, *William Howard Taft, Jury-Basher, L.A. Daily Journal*, Nov. 6, 1995.

judge is powerless to dispel, and under the hypnotic influence of which the counsel is able to lead the jurors to vote as jurors for a verdict which, after all the excitement of the trial has passed away, they are unable to support as men and women.

Another problem is the difficulty of securing jurors properly sensible of the duty which they are summoned to perform. In the extreme tenderness the state legislatures exhibit toward persons accused as criminals, and especially as murderers, they allow peremptory challenges to the defendant far in excess of those allowed to the state. This very great discrepancy between the two sides of the case allows defense counsel to eliminate from all panels every person of force and character and standing in the community, and to assemble a collection in the jury box of nondescripts of no character, weak and amenable to every breeze of emotion, however maudlin or irrelevant to the issue.

Some people may consider the preceding remarks a gross overreaction to the "not guilty" verdict in the O. J. Simpson case. Others may think these remarks are right on the money. In any event, they were made on June 26, 1905, as part of a Yale Law School commencement address, long before defense lawyers had the assistance of any experts in selecting a jury and long before anybody accused defense lawyers of "playing the race card."

The speaker on that day some ninety years ago (I have substituted "men and women" for "men") was a lawyer who had already acquired considerable stature—and was to achieve a good deal more. His name was William Howard Taft. His trashing of juries, and the American system of criminal justice generally, contributed to a remarkably successful political career culminating with his election to the presidency. On top of that, some years later he was appointed Chief Justice of the United States.

Shortly after the Simpson jury rendered a "not guilty" verdict, I wrote an op-ed piece in a legal newspaper quoting Taft's jury-bashing comments as a graphic example of how ancient this American sport really is. I noted that if one had not known who had made these remarks one would have assumed they were aimed at the jury that acquitted Mr. Simpson. Professor Gerald Uelmen, a legal scholar with an historical bent (and one of O.J.'s lawyers), then contributed an article to the same newspaper, pointing out that the parallels to the aftermath of the O. J. Simpson case were even stronger than I had realized.

Uelmen made a persuasive case that the genesis of Taft's 1905 jury-bashing remarks lay in his experience as a young prosecuting attorney twenty years earlier in his home town of Cincinnati, Ohio—especially his dealings with and hostility toward a prominent local criminal defense attorney, Tom Campbell. (Taft was shocked and dismayed when one of Campbell's clients, a stable boy prosecuted for strangling his boss, was convicted of manslaughter rather than murder.)

In 1884 Taft, then a young assistant prosecutor, told the Cincinnati Bar Association that much of the blame for the recent rise in crime was attributable to "the wiles of criminal lawyers" who manipulate continuances and put on perjured testimony. He then warned his audience: "It is well-nigh impossible to convict a man who has money in this country under our present system of prosecution." (Now *there* is a statement that reads as if it were uttered in the wake of the O.J. acquittal.)

That same year, newspapers editorialized that the lesser verdict in the stable boy's case sent a message to the "criminal class" that if you can afford to retain the services of a clever lawyer and get a pliant jury you can escape the snares of justice. At a mass public meeting, a local judge called for the jurors who rendered the verdict to be expelled from the city, along with the lawyer (Tom Campbell) who represented the defendant.

The crowd then adjourned to the city jail, where an attempt to lynch the defendant failed. The next night, the crowd returned. Finding the jail guarded by state militia, the crowd vented its wrath on the county courthouse, burning it to the ground. When the smoke cleared, 45 were dead, another 125 were injured.

Who was to blame for this outrageous event? A subsequent grand jury inquiry placed the blame squarely on the jury that had rendered the unpopular verdict and, more generally, on defects in the criminal code which exempted so many from jury duty and made it so difficult to secure intelligent jurors in criminal cases. Blamed, too, were criminal defense lawyers like Tom Campbell, who dupe and corrupt ignorant jurors. Indeed, Taft led a team of lawyers who sought to disbar Campbell. (The lawyer was exonerated.)

Neither Taft nor any committee of the bar criticized the local judge who had stirred up the mob. Nor was any mention made of inflammatory newspaper reports of the case.

Taft's attack on juries and criminal defense lawyers in the 1880s and 1900s met a warm reception—for the same reason the trashing of

juries and defense lawyers was warmly received in the aftermath of
O. J. Simpson's acquittal. In all three instances people believed they
were living in a period of "crime crisis." When Taft attributed much
of the crime crisis to the "wiles of criminal lawyers" in 1884, forty-two
men were in the county jail awaiting trial on murder charges. When
Taft attacked juries, defense lawyers—and the Bill of Rights generally—in his 1905 commencement address, the murder rate had
soared 500 percent in the past twenty years.

(According to Taft, the problem was that although there had been
a startling increase in the annual number of murders, the number of
executions per year had remained about the same. The clear inference
was that the execution rate should keep pace with the murder rate
and also increase 500 percent. In Taft's time, we were executing some
110 people a year. That number seemed small to Taft, but the *total
number* of people we have executed from 1976 to 1995 is approximately 300.)

In the 1880s and 1900s, as in the 1990s, it was easy to convince people that the crime problem was so serious that the policy of the Bill of
Rights was too inconvenient to be taken seriously and should best be
passed over in silence. Then, as now, it was tempting to blame the
intractable crime problem on dishonest defense lawyers, ignorant
jurors, sob-sister probation officers and parole boards, or the privilege
against self-incrimination or some other provision of the Bill of Rights.

The O. J. Simpson case raised serious questions about whether we
take the Constitutional guarantees against unreasonable searches and
seizures seriously today. Without bothering to apply for a search warrant, the police climbed over the fence onto Mr. Simpson's property
(because, they said, they wanted to help and comfort him). It's hard
to imagine that either the experienced prosecutors who handled the
Simpson case or the two experienced judges who rejected Mr. Simpson's efforts to suppress the evidence (Judge Kathleen Kennedy-
Powell, who denied a pre-trial motion, and Judge Lance Ito, who
affirmed Kennedy-Powell's ruling before the trial commenced) really
believed Detective Philip Vannatter's explanation for why he scaled
the wall of the Simpson estate. (As Boston criminal defense lawyer
and *National Law Journal* columnist Harvey Silverglate pointed out
after the Simpson acquittal, ironically, had the evidence obtained as a
result of the highly questionable entry onto Simpson's property been
suppressed, "it might have robbed the defense of the core of its claim
of a racist frame-up.")

As might be expected, I had many talks with colleagues about the "trial of the century." I was taken aback when several law professors I had always labeled "liberal" told me it was a good thing that no judge had suppressed the evidence found as a result of that legally shaky search, because if any judge had done so the uproar would have been so great that the "exclusionary rule" (the rule that evidence obtained in violation of the Fourth Amendment protection against unreasonable searches and seizures must be excluded from consideration) might not have survived. I was even more shocked at the possibility that they may have been right.

I do not think most Americans know, or would care if they did, that according to the most careful study of the available empirical data, the general level of the exclusionary rule's effects on criminal prosecution is marginal at best. Most of its impact is concentrated in drug and weapon possession cases, the prosecution of which depends heavily on physical evidence. The impact of the rule is especially small in robbery, rape, and homicide cases.

Nor do I think the majority of Americans know, or care, that according to the most intensive study of police perceptions and attitudes about the exclusionary rule, the police would have great difficulty believing that search and seizure standards can have any real meaning if the government could profit from violating them. Regardless of what "substitute remedies" might be provided, the police are bound to view the elimination of the exlusionary rule as an indication that the Fourth Amendment is no longer a serious matter. Moreover, since the exclusionary rule has become functionally identified with the Fourth Amendment, police doubts about the importance and relevance of search and seizure standards are likely to be stronger if the rule is abolished than they would be if the rule had never been imposed in the first place.

I can hear the critics of the exclusionary rule now. Forget about statistics, I can hear them say; *one* lost murder case because of the exclusionary rule is one lost case too many.

But doesn't the Fourth Amendment embody the judgment that *sometimes* at least securing all citizens "in their person, houses, papers, and effects against unreasonable searches and seizures" *outweighs* society's interest in apprehending and convicting criminals? I realize that the amendment has both the virtue of brevity and the vice of ambiguity. But doesn't it mean *something?* Is not its very purpose—and that of the Bill of Rights generally—to identify values that *may not* be sacrificed to expediency? And to stand in the way when the job of combating crime and convicting the guilty seems such a pressing concern, as it will in every era, that we may be lured by the temptation of expediency into forsaking our commitment to protecting individual liberty and privacy?

I can hear the critics again: What you say may be true in ordinary times. But we are living in times of great danger. We are losing the war against crime. We can no longer afford a "civil-liberties binge." We must strengthen the "peace forces" against the "criminal forces."

When, may I ask, *were* we living in "normal" times? When weren't we losing the war against crime? When wasn't our society in a "state of emergency" concerning crime? When *could we* afford to take procedural safeguards seriously?

In 1910 the president of the California Bar Association proposed, in order to meet what he called "the expanding social necessity," that the requirements of a unanimous verdict of guilty in criminal cases be reduced to three-fourths. This, he added, would still "give the defendant three-fourths of the show."

The following year, in a hard-hitting *Atlantic Monthly* article entitled "Coddling the Criminal," a New York prosecutor deplored "the appalling amount of crime in the United States as compared with other civilized countries." What was his proposed solution? We must remove two formidable law enforcement obstacles, he insisted—the protection against double jeopardy and the privilege against self-incrimination.

In 1920, Edwin Sims, the first head of the newly established Chicago Crime Commission, added his voice to the insistent demands for "action" that would reduce crime. He had the figures: "During 1919 there were more murders in Chicago than in the entire British Isles." Who was to blame? Sims focused on "the tender solicitude for the welfare of criminals publicly expressed by social workers" because they give thousands of criminals "the mistaken impression that the community is more interested in them than it is in their victims."

In 1931 the famous criminologist Harry Elmer Barnes predicted that as grim as the crime picture was it was likely to get worse because the repeal of prohibition might trigger "an avalanche of crime"—as thousands of crooks chased out of the booze business returned to their old rackets. The only effective check Barnes could think of was "turning our cities over for the time being to the U.S. Army and Marines."

Two years later, the public had become so alarmed at the apparent increase in crime that a U.S. Senate investigating committee scoured the country for information which could lead to a national legislative solution. Several witnesses proposed a "national vagrancy law," whereby "well-dressed crooks" would have to prove they were earning an honest living. A veteran criminal court judge maintained that permitting the state to appeal an acquittal would give the prosecution a "fair break." A high-ranking police official proposed that an "expert adviser" retire to the jury room with the jury "to advise them on those technicalities that had been implanted in their minds by a very clever defense lawyer."

I have dwelt on the first third of this century because the U.S. Supreme Court pretty much kept "hands off" state criminal procedure during that period. We know now that the prevailing police interrogation methods of the 1920s and 1930s included the application of the rubber hose to the back or the pit of the stomach, kicks in the shins and blows struck with a phone book on the side of the suspect's head. These techniques did not stem the tide of crime. Nor did the use of illegally seized evidence—no questions asked—which most state courts allowed in the 1930s, 1940s, and 1950s. Nor, until they were invalidated by various courts, did the "public enemy" or "national vagrancy" laws or the many criminal registration ordinances stimulated by the U.S. Senate investigating committee headed by Royal S. Copeland of New York put a dent in crime.

When I hear about attacks on various provisions of our Bill of Rights, or on our criminal justice system generally, I am reminded of a story, apocryphal no doubt, about a certain aging promiscuous actress. When asked what she would do if she could live her life all over again she is supposed to have replied: "The same thing—with different people."

I venture to say that nowadays too many law enforcement officials, too many politicians, and too many media people are doing "the same thing—with different people." They are using more recent crime statistics, mentioning the names of different cases, and sometimes focusing on different targets (the federal courts rather than the state courts or parole boards rather than social workers), but they are reacting the same way they reacted in past generations.

They are proclaiming great emergencies and announcing lack of confidence in the capacities of ordinary institutions and traditional procedures to deal with them. They are explaining our failure to cope successfully with the "crime crises" in terms of betrayal. They are permitting a mood of irritated frustration with complexity to find expression in "scapegoating."

For as long as any living American can remember, there has never been a time (at least according to law enforcement officials, politicians, and the mass media) when we weren't experiencing a "crime crisis"—when we weren't being told that so far as the rights of the accused were concerned, "the pendulum has swung too far to the left." Any time during the last hundred years—whatever the time— was *not* the time to take the Bill of Rights seriously. Rather it was, or seemed to be, a time when (as usual) criminal procedural safeguards had already been stretched to the breaking point.

I venture to say that no person alive today will live to see the day when the public is not alarmed and indignant about crime—when we are not in a "crime crisis." If we want to take the Bill of Rights seriously, we better do so now.

The Trial and the City

A Nasty Parody on Multiculturalism

HARVEY COX

Many years ago the celebrated philosopher-historian of urban life Lewis Mumford wrote, " . . . the great function of the city is to permit, indeed to encourage and incite, the greatest possible number of meetings, encounters, challenges between all persons, classes and groups, providing as it were a stage upon which the drama of social life may be enacted, the actors taking their turns as spectators and the spectators as actors."

Mumford died in 1990. But it is hard to avoid wondering how he would have viewed the O. J. Simpson affair. The city a spectacle of encounter between races, classes, and genders? A drama with audience and participant, fact and fiction blurring? This case provided both in superlatives. Who can forget the absorbing chase along the freeways, watched—it has been reported—by 95 million American spectators? Even the endless and tedious television trial failed to discourage a dogged audience of overnight experts on court procedures. Then add the victims, a perfectly proportioned fashion plate and her mysterious waiter-sometimes-actor companion. Mix in a well-mannered racist police officer who was sniffed out only because he had contributed some realistic local color to the writer of a forth-coming cop show. Top with the weekly euphoria of the *National Enquirer* and the usually more restrained newspapers and magazines that increasingly came to resemble it; the potent blend of courtroom tactics, leaked interviews, and scientific charts on DNA; the rival theories and speculations. Then cut to the unprecedented national breath-holding as tens of millions of eyes watched O.J.'s face while the verdicts were read. Here was encounter, drama, and spectacle with a vengeance. But I doubt it was what Mumford had in mind. It was, in fact, a grotesque caricature of the City he fondly hoped would one day appear on earth.

How did the Simpson trial correlate with existing images of the City—and of Los Angeles in particular—that we carry around in our heads? Throughout our history Americans have nourished a love-hate relationship with their cities. Quoting the Sermon on the Mount, Governor Thomas Hutchinson assured the first settlers of Boston that God expected them to build a "city set upon a hill" that was to be a beacon and an example to all mankind. A little farther south, William Penn envisioned a "city of brotherly love" that would exemplify the Quaker virtues of tolerance, simplicity, and gentle persuasion. Cities—some of them mere villages at first—with names like "Providence," "Concord," and "New Harmony," dotted the American landscape. (It is even said that in the state of Arkansas there exists a small city called "Hope.")

But there is another side. As Morton and Lucia White reminded us thirty years ago in *The Intellectual Versus the City,* Americans have also always harbored a withering suspicion, mixed with a profound contempt, for the city. Beginning as early as Thomas Jefferson's ideal of a republic of sturdy rural yeomen, and stretching to Frank Lloyd Wright's thoroughly antiurban plans for "Broadacre City," urban life has been looked upon with hostility. Jefferson wrote, "I view great cities as pestilential to the morals, the health and the liberties of man." It seems possible that the witnesses who paraded through the O. J. Simpson trial might well have confirmed his judgment.

The City as glorious ideal. The City as pestilential curse. The shimmering pinnacle of peace and harmony. The loathsome cesspool of "human junk." In the Bible, one finds both extremes. There is the corrupt Babylon and the Sybaritic cities of Sodom and Gomorrah—whose destruction by flames has often been read not only as a cautionary tale against vice but also as a grim warning about cities in general. But one also finds the glorified New Jerusalem with gates of pearl and streets of gold, in which there are no more tears and which, in the final pages of the New Testament, descends from heaven at the climax of human history. Unlike some of the Asian religions, in which the absorption of the self into the ocean of nirvana is the ultimate epilogue, in the Bible the grand finale is a city. Perhaps in part because of this enigmatic religious heritage, although the City has always symbolized something for Americans, just what it symbolizes has always been confused and self-contradictory.

Los Angeles is the principle case in point. Years ago at least some Americans used to hope that it represented the future. Then they were not so sure. Now they are afraid that it just might. And for millions of these Americans, the trial of Orenthal James Simpson was simply Los Angeles writ large. If the city has been excommunicated as a depraved Sodom-and-Gomorrah-style threat to morals, here it was: a stunning white wife who favored scanty swim suits; slit throats and multiple stab wounds trailing splotches of blood; enticing hints of cocaine; fast cars and exclusive restaurants. A melting pot? Try a black defendant, an Asian-American judge, a salt-and-pepper jury, a team of black and Jewish defense lawyers, and a puzzling somebody named Kato Kaelin. It was the dream of a multicultural metropolis redesigned by Stephen King. But, after all, it was happening in a city, and the city was Los Angeles. So what could you expect?

If the O. J. Simpson trial was a nasty parody of multiculturalism, then it should also be remembered that when it comes to that much-debated topic, Los Angeles—like America—has been through several stages. The difference is that in Los Angeles, like everything else in that city, the phases of multiculturalism have been more exaggerated. It was a Spanish Catholic priest, Father Juan Crespi, who along with the explorer Gaspar de Portola, is credited with being the "founder" of Los Angeles in 1769. There was, of course, already an Indian village on the spot. But that did not discourage the Spaniards from renaming it "Nuestra Señora la Reina de los Angeles," after the Blessed Virgin Mary in her highly developed Latin role as co-monarch with Christ and Queen of the heavenly realms. It is unlikely that the Indians had much of a feel for the celestial Sovereign after whom their pueblo was rechristened. But it would not be the last time that Los Angeles would be endowed with an image that hardly fit the facts.

It was not until 1781 that the first permanent settlers trudged up to Los Angeles from Mexico. But with their arrival, the town was instantly transformed into a multicultural microcosm. There were twelve families of forty-six persons in all. They included people of mestizo, black, and Spanish ancestry. The city's cosmopolitan coloration was there from the first day and held sway more or less until the next great event in its life, the conquest of California by the United States in 1846. This was quickly followed by the discovery of gold in 1848, and the coming of the railroads in 1869, whose construction required the importation of Chinese workers. By 1900 the city had just over 100,000 residents. In 1911 the first moving picture was made in Hollywood, then one of the city's suburbs. But from the beginning Los Angeles was what it remains today, a city that is half real and half fictional, both the producer and the object of concocted images and contradictory visions. After all, the city was populated by people who came from somewhere else because they were looking for something different. If they did not find what they were looking for, they invented it.

In the early decades of the present century, Los Angeles was becoming the goal of a vast army of immigrants. Its drawing power was supplied by one of the biggest booster campaigns ever to trumpet the alleged virtues of any American municipality. Only the 187th largest town by the 1880 census, and lagging far behind San Francisco, it had doubled its population twice by 1900 and was well on the way to surpassing its northern rival. For some, its meteoric ascent was inexplicable. It lacked drinking water, a seaport (the San Pedro harbor was only completed in 1914), or anything else that might commend it to prospective investors. Nevertheless, real estate developers passionately promoted moving to Los Angeles as the secular equivalent of being born again. It was the place to begin life anew in a land munificently blessed with the only thing it did have in plenteous supply—sunshine. It was a city where piety and the hard sell met. As the journalist Morrow Mayo once wrote, "Los Angeles, it should be understood, is not a mere city. On the contrary, it is, and has been since 1888, a *commodity;* something to be advertised and sold to the people . . . like automobiles, cigarettes and mouth wash."

But there was something other than sunshine that Los Angeles was also touted for. Oddly, for a city that began with exclusively Indian, black, and Spanish settlers, and which had no Protestant church until 1850, by the beginning of the twentieth century it was advertised as the last citadel of Anglo-Saxon racial purity. It was lauded as a barrier reef against the successive waves of swarthy European immigrants who were streaming into the cities of the east coast. Before the turn of the century Boston had already elected its first non-Brahmin mayor, and Irish-American political machines were flexing their muscle in several other cities. Not so in Los Angeles, where the previous Spanish culture had been dissolved into the "mission myth" of gentle Franciscans and grateful natives, while the white Protestant majority grew larger every day.

There was already a small but growing community of African Americans in Los Angeles by the turn of the century. But there were not enough black citizens to discourage Joseph Widney, one of the first presidents of the University of Southern California, from hoisting over the city the standard of a white bulwark. Widney published his *Race Life of the Aryan People* in 1907. It is a rhapsodic celebration of Los Angeles as the future world capital of Aryan supremacy, a "new Rome" whose virile sons and daughters would one day lead the world.

But Widney's dream evaporated before the ink on the pages of his manifesto was dry. Between 1900 and 1910, 5,500 blacks, 5,000 Mexicans, 4,000 Japanese, and over 30,000 Europeans also arrived. By 1910 these "non-whites" and immigrants constituted fully 22 percent of the city's population. From Widney's perspective, this new Rome—like the original one on the seven hills—now found itself with the barbarians within the gates. Only this time, they had not waited four centuries to make their appearance. For those who shared Widney's dream, the city of the angels was already what it would be in the scripts of the *noir* film writers two generations later, a Sunset Boulevard of broken dreams.

Los Angeles, which with the help of Hollywood was quickly becoming the image-manufacturing center of the world, had never been able to live without a propelling image of itself. Now a relentless and sometimes desperate quest for the new image went on. Then, shortly after World War II, it appeared like a divine theophany: Los Angeles was ordained to be the multicultural capital of the globe, the cosmopolitan megalopolis of the Pacific Basin. It would become the vibrant showcase of America's luxuriant pluralism, a vast display room where the descendants of the once-excluded "coolies," friendly and talented blacks, fiesta-loving Latinos, and the now vastly outnumbered descendants of the Okies and Arkies would learn to appreciate each other's cuisine and street festivals.

Certainly the ingredients were there for a composite city. They still are. If current demographic trends continue, by 2010 Latinos (or as the census takers call them, Hispanics) will increase from 14 percent to 40 percent of the city's population. Non-Hispanic whites will decline from 75 percent to 40 percent. The black population will remain constant at about 10 percent. Asian Americans, a category which includes people of Japanese, Chinese, Vietnamese, Korean, and Filipino extraction, are expected to reach nearly 10 percent in the first years of the next century.

But it takes more than just ingredients to make a multicultural stew. Sadly, just as Widney's white Etruscan republic collapsed before it began, the vision of Los Angeles as a multicultural Shangri-la was disappearing as it was being concocted. During World War II there were the street attacks on the Latino zoot suiters. Then, as soon as the postwar boom was over, the trouble started in earnest. There were the Watts riots, the imposition of a kind of architectural apartheid on the design of the city, and the fiery response to the acquittal of the police in the Rodney King affair.

In this quickly shifting kaleidoscope of images, O. J. Simpson was a man behind his time. He was designed to fit remarkably well into the picture of the multicultural Olympus the previous wave of Los Angeles portraitists were trying to draw. He was, as many have observed, carefully projected on television as the big, black man whites need not be afraid of. See, he was smiling. He even carried a briefcase as he loped gracefully through the airport. This was the kind of black man who could be welcomed into your neighborhood, thus erasing forever any lingering suspicion that you might be a closet racist.

But it was too late, and in many ways the Brentwood murders and the subsequent trial were already anticlimactic. True, there was blood on the Bronco, but there had been lots of blood elsewhere. The airbrushed photograph of Los Angeles as the city of harmonious intergroup mutuality had already faded. Its final consignment to the dustbin occurred perhaps with the publication of the news photo of the young Korean brandishing a rifle as he stood on the roof of his family's store during the riots that erupted after the Rodney King affair. The brew had already gone sour. The murder of Nicole Brown Simpson and Ronald Goldman, and the subsequent trial of the nationally famous running back and Hertz spokesman marked only the dramatic crashing in flames of what had already been a long spiraling fall.

So what about the next phase? In 1985, before anyone had heard of Rodney King and long before O. J. Simpson became prisoner #4013970 in the county jail, then-mayor Tom Bradley appointed something called the "Los Angeles 2000 Committee," consisting of "85 diverse citizens" who consulted with "150 business and civic leaders," and with the RAND Corporation. In 1988 the committee published a handsome and creatively illustrated 92-page booklet entitled *LA 2000: A City for the Future.* It is divided into six chapters with subsections covering growth management, the environment, education, the economy, governance, transportation, and several other topics. It is an almost ebulliently upbeat prospectus for the city, whose future is portrayed as a "dream" which, if everybody works together, "can be struggled for with courage and zest—just as, after all, other citizens of this city in times past made their Los Angeles dream come true." Now, nearly a decade later, the report provides a fascinating insight into how the elite of one paradigmatic city wanted to think of the future. Its conclusion seems to be that if Los Angeles is in fact the city of the future, and if cities are the future of our whole species, then we can rest assured that we are all in good hands.

But what about the dark stains on the sidewalk in Brentwood? It takes a careful reader of *A City for the Future* to find them foreshadowed. Tucked away in the middle of a cheerful section entitled "Liveable Communities," embellished with line drawings of artists, jugglers, acrobats, dancers, and a child with a cluster of balloons, the careful reader uncovers this:

> No community can be considered truly liveable unless it is reasonably safe from crime. An overwhelming percentage of respondents to the RAND survey named crime as the worst things about Los Angeles: conversely, they indicated that being crime-free was what they most wanted in their communities.

The paragraphs that follow are among the only grim ones in a report that brims with great expectations. They suggest that although the complex causes of crime are certainly not exclusively Los Angeles phenomena, still, because of the city's "tremendous disparities between wealth and poverty," a "vicious cycle of poverty, dropouts, and illiteracy" has "limited opportunities for upwardly mobile jobs." It pleads for "long term" solutions, for which it refers the reader to the chapters on "Enriching Diversity" and "Individual Fulfillment."

Mike Davis, the author of *City of Quartz,* one of the most disturbing studies ever written on the cultural geography of Los Angeles, described the city in these hard-edged terms in an article published two years before the O. J. Simpson affair:

> The city bristles with malice. The carefully manicured lawns of the Westside sprout ominous signs threatening "Armed Response!" Wealthier neighborhoods in the canyons and hillsides cower behind walls guarded by gun-toting private police and state-of-the-art surveillance systems. Downtown, a publicly subsidized "urban renaissance" has raised a forbidding corporate citadel separated from the surrounding poor neighborhoods by battlements and moats.

Davis presents ugly evidence of a new partnership among architecture, urban design, and the police apparatus. In this pattern, a sort of civil war between the middle and privileged classes on the one side and the poor on the other is codified in the structure of urban space itself. Fortified cells are connected with each other by fast roads while police skirmish constantly with criminals in the dark interstices everyone avoids where possible. For Davis, Los Angeles—to be followed inevitably by other American cities—is developing into a cluster of highly policed Bantustans interspersed with moated islands of privilege.

For many, this balkanization—though regrettable—works, at least most of the time. True, the Los Angeles County District Attorney's Office prosecutes 70,000 felonies a year. That is just about 200 per day. But most do not take place in Brentwood. Reputed to be one of the quietest communities in the West Side, it includes the private home of the mayor and the district attorney. It has an active property owners' association. For many Angelenos, the most shocking thing about the murders of Nicole Simpson and Ronald Goldman was not their brutality, but that they happened in Brentwood, in a part of Los Angeles where homicides were just not supposed to take place.

Recent statistics strongly suggest that urban crime rates in America are on the decrease. Still, the perception that violence stalks us everywhere, even in allegedly "safe" neighborhoods, persists. The irony of the O. J. Simpson trial is that its final outcome only compounded the ambiguity of Americans' views of the city and crime. Simpson was no hooded teenager in baggy pants and sneakers. He was not the kind of black man many white Americans cross the street to keep from encountering. Stuck with a multiracial society which is most vividly evident in the cities, many whites would desperately like to believe that all African Americans, if they just straightened up and bore down, could succeed and buy homes in the Brentwoods, Wellesley Hills, and Shaker Heights of America. Maybe then you would not have to admit to your lingering racism and cross the street when the parkas and sneakers approach. But here, despite all the precautions, and despite the fact that O. J. Simpson was one of the most successful black men in America, the nightmare still struck, and in a peaceful bedroom community.

Then, as if to make the matter even more baffling, O.J. was acquitted. What did *that* mean? Did he really do it, but the jury let him off for any of a number of reasons—tainted evidence, racial politics in the jury room, the fumbling of the prosecution? In that case the criminal justice system was in even worse trouble than we had imagined. But if he really did not do it, then who did? This was, if anything, an even more frightening puzzle. It meant that the murderer or murderers were then still at large, elusive, mysterious, faceless, lethal, and ready to strike again. Even in Brentwood.

Lewis Mumford ends his magisterial work *The City in History* with the following measured but somehow reassuring words:

> In order to defeat the insensate forces that now threaten civilization from within, we must transcend the original frustrations and negations that have dogged the city throughout its history. Otherwise the sterile gods of power, unrestrained by organic limits or human goals will remake man in their own faceless image and bring history to an end.

Let us not, then, read into the Brentwood murders and the Simpson trial more significance than they deserve. Cities have always been the places where the best and the worst of the human enterprise, its cruelest cutthroats and its soaring cathedrals, have uneasily cohabited. Whatever the mix, as Mumford also says, "The final mission of the city is to further man's conscious participation in the historic process . . . and it remains the chief reason for the city's continued existence." As we near the end of a century that has witnessed unprecedented cruelty, irrationality, and disregard for human life, we must not allow even a crime as ruthless or a trial as divisive and fatuous as this one to derail us from the work our species has to do.

The Good News

STANLEY CROUCH

Race is such a large decoy that it almost always causes us to get very important things wrong. That is why I don't accept the idea that the verdict in the O. J. Simpson double-murder case, and the heated counterpoint of celebration and condemnation, mean the country is now in greater racial trouble. As Americans, we are all members of an improvising social experiment that is always in some sort of trouble. Ours is a country that learns whatever it learns by bruising its ideals in combat with human shortcomings, from the public to the private sector, the mass to the individual. In the long goodbye to those no-good things that we are eventually forced to address, context by context, nothing slips the noose forever. This means that we have serious scars and lumps on our heads from the crashing of idols in every line of high-profile endeavor. "Say it ain't so" is the dark, hot, minor strain of the national anthem.

Yet we always cool off. That's part of our style and part of the heroic drama that defines the evolution of our nation. It happens once the sort of emotion we feel for our individual and group identities wears itself away. We then cease hiding under our beds, where

228

we try to ignore the mature responsibilities demanded by the blues that periodically knocks at the national door, the blues dressed up in new duds and full of classic devilment. So what we are facing is just another situation in which those looking for something to get happy about and those looking for the opportunity to express their rage about some condition of purported oppression have gotten their moment. Such occasions inevitably work out for the national good because they demand that we face the complexities of our nation and grow up.

A chance to mature is exactly what was put before us in the case that began in a high-rent district with Nicole Brown Simpson's nearly decapitated corpse lying in sticky red death not far from the body of Ronald Goldman, the male model and weight-lifting waiter who came to deliver sunglasses and found himself in a losing struggle with the savage blade of murder. We were given fresh access to the kind of human tragedy that is not limited by race or social class or profession or good looks or athletic prowess or intelligence or sex or, apparently, golden luck. As the media lapped up every drop of blood, fingered every swelling, sniffed out every scent of illicit sex, and listened for every puff and snort of drugs, we came to know brutal and decadent secrets that were bribed or coaxed or forced up from the world of whispers.

In terms of our human understanding, the Simpson verdict crosses a terrain in which something is both amiss and affirmed in our national mythology. Once we cut ourselves loose from Europe, we made that mythology up as we went along. It had to stretch from the backwoods to the cities to the plains, North, South, East, and West. It had to be big enough to handle people from backgrounds as different as those of Jefferson, Lincoln, Douglass, Edison, and so on. We needed a cultural myth to explain the flesh-and-blood illumination that arrived from the crude background as well as the smooth. But what we settled for in our weakest moments may well have put far too much emphasis on squeaky-clean human symbols, since we are almost always pulled up short by the tattling of private tales or by the public exposure of caked or fresh dung in the drawers of widely admired figures.

Fused to our human symbols were our newspapers, which, if they weren't muckraking, did their assumed duty by hiding that dung from us. People in the business figured we couldn't stand the truth, and they didn't mind reporting only as much of it as they thought we could take. Censorship functioned in the name of "good taste." Whenever in doubt, we moved into the recasting of a basic American vision, which is that the common person, the innocent, the mistreated or misunderstood, will pick up where others have failed at truly realizing the meanings of our democratic ideals. This person will not be corrupted by the narcissism that comes with large monetary success, excessive power, and inordinate admiration by the mob. This person, one calloused big toe standing on pointe at the peak of the moral pyramid, will have a messianic effect on our belief in our system.

That is where the Negro comes in, and where, at our moments of greatest desperation, we secretly make our most serious bets on something better rising out of something bad. If the Negro can stand the pressure of sustained and unfair opposition, then we all can. If the Negro can get up to the top and hold in place everything this culture has found so charismatic, we have a much greater chance of bringing off this social experiment, especially since the African American's history on this land reaches back beyond the Mayflower. The patience, the grace, the rhythm, the humor, the discipline, and the heroic majesty historically found in the best of Negro life have always provided some sort of an antidote to the disorder that, as Ralph Ellison observed, is ever a danger to our society. That is why identification with Negro aspirations and Negro style has been so important to the development of this country's democracy and its culture. The Negro has tested our democracy and been central to what we mean by the spirit of America when it sings, when it dances, when it talks to the cosmos, when it gives a certain texture of rhythm to English or exhibits the long memory so essential to our recognition of the tragic losses that have formed the hill of corpses upon which we stand and are able to see beyond the worst of our human limitations while acknowledging their every nuance.

The Simpson case tested all of our contemporary democratic mythologies about good and evil, about race and fairness, about law enforcement and the criminal courts and justice. The Negroes who disturbed so many by celebrating, by cheering, and by dancing were responding to a dream of American possibility quite different from that assumed by the media. It was all, given the brilliance of the defense, much, much deeper than "a brother beating the system."

The multiethnic selection of citizens that magically disappeared and conveniently became an all-black jury—even in the minds of outraged liberals—delivered a verdict that had nothing to do with racial solidarity or jury nullification. Those jury members were neither that simpleminded nor that incapable of understanding what was on display as evidence. The jurors might well have recognized that they were in the presence of a level of lawyering that none will probably ever see in the flesh again, day by day, witness by witness, exhibit by exhibit. That, above all else, is what they responded to in such a swift stroke.

As far as color goes, we all saw just what our country has come down to, which is not some imbecilic racial divide but interracial teams working both sides of the basic arguments. Just as there are now highly visible so-called minorities in both major political parties and either heading or inside the administrations of almost every important city, the prosecution and the defense in this epic trial comprised integrated teams. For all of the discussion about sinister developments in black and Jewish relations, we saw prosecutor Marcia Clark, a Jewish woman, whose central partner was Christopher Darden, an unarguably grassroots Negro, both backed up by a remarkably diverse group of people appearing as witnesses, police officers, and experts. The same was true of the defense team, which was first headed by the extremely smooth Robert Shapiro, whose demotion in favor of Johnnie Cochran may reveal as much about his post-trial sour grapes as anything else. If, say, Shapiro is the kind of guy who is accustomed to being far brighter than most people he encounters, it must have been quite an experience for him to observe in Cochran a level of argument, eloquence, delineated passion, and superbly paced execution that he will never feel or hear coming out of his own body. He might well have smarted quite deeply as his initial celebrity was gradually but completely overshadowed by Cochran's. That smarting might have reached its supreme intensity near the end, when Shapiro found himself so far down in the public polls that he was loudly booed at a basketball game and approached in restaurants by social wild cards ranting about his betraying the genocidal horrors of World War II.

In fact, there may have been no issue larger in the overview of it all than betrayal. Riled feminist ideologues freely accused Negro females—on and off the jury—of betraying their battered and butchered blond sister. (This uncriticized demand for solidarity is ironic, given that Negroes were condemned for their purported racial unanimity in the wake of the verdict.) The solidarity of victimhood should have transcended the looming presence of a remarkable doubt. The dark welts on the souls of athletic heroes and media figures are not new to us, whether we are talking about an O. J. Simpson or a Jessica Savitch. But this time, we had our sensibilities and whatever innocence we could claim pushed right into hard facts about law enforcement, about the risky deals a prosecution team will make with the devil, about the kind of sloppiness in evidence collection and assessment that seems to pass by quite easily in most instances. In the aftermath, we got a chance to see how all of those people who so cynically dismiss "the system" with examples like Watergate, FBI hanky-panky, the serpentine antics of the CIA, Oliver North, the savings-and-loan scandal, the Clarence Thomas–Anita Hill hearings, and so on were suddenly and haughtily able to set aside every example of police misconduct and suspicious evidence in the Simpson case.

Those same people—*all of whom should know that juries almost automatically acquit when the police are caught lying or red-handed*—turned in the other direction, dropped their pants, and contemptuously mooned the verdict. Turning back around, these people asserted that the forensic evidence should have transcended everything else. They seemed to forget that Americans have a dual attitude toward the kind of technology that lay beneath the DNA evidence. We suspect machinery just as much as we love it, primarily because our society is one at war with the potential anonymity imposed by our technology. So when a good-enough lawyer plays into that aversion to the technological, he or she isn't so much summoning up the ignorant impatience of the jury as pulling forth a basic aspect of its American feeling: our fear that our humanity will be compromised by our toys of mathematical definition and measurement. As lovers of the underdog, as people from one group or another who have had the deck stacked against us at some distant or recent time, we don't always take too kindly to statistics and often refuse to be bullied by experts.

Sometimes, like the sort of farm boys whose down-home logic thwarts city slickers, we just want to know why some blood left on a fence for several weeks contains a chemical found in police labs. (Is that a statement on the preservative powers of smoggy Los Angeles weather?) We just want to know why there is no blood trail leading to or away from the infamous bloody glove, which was described by Mark Fuhrman as being "moist or sticky" when it was found during his foraging for evidence all by his lonesome—seven and a half hours after it was supposedly dropped by the murderer. We would like to know how even a former superathlete and seriously mediocre actor could park, leap over a fence, bang into a wall three times, drop a glove, run upstairs, shower, change clothes, and come downstairs deporting himself as just another guy a little late for a limousine ride to the airport. As a deeply disturbed Mario Cuomo observed, there was more than enough to raise a "reasonable doubt," but endless white Americans were distraught because the jury took that doubt's specifically instructed meaning so seriously. Those howlers would have preferred that the jurors ignore the law. They felt betrayed.

There are also those who feel betrayed by Simpson's upper-class life to such an extent that a special kind of racism has been put back into play, one that used to slither off the term *uppity*. It now allows William Safire to write in the *New York Times,* "The wealthy celebrity who lived white, spoke white, and married white wrapped himself in the rags of social injustice and told his black counsel to move black jurors to vote black." Safire was following the pompous lead of *Time* magazine's Jack E. White, head mulatto in charge of darky corrections, who wrote, "Never one to speak out on civil rights, [Simpson] seemed to shed his racial identity, crossing over into a sort of color-less minor celebrity as easily as he escaped from tacklers—or from the black wife he traded in for a white teenager."

Twenty-five years ago, no writer, black or white, would have been allowed to impose such a limited vision of "authenticity" on a Negro. Individual freedom was then the issue, not joining a movement, not maintaining a style that would make certain white people feel more comfortable in the exclusive and fraudulent franchise of their "white-ness," which includes expensive property, privilege upon privilege, the money to do battle with the legal system on equal ground, the proper enunciation of the English language, and freedom of social choice. In this era, when Woody Allen was in the middle of his big mess with Mia Farrow, he wasn't asked to reinstate his foreskin because of the women he's chosen over the years. No one asks Allen to suppress his urban neurosis in favor of the elegant worldliness of Leonard Bernstein. Nor is Susan Sontag told to emulate Fanny Brice in order to truly represent the group. Sylvester Stallone isn't under attack for his lovers or where he lives or whose company he travels in. The only ethnic under that pressure is the Negro, whose unlimited variations on Americanness must now meet not the infinite meanings of our national humanity but some short-order ethnic recipe written up and agreed on by supposed insiders and outsiders.

As we look back on this trial from some point in the future, we will see beyond such recipes and remember certain purely American things that are signal examples of the way our country is going. Ours is no longer a culture dominated by one race taking up all the seats in high places. We will remember Judge Lance Ito—Eagle Scout and son of parents who did time in American concentration camps—letting both sides have a lot of rope but surely favoring a prosecution that still couldn't serve Simpson's head on a platter. We will remember Johnnie Cochran doing an extremely witty variation on Marc Antony's speech over Caesar's body, pivoting on the phrase "but Christopher Darden loves me." We will remember Marcia Clark coddling Mark Fuhrman through his testimony and F. Lee Bailey getting the rogue cop to say the things under oath that would make him unarguably a perjurer. We will remember Rosa Lopez cringing under Darden's smoldering questions. We will remember Dennis Fung's perfectly modulated voice losing all confidence and starting to quaver as Barry Scheck systematically turned his expertise into confetti. We will remember the way Henry Lee sat there and spun out parables while speaking with such clear, technical authority that it seemed as though the ghost of Charlie Chan had been brought to life with a deeply human three-dimensionality the Hollywood scriptwriters never achieved. We will remember the enlarging pie pans under Marcia Clark's eyes as the months passed and then the extremely chilling way she ended her summation with the voice of Nicole Brown Simpson calling 911 for help. We will remember the rising and falling of the case, each side seeming to be losing at one point, winning at another. Then we will remember the final arguments.

By the end, it came down to black and white, Negro and Jew, Christopher Darden and Marcia Clark up against Johnnie Cochran and Barry Scheck. The astonishing one was Cochran. Whatever we must say about this lawyer so foolishly allowing Nation of Islam goons to guard him, or his demagogically attempting to recruit black reporters for the defense point of view, we should also remember that, in the heat of battle, especially during the ninety minutes that followed the dinner break on the first of two days of defense summations, the man was so extraordinary that Brooklyn district attorney

Joe Hynes said that, in thirty years as a professional, he had never witnessed such a tour de force in the arena of advocacy.

Cochran's command of American sound and rhythm was perfectly orchestrated within the context of an argument that tore down the prosecution's case as he ripped apart the state's speculative logic and showed how the testimony of one police officer after another was full of specious contradictions. He convincingly revealed the holes in certain evidence and unmasked the potentially sleazy motives behind the actions of the cops at Simpson's mansion. Part of his compelling virtuosity was the way in which he mixed various straight and street accents, crossing and recrossing the ethnic divide, reaching for an idealistic judicial diction, parodying the voices of the cops and backing things up with superb pauses and brilliant emphasis, then closing out with the repetitions and inflections of the best and more subtle African American pulpit talk. Cochran was so remarkable that, at one point, Ito himself repressed a smile at the quality of the summation he was hearing. The dark-skinned and handsome Cochran, ever immaculately dressed, jumped froggy and brought that Negro American swing to court. One understood right then why Los Angeles lawyer Mike Yamamoto says that to bellow and whine about "the race card" is to deny the fact that this man proved, day by day, that he is the best lawyer in the whole town.

For all that we might find fault with on either side, there is no denying the bottomless humanity we witnessed. There is also no denying that if all we learned as a nation about police misconduct, irresponsible prosecution teams, and sloppy crime laboratories moves us closer to bettering the liberty of the people through the agencies created to protect them, then Nicole Brown Simpson and Ronald Goldman will not have died in vain, regardless of who may have killed them. Lying murdered in Beverly Hills, their bodies brought elements into play that let us see how vulnerable we all are to the most brutal treatment, and how much we still have to do if we want to move this country closer and closer to justice. Along the way, we will continue to grow up, since the immature can never handle the inevitable blows of the blues. However we get there, as the trial never failed to let us know, we will achieve our American ideals only through multiracial teams of both sexes, calling upon the fullest range of our national humanity.

Appendix

A Quick Primer on the Civil Trial

Despite his acquittal on criminal charges, O. J. Simpson still faces civil trial of the wrongful death lawsuits filed by the families of Nicole Brown Simpson and Ronald Lyle Goldman. Originally, there were three separate lawsuits—one from the Brown family, another from the father and sister of Goldman, and a third from Goldman's mother. These lawsuits have been consolidated into one and the case is currently scheduled for trial on September 9, 1996, in Santa Monica Courthouse. The presiding judge is Superior Court Judge Alan B. Haber.

As originally worded, the Brown family's wrongful death complaint read as follows:

> On or about June 12, 1994, Orenthal James Simpson . . . planned and prepared to assault, batter, and murder Nicole Brown Simpson and did thereafter brutally, and with malice aforethought, stalk, attack, and repeatedly stab, and beat decedent Nicole Brown Simpson.

Civil jury trials differ from their criminal counterparts in three important regards. First, the plaintiffs must prove that Simpson committed the murders only by a preponderance of the evidence, and not beyond a reasonable doubt. This means that the jury may find for the plaintiffs if they think the evidence, taken as whole, makes it more likely than not that Simpson committed the murders.

Second, civil jury verdicts need not be unanimous. In California, a vote of 9–3 is sufficient to resolve the case.

Third, Simpson can be required to testify at his civil trial. In a civil trial, a defendant may invoke the Fifth Amendment privilege against incriminating himself only if there is some likelihood of pending criminal charges flowing out of the same events on trial. Since Simpson has already been acquitted of the murders and can never be tried again in a criminal court for murder, he is not in danger of incriminating himself by testifying at the civil trial.

Trial location is another factor that may affect the civil trial. Whereas the criminal case unfolded in a downtown Los Angeles courthouse before a mostly African-American jury, the civil jury seems likely to take place in Santa Monica before a more white and affluent jury.

The cast of lawyers for the civil trial will be different. Gone are the prosecutors—plaintiffs in a civil action are represented by private attorneys and not by the District Attorney's office. Fred and Kim Goldman, the victim's father and sister, are represented by Daniel M. Petrocelli of the toney Los Angeles firm Mitchell, Silberberg and Knupp. Sharon Rufo, mother of Ron, is represented by Michael A. Brewer. During the depositions, John Q. Kelley of New York represented the Brown family.

Simpson's lawyers include Robert C. Baker, Robert Blaiser, and Daniel Leonard; Blaiser was a member of the so-called Dream Team. Leonard comes from F. Lee Bailey's Boston law firm of Bailey, Fishman and Leonard.

The first person to give a deposition in the civil suit was model and ex-Simpson girlfriend Paula Barbieri on December 15, 1995. Barbieri testified that she broke up with Simpson via answering machine the morning of June 12, 1994. Nicole Brown Simpson and Ron Goldman were murdered later the same day.

On December 20, Judge Haber ordered Simpson to turn over his financial records to the plaintiffs. Judge Haber noted that plaintiffs were entitled to those records since they met "their burden, period" of showing substantial evidence of guilt.

On January 22, 1996, Simpson began giving his deposition at the law offices of Goldman family attorney Petrocelli. This marked the first time that Simpson had testified under oath regarding the murders. Transcripts of Simpson's deposition, which took ten days to complete, are now publicly available.

Lawyers for the victims' families made frequent use of Nicole Brown Simpson's diary to question Simpson about numerous instances of physical abuse. In one entry, Nicole Simpson recounts her husband as shouting, "Let me tell you how serious I am. . . . I have a gun in my hand right now. Get the f— out of here." The diary goes on: "I got real scared and grabbed Sydney [their daughter] and the cats and a bag for her and a bottle and a pair of sweats and got the hell out of the house."

When asked about this and other diary entries regarding abuse, Simpson denied that they happened. He accused Nicole of fabricating charges of abuse in a lawyer-inspired plot to void the couple's prenuptial agreement. To the extent his ex-wife ever suffered any bruises or marks, Simpson attributed them to defensive action he took during "rassling" matches provoked by Nicole's attacks on him. At one point in the deposition Simpson even referred to himself as a "battered husband." He flatly denied ever striking, slapping, choking, beating, or physically hurting her.

Simpson also denied being obsessed with his ex-wife following their separation and divorce. However, he did admit to looking through a window and seeing her engaged in a sex act on the living room couch with another man. Simpson acknowledged being upset by what he saw but only because his children were asleep upstairs.

As to the night of the murders, Simpson for the first time denied ever telling limousine driver Allan Park that he had overslept. Simpson placed himself in the shower, when Park first began buzzing on the intercom. Earlier that evening, around 10 P.M., according to Simpson's account, he had been chipping golf balls on his front lawn. This led to a series of questions about what happened to the golf balls he would have hit—who retrieved them and when?

Simpson's first reactions to news of his ex-wife's death were also a subject of examination. In earlier statements to police, Simpson stated that he cut his finger in a Chicago hotel room when he broke a glass in distress upon hearing that Nicole was dead. But in the deposition Simpson now says that he cut his finger when he picked up a shard of broken glass in the hotel bathroom.

While still in Chicago, Simpson called the Brown family but was apparently shouted at and hung up on by Denise Brown, Nicole's sister. In a most interesting section of the deposition, Simpson then acknowledged making several phone calls before returning to Los Angeles in an unsuccessful effort to reach Kato Kaelin. Earlier in the deposition, Simpson had characterized Kaelin more as an acquaintance than a friend and so the question was why he singled out Kaelin for calls within an hour after learning of Nicole Brown Simpson's murder. Simpson's telling response was that Kaelin "had talked about some noises the night before." Goldman family lawyer Petrocelli then grilled Simpson on why he "associated" Kaelin's report of noises with Nicole's murder and whether it was his intention to go over his story with Kaelin. Simpson lawyer Robert Baker then intervened, denying that Simpson had ever said he "associated" Kaelin's report of noises with the murder and this provocative line of questioning ended with Simpson's denying that he had any intention of going over his story with Kaelin.

Simpson characterized himself as being in great pain over his wife's death when he flew back to Los Angeles and returned to his estate. Nonetheless, he acknowledged that he and friend Robert Kardashian shortly returned to the airport to retrieve a bag of prized golf clubs that had somehow been left behind.

As to the low-speed Bronco chase, Simpson said he wished to visit Nicole Brown Simpson's grave but police presence at the cemetery foiled his plan. He acknowledged taking a gun with him into the Bronco because he was contemplating suicide. But he said he never cocked the gun.

Copyright Acknowledgments